When the Bank Says No!

Creative Financing for Closely Held Businesses

Lawrence W. Tuller

LIBERTY HALL
PRESS™

LIBERTY HALL PRESS books are published by LIBERTY HALL PRESS, an imprint of McGraw-Hill, Inc. Its trademark, consisting of the words "LIBERTY HALL PRESS" and the portrayal of Benjamin Franklin, is registered in the United States Patent and Trademark Office.

FIRST EDITION
FIRST PRINTING

© 1991 by LIBERTY HALL PRESS, an imprint of McGraw-Hill, Inc.

Printed in the United States of America. All rights reserved.
The publisher takes no responsibility for the use of any of the materials or methods described in this book, nor for the products thereof.

Library of Congress Cataloging-in-Publication Data

Tuller, Lawrence W.
When the bank says no! : creative financing for closely held businesses / by Lawrence W. Tuller.
p.   cm.
Includes bibliographical references and index.
ISBN 0-8306-3590-4
1. Close corporations—Finance—Handbooks, manuals, etc.
I. Title.
HG4027.3.T85   1991
658.15′9—dc20   90-24558
                                                 CIP

For information about other McGraw-Hill materials,
call 1-800-2-MCGRAW in the U.S. In other countries
call your nearest McGraw-Hill office.

Vice President and Editorial Director: David J. Conti
Technical Editor: Lori Flaherty
Production: Katherine G. Brown
Book Design: Jaclyn J. Boone

Contents

To Helen Betlach,
who has never lost faith.

Acknowledgments

DAVID J. CONTI, VICE PRESIDENT AND EDITORIAL DIRECTOR, AT MCGRAW-HILL'S Liberty Hall Press is principally responsible for this book being written. It was his idea. H. Michael Snell also deserves credit because, without his encouragement, I wouldn't be writing at all. And finally, a special thank you to all of my friends, business associates, and clients who have suffered the demeaning experience of trying to raise capital from bankers. Without them, this book would be meaningless.

Preface

THE LEVEL OF FRUSTRATION I EXPERIENCED WHEN TRYING TO RAISE CAPITAL through commercial banks for my own operating companies has only been surpassed by the anger, confusion, and distrust expressed by my clients taking the same tack. The age-old maxim about banking still seems to be true. *If you don't need money, any bank will lend it; if you do need money, no one is interested.* Even if a bank is willing to lend, the rapidly deteriorating financial condition of most U.S. banks makes one quickly realize that searching elsewhere for capital remains a far saner choice. Until now, however, a single compendium of alternative financing options for small and midsized businesses has not been available.

This book remedies the situation by providing a comprehensive, up-to-date digest of more than 20 different varieties, sources, and methods for raising capital other than borrowing from a commercial bank. Not only can it assist you in determining which sources will be the best fit for your needs, but the advantages and risks of each is thoroughly evaluated. To help you make the right contact, names and addresses of prominent sources are included in the appendices.

It has taken many years of working with financial markets to compile the comprehensive coverage included in this book. Often, without a ready reference of alternatives, I have approached financing solutions the same way many other entrepreneurs have—by trial and error. This has been a costly and time-consuming mistake. A single source of options would have been helpful many times. The purpose of this book is to provide you with just such a source and to make it easier for entrepreneurs and managers to raise the capital they need.

A great many clients, friends, and associates, some of whom have made their careers in the financing game, have contributed to this book. Without their help and guidance it would have been impossible to condense so many sources and methods in one place and still make the text comprehensible.

As you delve into the world of financing, remember the cardinal rule: money is always available if you look in the right places.

Lawrence W. Tuller

Introduction

THIS BOOK WAS WRITTEN WITH THE FERVENT BELIEF THAT OWNERS AND managers of closely held companies can, and should, use creative financing resources to continue the profitable expansion of their business without succumbing to the inappropriate, restrictive demands of commercial banks. It explodes the common myths that elevate the commercial banking industry to unwarranted heights of public confidence and clearly describes why closely held companies are far better off looking beyond the banking industry for capital. It also pinpoints ways to arrange financing for projects rejected by commercial banks.

Descriptions of current federal tax regulations affecting the structure of financing alternatives are included to prevent you from wasting time and effort approaching the wrong sources. Tricks in preparing and presenting various types of financing plans, bid packages, and prospectuses to reduce the likelihood of rejection are covered in detail. Also, information on selecting qualified professional advisors is included. A few of the unusual types and sources of both short-term and long-term financing found in the book include:

- Government contracts
- Small Business Administration
- Economic Development Agency
- Eximbank
- Other government agencies
- Foreign banks

- Private foundations
- Public stock issues
- Passive or active partners
- Limited partnerships
- Municipal revenue bonds
- Customers and suppliers
- Joint ventures
- Investment banks
- Venture capitalists

Knowing what type of capital to look for and where to find it are not enough. How the funds are applied has a major impact on choosing the right financing combination. To this end, special capital sources are described for specific purposes, including the best combinations to:

- Purchase machinery, equipment, and real estate
- Sell assets and lease them back
- Bring research and development projects to market
- Acquire another company or product line
- Export products and services
- Establish a facility overseas

Many financing sources are only interested in participating in helping a company grow if it is profitable and growing. That leaves financially troubled companies out in the cold. Although all distressed businesses are not salvageable, many are. Chapter 14 contains several options for restructuring a financially distressed company to stop the bleeding and open the door to additional outside capital. Some uncommon ways of using the bankruptcy code to encourage new financing are also described.

As everyone who has ever tried to raise business capital knows, there is no surefire way to do it or single source to consult. Every business is different. Each application of funds has a slightly different twist. Changing economic factors in an industry, the nation, and the world dictate different approaches at different times. Political exigencies in local, state, national, and global arenas influence the availability of funds for different uses.

To confuse the issue even more, the sources of capital themselves keep changing. New government programs are introduced to help small businesses expand, enter the export market, and invest overseas. The health of the financial community, and the regulations governing what can and can't be done by a specific type of financial institution, affect the willingness of a lender or investor to put money into a business. Global economic conditions determine where, and how much, foreign investment finds its way into domestic companies. Finally, continued tampering with income tax regulations creates unpredictable hazards for everyone.

Therefore, any comprehensive list of financing sources today will, by definition, be at least partially outdated tomorrow. For this reason, most recommendations are as flexible as possible. Common, unchanging rules and concepts of financing are stressed, and the advantages and risks of alternate sources are emphasized.

Creative financing requires business owners and managers to be flexible. They must be willing and able to adapt rapidly to changing conditions in financial markets. No single source will always be the best for a given application. By knowing the variety of creative financing methods available for different purposes, however, a business owner or financial manager should be able to pick and choose those structures and sources best suited to his or her requirements.

History has shown that there is always a way to raise capital when it is needed. You don't have to be a financial genius to do it. It takes perseverance, creativity, and the determination not to be deterred by bankers or anyone else. There is always more money in the financial pipeline than there are places to put it. The secret is to know where to look.

1

Why bankers can be hazardous to your business health

WHEN THE OPPORTUNITY TO OPEN A SECOND FACILITY IN BOSTON AROSE, Jack Snow, the owner of a computer sales and service company, beat a path to his friendly banker. Equipment and working capital at the new computer center would cost him $1 million. With his excellent credit record at the bank—always paying back short-term loans ahead of schedule—Jack thought that borrowing $1 million on a five-year note would be a snap. Collateral would come from his present inventory and receivables, and a personal guarantee could be easily secured with company stock. There should be no need for additional equity. Although his balance sheet would be thin, the deal was certainly do-able. But not to the banker. He turned Jack down flat. Suggesting instead that the entrepreneur consider recapitalizing to improve his debt/equity ratio. Unfortunately, the bank couldn't help with that either.

Frustrated and disenchanted, Jack dropped his plans for expansion and resolved to find a new bank as soon as possible. Baffled by the banker's mystifying terminology and logic, Jack was determined to learn more about financing alternatives before trying another expansion scheme.

Jack Snow needed answers to the same questions that confront all business owners whenever they need extra cash:

1

1. What form of financing is best suited to the company's needs?
2. What are the available sources for this capital?
3. What must be done to get the money?

The ensuing chapters of this book arm business owners with answers to these questions. Before getting to these answers, however, it's important to understand why you should not use commercial bank loans except for very short-term working capital peaks.

Avoiding commercial banks

Almost without exception, when additional outside cash is needed for any reason, a business owner thinks first of a commercial bank loan. The billions spent annually on media advertising by the commercial banking industry conjures up an image of a sincere, well-meaning bank executive, eagerly reaching out with a handful of greenbacks to help the small business owner with his cash problems. Propaganda from Chase Manhattan, Citicorp, Bank of America, First Chicago, and other local and regional commercial banks attempts to persuade the unwary business owner that he can have whatever he wants now—not tomorrow—by earning profits—but now, right now, by going into debt. The dissemination of promotional propaganda is hard to resist. More than one entrepreneur has been taken in, only to learn at a later date that he has abdicated control of his own business to this now, not so friendly, commercial banker.

To understand the insidious nature of commercial bank debt, one need only look to the catastrophe that occurred in the farm belt over the past two decades. Falling prey to the bank credit binge of the seventies and eighties, the small, family-owned farm has all but disappeared from the American landscape. Succumbing to the credit lie, farmers paid dearly for the privilege of borrowing money without reasonable expectations of being able to pay it back. Commercial banks charged exorbitant interest rates and demanded short payback periods. When bad weather, changes in the political winds, and overproduction made crops and prices falter, these same commercial bankers stepped in for the kill. Families farming the same land for generations suddenly found themselves not only out of work, but off their land. Foreclosures became the game of the day.

Farmers were not the only ones who suffered the evils of overextended credit. Commercial banks also failed. But how could that happen? Commercial bankers are notorious for their conservatism—almost as conservative as the farm community they served. Certainly they must have investigated the ability of the farmer to repay the loan before granting him funds. Not so. Bank greed and consumer ignorance combined to make commercial bankers in the farm belt the laughing stock of the industry.

And imprudent commercial bank financing has changed the face of the agricultural industry. It remains unlikely that small family farms will again pepper the rural landscape in the foreseeable future.

So how can the private business owner guard against a similar fate? By clearly understanding the rules that commercial bankers play by, and thus dispel the banking myths encouraged by the financial community.

There are three fundamental, but mythical, principles underlying the efficacy of commercial banking:

1. A commercial bank is a safe place to put your money and will always be around.
2. Bankers are honest and above reproach.
3. Bankers are experts at playing the financial game.

Without universal confidence and trust by the public, the banking system would soon collapse. Since the abandonment of Bretton Woods in 1971, the paper money we all use is, in fact, worthless. It only has value as a transaction commodity if we believe it will always be here. If we take a dollar today in exchange for a product or service, we expect to be able to use that dollar to buy other goods and services at a later date. If one day all green currency was outlawed and only newly printed red paper accepted by a bank, either as deposits, or in payment of obligations, we would quickly burn our green bills and scurry around trying to accumulate red bills—which would, of course, be impossible because the banking system would own them all. In 1990, this is exactly what happened in Argentina, leading to civil disturbance and political instability.

But we all know this won't happen here. We are confident that our banking system will maintain stability in the financial marketplace and will continue to accept green paper as deposits and payments. This trust in banks has enabled the American free enterprise system to survive economic and political tragedies debilitating other countries. Argentina, Brazil, Mexico, and recently Poland, are examples of banking systems collapsing without the confidence and trust of the public. Inflation-driven currency devaluation has all but bankrupted these countries, and the primary force behind their rampant inflation rates is the mismanagement of, and lack of confidence in, their banking systems.

The entire American financial system is predicated on the belief that if a person, company, or bank promises to pay in the future, it will fulfill that promise. This is the fundamental principle of credit. I sell you a product today with the understanding that you will pay me for it next week. If you don't pay, I have lost. The same condition supports the banking system. I deposit my green paper in a bank and the bank promises to pay it back to me, with interest, at a later date. If the bank doesn't pay it back, I have lost.

Similarly, if a bank loans me $1,000 today, and I promise to pay it back in six months but don't, then the bank has lost. If enough of these losses occur, either myself or the bank will be bankrupt. The system works because the bank and I trust each other. We can only trust each other if we believe each of us is safe, and will be around and still solvent when the time comes to pay up.

But what if a bank is not safe? What if, for some reason, it goes out of business—bankrupt—before it returns my deposits? Obviously, if people believed that could happen, the entire system would be undermined. No one would give the bank his or her money to hold, and the banking system would collapse. To prevent such fears, the federal government set up the Federal Deposit Insurance Corporation (FDIC) to automatically insure depositors against potential losses. Of course, we never expect to need this insurance because we have been taught that banks are safe and will always honor their obligations.

Recent history has debunked this assumption, however. In the past decade, hundreds of banks throughout the country have failed. In fact, so many have failed, that the FDIC is practically bankrupt itself. One of the measures of a bank's financial strength, and hence a criterion for judging how safe it is, comes from bond ratings. In 1980, nine of the largest banks in the country warranted the highest AAA rating. In 1988, not one bank retained an AAA rating. For example, Standard and Poor's downgraded Chase Manhattan's senior debt from AA- to A; Manufacturer's Hanover Trust from A- to BBB; and Bank of America from BBB to BBB-, which is only one notch above the rating for junk bonds. In early 1990, the Bank of New England announced substantial loan write-offs and their ability to continue as a viable entity still remains in doubt. So, one has to ask how valid is the belief that banks are safe?

The honesty myth

The second banking myth—that bankers are more honest than other business people—is equally fallacious. Quite the contrary. Recent history has proven that the temptation to steal is more prevalent in the banking industry than nearly anywhere else. It's far more serious when a banker steals, however, because most of the money in banks belongs to other people—namely you and I. When a banker steals from his bank, he is stealing from us.

One has only to read the headlines over the past 10 years to learn of corruption in the banking industry. Some of the frighteningly large number of bank failures in the 1980s have been attributed to defaulted loans. But many others are a result of bank presidents, or other bank officials, absconding with bank funds. In 1988, there were more than 4,000 savings and loan institution cases awaiting court dockets dealing with mismanagement by bank officers. Most of these cases have to do with the outright theft of funds by these bank officials.

Less dramatically, loan officers of commercial banks throughout the country routinely obscure the facts from borrowers about terms and conditions of loans. This deceit is just as dishonest as stealing cash. When a borrower believes his loan agreement specifies a due date three years hence, but the bank calls the loan next month, under a confusing and frequently misunderstood provision never explained to the borrower, that is the pinnacle of dishonesty.

The pedestal myth

The third banking myth is that bankers are expert players in the financial game. Because of the aura of power attributed to money, and successful banking propaganda cloaking the workings of money manipulations in a robe of mysticism, we are intentionally led to believe that bankers must be special people. They must have more intelligence and power than the average person, or they wouldn't be in banking. And they certainly must know more about the inner sanctum of the financial world than the uninitiated business owner. This aura of power and mysticism enhances a banker's standing in his community and commands the respect of others far more savvy in business matters. This myth easily camouflages the truth and reinforces the bank's power in the business community.

But this myth can be easily dispelled. After reading this book, ask your friendly banker how prime rate is established, or how much profit the bank makes on credit insurance, or why his bank charges $25 for an overdraft check when processing the check costs the bank less than $1/10$ of a cent. See what answers you get. Unless you happen to be dealing with an unusually sharp banker, he will try to bluff his way through the answers, never admitting he really doesn't know. This should explode any misconception about his superiority in financial matters.

These are the three myths that the banking community would like us to believe. As long as the public falls for them, bankers are protected. Once they are exploded, there is no longer any reason to believe banks or bankers are sacrosanct.

Ten rules of borrowing

If you still feel the need to ask for a loan from a commercial bank, the following 10 rules of borrowing should give you an advantage in dealing with that friendly banker.

Rule #1—repayment priority

The first rule to remember is that the top priority of commercial bankers is to get the loan repaid. Making a profit becomes a secondary consideration. A commercial banker will only worry about profits when he can rest assured that his loan will be repaid. With this mentality, collateral is far more important than interest rate. Consequently, a commercial bank loan will often cost less than other types of financing.

Rule #2—convertible collateral

The second rule is that, because of the importance a banker attaches to being repaid, loan collateral must be readily convertible to cash. That's why bankers love to make loans secured by receivables—the most liquid business asset other than cash. This is also why they hate to make loans secured by machinery and equipment, which can be difficult to liquidate.

Rule #3—unilateral agreements

The third rule, and by far the most important to understand, is that commercial bank loan agreements are always unilateral. This means that a bank may, at any time, call a loan, with minimum notice to the borrower. Loan agreements are written with language that makes it impossible to avoid breach of contract, as long as you are conducting a business. Because the borrower is always in breach, the bank always has the legal right to call the loan. Such an arrangement makes borrowing on receivables, for example, extremely treacherous. The following case clearly illustrates how a commercial bank can directly cause a business to fail.

Mac Connel owned a small trucking company, Iowa Interlake Express Shipping, Inc., IIES leased a fleet of four trucks and hauled farm produce throughout Iowa and northern Missouri. As the business grew, so did receivables, and Mac found short-term cash flow shrinking. Approaching his local commercial bank for a working capital line of credit, the banker granted him a loan of $550,000, secured by 85 percent of the value of qualified receivables. Set up as a revolving line, as receivables were collected the loan balance declined, and as new receivables were generated Mac could borrow up to 85 percent of each account. One summer following a very wet spring, the Iowa corn crop was especially poor and IIES shipping volume dropped off. The bank, leery of Mac's ability to pay back the loan balance, decided the timing was right to foreclose. The loan officer notified Mac that the bank would no longer lend additional funds on new receivables. The following illustrates the effect on available cash in just the first month after the bank called the loan.

	With Operating Line	Without Operating Line
Receivables balance July 31	$650,000	$650,000
Shipments for August	300,000	300,000
Collections for August	(350,000)	(350,000)
Receivables balance August 31	600,000	600,000

	With Operating Line	Without Operating Line
Loan Balance July 31	$550,000	$550,000
Paybacks from collections	(300,000)	(350,000)
New loans from shipments	255,000	-0-
Loan balance August 31	505,000	200,000

The following compares cash that would have been available during the month of August had the operating line been left in place with how much Mac actually could use under the foreclosure action.

	With Operating Line	Without Operating Line
From collections	$ 50,000	-0-
From new loans	255,000	-0-
Total	$305,000	-0-

The second month was even worse. Of the $285,000 collected from receivables, $200,000 went to pay back the balance of the working capital loan, leaving only $85,000 for operating needs. By the time collections started coming in during the third month, Mac had already begun proceedings for a Chapter 11 bankruptcy filing.

This case might seem severe, but time and again, in virtually every industry, commercial banks unilaterally call working capital loans for a variety of reasons. In some cases, because a borrower experiences temporary economic difficulties. In others, because the bank's board of directors decides there are too many small loans outstanding and opts to foreclose rather than to support smaller businesses. In still other instances, a new loan officer might have a personal disagreement with the business owner, or perhaps the chemistry isn't right, or he or she might just get up on the wrong side of the bed one morning and make the unilateral decision to flex the bank's muscle. Very seldom do commercial banks feel any sense of responsibility or loyalty to their borrowers, and the unilateral features of loan agreements always put the bank in the driver's seat.

Rule #4—banker's qualifications

Rule number four has to do with the type of person very often employed as a commercial bank loan officer. Simply put, most loan officers have no experience in any form of business outside a commercial bank. By definition, this means that when you present rational, businesslike propositions, either to qualify as a good credit risk or to increase an outgrown line of credit, the arguments fall on deaf ears. Don't expect the typical loan officer to understand your rationale describing why the business needs additional cash, what caused the latest blip in its growth curve, or how competition forced a general price reduction. Such occurrences, normal in every entrepreneur's business day, are foreign to commercial bankers' experience. A banker knows only about his or her little world as a bank loan officer. Nothing more, and sometimes, a great deal less.

Rule #5—personnel turnover

Rule number five cautions that commercial bank loan officers rotate like a revolving door. Just when you get to know one of them and think you have an inside track for the next loan application, a new face appears behind the desk. That friendly banker you took to the ball game last month—at great personal inconvenience and cost—has either been moved to a different department or branch or has been fired. Yes, even bankers get fired occasionally. All the romancing and coddling over the past year has been wasted effort. Now you must start all over again, and this time it's obvious from the beginning that you don't even like each other. Which brings us to rule number six.

Rule #6—the nice guy role

Rule number six states that, contrary to normal business practice, the success or failure of a relationship with a commercial bank is directly dependent on how adept a business owner is at playing the nice guy role. Bankers can't stand up to the rough and tumble business world outside their solid oak doors. With the supercilious attitude that comes with financial power, rests an absolute belief that the bank is always right and the customer always wrong. To overcome this barrier, a business owner must always put on a happy face when entering a banker's office. Like him or not, you dare not say or do anything, or act in any way, that might be construed as antagonistic, adversarial, or independent. You must at all times treat the loan officer and his or her superior with respect and admiration.

Now that seems downright parochial. Yet, more often than not, that's how it works. Take the case of Mary Joe Randall, sole owner of Accuware Accounting Systems, Inc. Mary Joe's software company was beginning to expand into related computer software products—spread sheets, utility managers, and word processing. She needed to raise about $1.5 million in long-term capital to provide free training sessions for customers of her new software. Such free training had become her trademark in the accounting software field. Mary Joe was known as a tough, no nonsense, but fair, business manager. She had won the respect not only of her employees, but of her customers, suppliers, and competitors as well. Her business acumen kept her out of the banks during all those years that she was building the company, so she didn't have any hard-core experience in dealing with commercial bankers. But now she needed outside capital, and her first trip was to the commercial bank where she maintained her six, and sometimes seven-figure checking and savings accounts. Armed with a financing plan and accompanied by her CPA, she approached the loan officer, Fred Wycoff.

Wycoff seemed like a pleasant enough person, but Mary Joe quickly surmised that he had no knowledge of computer software and little, if any, knowledge of accounting. After playing the acquiescent yes-girl with the banker for a couple of hours, she finally grew tired of the game and asked him point blank how he could possibly pass on the viability of her request without any knowledge of her business. Why didn't he take a night course or something to get smart? Within five minutes, Wycoff informed Mary Joe that his bank was not interested in loaning her the money.

Furious, Mary Joe and her CPA left, and on the way out she asked her long-time professional friend what had happened. "Pretty simple, Mary Joe. You blew your cool. Nobody talks to bankers that way. I warned you ahead of time you had to soft-soap the guy if you really wanted the loan."

Infuriated at the lack of courtesy and apparent incompetence of the loan officer, Mary Joe wrote a seething letter to the bank president. In five weeks he replied, with two paragraphs, stating how sorry he was that Mary Joe was disappointed and how he hoped she had more success with her new bank.

Rule # 7—the demand note

Rule number seven warns that commercial banks do not like to loan money on anything other than a demand note. Because getting repaid is the primary objective in the loan business (Rule #1), banks are reluctant to enter into any contractual agreement tying up their money for long periods of time. That's why even though a borrower might be willing to secure the loan with collateral value in excess of borrowed funds, a com-

mercial bank will nearly always want a demand note in addition to any
security agreement. Because a demand note means that the balance of the
loan must be paid on demand by the bank, the debt becomes short-term,
regardless of how the loan documentation reads. Of course, bankers are
careful not to stress this feature to customers. If they do agree to an installment loan, or other long-term instrument, they would like us to believe
that, as long as monthly, quarterly, or other specified payments are made,
the loan balance will be left intact. With a demand note, however, the bank
can always call the loan—unilaterally.

Commercial bankers do not regard such devious behavior as irregular
or unethical. On the contrary, they place the responsibility for understanding the ramifications of demand notes squarely on the borrower. He's the
one who signs the note, and we all know we shouldn't sign any document
we don't understand and agree with. The truth is, however, that in the
heat of the battle, desperately needing additional funds, unless the potential consequences of executing a demand note are clearly and unequivo-
cally explained by the banker, the average business person will only
casually recognize its implications. And this is just as clearly devious
behavior as if a seller of lawnmowers doesn't explain to the consumer that
if the instructions in small print specifying required maintenance procedures are not followed precisely, the machine will fall apart in three
months. *Caveat emptor* applies to borrowing money just as much as it
does to buying merchandise or anything else.

Unwary borrowers seldom question the veracity of a commercial
banker, however. Most people believe that because bankers are entrusted
with our money in savings and checking accounts, they must be honest.
By definition, honesty requires open and straightforward explanations of
easily misunderstood loan provisions. Unfortunately, bankers do not practice honest business dealings, any more than retailers, manufacturers, or
service persons. In fact, deceit in the commercial banking community is
far more prevalent than in other industries: which leads to rule number
eight.

Rule #8—bankers lie

Rule number eight states that lying is a general practice in the banking
community. This might be too harsh a criticism of an entire industry. Certainly some bankers try hard to be honest and open in their dealings and
go out of their way to be certain that the customer knows and understands
what he's getting into. But this exception does not cleanse the banking
industry as a whole. Lying comes in many forms: stating outright false-
hoods, covering up practices that a borrower has a right to know, omitting
explanations of certain terms and conditions from a deal, or implying that

something will happen when the odds are astronomical that it won't. Any, or all, of these deceitful practices seem to be so widespread that one can only surmise a pervasive infiltration of duplicity throughout the industry. Take, for example, the credit life insurance and disability insurance a bank tries to encourage you to buy when you borrow money in the form of a mortgage, installment loan, or other long-term debt instrument.

Assume you borrow $10,000 to purchase a piece of equipment. The terms of the loan call for 13 percent interest and a five-year amortization schedule. You agree to purchase credit life insurance from the bank, costing $1.25 per month per $1,000, and disability insurance at $2 per month per $1,000. The credit life insurance will pay off the balance of the loan should you die during the next five years, and the disability insurance will continue to make loan payments should you become disabled and not capable of earning income. Further, assume that the bank has talked you into an installment loan. The total amount owed would be calculated as follows:

Original loan balance	$10,000
Credit life insurance -	
$1.25 × 10 × 60 months	750
Disability insurance -	
$2.00 × 10 × 60 months	1,200
Total amount financed	$11,950
Interest charge -	
$11,950 × 13% × 5 years	7,768
Total amount due	19,718
Monthly payment -	
$19,710 / 60 months	$328.63

By taking both insurance coverages and using the same installment method for calculating interest, you are now actually paying more than 19 percent interest for a $10,000 loan. This is okay, provided the borrower understands exactly what he or she is paying for and why. If the borrower still decides to go ahead with the transaction, at least it's with full knowledge. For the unwary, however, there are several things wrong with this deal.

1. For most people, rapidly declining five-year term insurance policies for $10,000—both life and disability—can be purchased directly through an insurance agent at a significantly lesser rate than a commercial bank charges.

2. The bank receives a rebate from the insurance carrier of up to 40 percent of the premiums on policies it places, but it keeps this fact secret.

3. Financing for $10,000 worth of equipment can be obtained at a significantly lesser interest rate elsewhere on a straight simple interest calculation, resulting in a substantially reduced total cost to the borrower.

Most commercial bankers are seldom straightforward enough or willing to take the time to explain all these matters to the borrower, and that's dishonest.

Rule #9—banks are poor credit risks

When a business owner presents his loan application and financing plan to a commercial bank, the first thing a banker looks at is the borrower's balance sheet; not his income statement or his cash flow schedule, but the balance sheet. And the first thing he looks at on the balance sheet is the borrower's debt to equity ratio: How much debt is being carried relative to the equity that the owner has in the business. Banks prefer to see a ratio of less than 1 to 1—preferably about 1 to 2, or less. Occasionally, they'll consider a slightly higher ratio, depending on the business and how well they know the borrower.

Turn this around, however, and look at a typical commercial bank's debt to equity ratio. The current Federal Reserve requirement is for a bank to maintain equity capital of 5 percent; that means a ratio of 20 to 1. Some banks slip below this ratio. A few go up to 6 percent which calculates to a ratio of 16.67 to 1. Can you imagine what response you'd get if you presented such a balance sheet on your loan application? You'd be laughed right out the door.

There's a sound business reason for any company to keep its debt to equity ratio at 1 to 1 or below. In a severe business downturn, or other emergency, with debt equal to, or less than, its equity balance, a business stands a good chance of being able to continue to meet its debt service payments and weather the storm. If it's true for a business enterprise, why not commercial banks? Time and again banks fail because they make bad loans. When a receivable cannot be collected on schedule, the bank's cash flow dries up and it cannot pay back moneys to depositors while meeting its own astronomical debt service payments. If the federal government really wanted to stop bank failures without bailing the banks out with taxpayers' money which is currently being done in the savings and loan (S&L) industry, banking regulations would require federally chartered banks to have at least as good a debt to equity ratio as they demand from their customers. But they don't; and that's why commercial banks are poor credit risks.

Two credible bank economists, Robert E. Litan of the Brookings Institute and R. Dan Brumbaugh, Jr. of Stanford University, have warned the Senate Banking Committee that about two-thirds of the FDIC's current bank reserves will be needed for banks that are weak or already insolvent. They claimed that, of the early 1990 $14.5 billion reserve, $9.5 billion will be needed to cover losses at banks that were already insolvent or close to it.

During each of the last three years, in addition to S&Ls, more than 200 commercial banks failed—a record since the Great Depression. A study conducted in 1989 found that 443 banks throughout the country had been losing money consistently since 1987. Although the American Banking Association scoffs at such figures, claiming they exaggerate the problem, it's clear to the intelligent business person, that the secret world of commercial banking is rapidly approaching its waterloo. With the insanely high debt to equity ratios sported by so many commercial banks, it is hardly surprising that insolvency is becoming a major concern. The only surprise is that more people in the business community, as well as individuals, haven't caught on yet, nor have they taken the requisite steps to safeguard their deposits before the entire system collapses.

Rule #10—excess collateral

A commercial bank will always ask for more collateral than the amount of the loan warrants. For example, a loan secured by demand notes and accounts receivable (often referred to as an operating line, working capital line of credit, or revolving line of credit), will normally equal 80 to 85 percent of qualified receivables. (Qualified receivables are usually defined as those not more than 60 days old.) So right away, 100 percent of receivables secure a loan equal to, at most, 85 percent of their value, plus the bank gets the added security of demand notes. It is not uncommon for a bank to require an additional pledge of other business assets as well, such as inventory, machinery and equipment, or even real estate. If there are already liens against these assets, the bank might take a second position behind the primary creditor. Not only that, many commercial banks also require personal guarantees from the business owner, especially if he has liquid personal assets such as securities investments, savings accounts, or certificates of deposit.

There is no rational reason for demanding this much collateral. In the first place, the efficacy of a loan should be judged on its own merit. Is the cash flow of the business sufficient to pay it back? Does the owner have a track record of sound management practices? Do either the business, or the owner, or both, have a good credit history? These are the important criteria for loaning money. If the answers are positive, and the owner is still willing to pledge his receivables, surely that should be enough. But it rarely is.

This is a ludicrous philosophy. The only reason for demanding any collateral to a loan is if the bank thinks the business might fail and be unable to repay the loan. But if a banker really believes that, why lend the money in the first place, and help the owner go broke? From the perspective of the borrower, granting collateral in excess of loan value can be suicidal. What if you need additional capital before the operating line is paid off? There won't be any assets to offer as collateral if the first bank has them all tied up. What if you sign a personal guarantee pledging personal assets and a family emergency arises requiring ready cash? With all your investments and savings accounts tied up with liens, there wouldn't be any cash available to handle the emergency. Enough "what ifs" can be conjured up to dissuade any reasonable entrepreneur from agreeing to overpledge collateral. Yet, many small business owners continually knuckle under to a commercial bank's demands. Don't do it. Know your rights. Get the money elsewhere rather than sacrificing your future.

Knowing the three banking myths and understanding the 10 rules of dealing with banks, a logical question might be asked: How can commercial banks get away with such flagrant violations of common business protocol? For two reasons: (1) because bankers think they have a monopoly on money; and (2) because of the fear factor.

Understanding the banking industry

A basic tenet in the American free enterprise system is that competition determines prices, quality, and service. The only exceptions to this rule arise when the government interferes in free markets with regulatory restrictions and covenants. Unfortunately, in spite of the much publicized free market philosophy of the Reagan years, government regulations remain a major force controlling markets. Electric, gas, and water utilities continue to be heavily regulated. Airlines, though free to set their prices in a market economy, must comply with strict federal safety and pollution regulations. Railroads, though partially deregulated, continue to be controlled by tariff, safety, and other regulations. Tax laws that influence new product development and international trade continue to change with the whims of big corporations and special interest groups.

Most industries, however, with the exception of federal and state pollution and safety standards, are fairly free to set their own pricing, quality, and service criteria. And these elements, which exert major influences on the success or failure of a given company, are controlled, to a large extent, by free market forces.

This is not true in the commercial banking industry, however. Commercial banking remains as much a closed community today as it was 40 years ago. Entrance requirements are stringent. Large money-center banks control industry pricing standards through variations in the fictitious prime rate. (Chapter 2 explains why the prime rate remains an unreasonable yardstick for most commercial banks.) Loan documentation and lending criteria hardly vary between banks. Slight variations in bank services give the impression of a competitive market, but in reality, they are little more than window dressing. Overall, it costs a commercial bank virtually nothing to get customer checks printed. Yet, prices for this service are uniformly high throughout the industry. The cost of processing overdraft checks is miniscule, yet fees of $25 to $30 per check are commonplace.

The 10 rules of banking apply to nearly all banks, regardless of their size or location. The uniformity within the banking industry remains unmatched in American business as an indication of the subtle monopoly of the industry. Where is that lone wolf banker willing to compete in the free market—and perhaps outstrip the profitability of his neighbors? What happened to the risk-taking entrepreneurship common in most other industries? Why do banks continue to regard their shareholders as incidental investors with no financial acumen? The facts clearly show that smaller American businesses have been taken to the cleaners by a monopoly as strong, or stronger, than the electric utilities ever dreamed of becoming, and that the federal government strongly supports the hoax that America's well-being can only be maintained by a monopolistic banking system.

Correspondent banking, prevalent throughout the country, effectively ties rural and small city banks to the apron strings of large, money-center banks. Branch banking places Chase, Citicorp, First Chicago, and First Interstate, for example, within easy reach of every major and minor market in the nation. And monopoly status continues to reward the commercial banking industry with profits unsurpassed by 90 percent of the American business community. As an indication of this, consider that new bank construction has been on a never-ending upward treadmill for 20 years. Most business enterprises, on the other hand, rent office space rather than tie up much needed capital in buying or building their own office building.

Changes in federal banking regulations permit these Goliaths to enter —and monopolize—money markets heretofore competitive. Investment banking, venture capital, consumer credit cards, insurance, real estate development, securities brokerage, pension and trust management, Foreign Sales Corporation management, and many other businesses competing effectively in a free market environment, are now within easy reach of commercial banks. The tentacles of monopoly banking have reached into virtually every corner of the financial community. Thankfully, there remain some independent sources trying to compete with these leviathans. And as long as some semblance of a free market system remains, there will probably be sources of funds for the closely held business other than commercial banks.

The fear factor

A second feature that allows commercial banks to dominate the business scene is the psychological fear both consumers and business people have of not being able to raise money when needed. Powerful banking lords make it clear in media advertising and in the halls of government that they control the purse strings of the nation. If anyone wants to raise capital, for any purpose, he must come to the commercial banker on bent knee. If anyone wants to put his money in an absolutely secure, safe place, he must use a commercial bank. If anyone wants a 100 percent guaranteed safe investment, he should buy bank certificates of deposit, bank money market funds, or a variety of other bank financial instruments. Commercial bankers work hard to convince the world of their honesty, integrity, and loyalty to customers. And they work doubly hard to convince us that if we don't go along with the banking fraternity, if we don't use their services, if we even try to short-circuit their grip on the financing markets, we will fail. In other words, commercial bankers have structured a web of deceit to cast a blanket of fear throughout the business world. Of course, they have been supported by the big business controlled media, federal government, and state legislatures, all of whom are indebted to the banking fraternity for their very existence.

The commercial banking system's enormous power gained by creating this web of fear is a frightening and serious problem in the American business community. By succumbing to this fear, private business owners, corporate executives, and consumers, are all in jeopardy of losing control of the very free markets they so desperately believe in. Left unchecked, it won't take long for banks to control, not only all of the financial services industries, but eventually retailing, agriculture, manufacturing, and even scientific research projects. Anyone in business recognizes that controlling money is the fastest and surest way to control a business or a market. If we allow the bankers' fear factor to overcome our natural reluctance to outside control, it won't be long before the independent business person loses his independence.

What you can do

It is a fiction to believe that a private business owner can negotiate a favorable loan agreement with a commercial bank, either up front or later on. Without economic or political clout, the small borrower remains at the mercy of the bank. A commercial bank should be the last place to look for new capital. The risk of losing everything is just too severe. And if there is any certainty at all in the business world, it is that economic conditions always change and, over time, if something can go wrong, it will. Most business owners work too hard and take enough risks in the market-place without being subjected to the whims of commercial bankers who know nothing about the vicissitudes or their businesses. Fortunately, there are ways to avoid almost the entire commercial banking industry. A variety of options exist for raising capital other than through commercial banks. The balance of this book will help the entrepreneur define, and locate, just such sources. Of the several possibilities, here are a few that are covered in the ensuing chapters:

- Loans and advances from customers and suppliers
- Asset based lender loans
- Mortgages
- State and municipal revenue bonds
- Foundation grants and subsidies
- Federal government loans and other funding
- SBA guarantees and direct loans
- Government export loans, subsidies, and guarantees
- Progress payment contracts
- International banks
- Public stock issues
- Limited partnerships
- Working and passive partnerships
- Joint ventures
- Mergers
- Investment banks and venture capital funds
- Private trusts
- Partial sales, liquidations, and spin-offs
- Conversion of owned assets to leases

Before beginning to source new financing, an understanding of the vocabulary and concepts underlying the mystical world of corporate finance can be helpful and that's what the next chapter covers.

2

Concepts, rules, and terms used in business financing

"HOW IN THE HELL AM I EVER GOING TO GET FINANCING TO BUILD THE NEW warehouse if I can't even understand what the guy at the mortgage office is talking about?", muttered Ned Colsaw on his way home from his first interview with the mortgage banker. "Before I go any further, I better try to get ahold of some kind of finance dictionary, or better still, have my CPA explain what's going on."

I had just returned from an especially hectic day preparing tax returns and soothing the ruffled feathers of two sizable clients at my tax practice in Southern Minnesota when Ned called. Sensing his frustration, I met with him that evening and tried to explain some of the unintelligible terms he had heard from the mortgage banker. Getting out position, long-term collateral, co-guarantor, and first position creditor were just some of the terms confusing Ned. It was then that I realized that the concepts, rules, and terms used in the financial community, while quite common to someone like myself who worked closely with lenders and investors, were not at all clear to many private business owners.

This chapter explains the most misunderstood concepts, rules, and terms used in business finance. A good grasp of these topics enables a business owner unversed in financing jargon to converse with lenders and investors. The macroeconomics influencing a decision to put money into a business are also reviewed.

How a lender or investor talks

The term *lender* as used throughout this book, refers to financial institutions, agencies, companies, and others who are in the business of providing debt capital. The term *investor* identifies those who provide equity or a combination of equity and debt capital. Lenders and investors are in the business of renting cash. It might be called equity or debt, but it's still rented cash that must be returned, with a profit, to the lender or investor. Grants and awards are obvious exceptions.

When a lender or investor talks about short-term, long-term, or mezzanine debt, demand notes, or risk capital, what does he mean? When he refers to hard asset security and soft collateral, prime rate, or liquidation pecking order, what is he talking about? And how about personal guarantees, co-guarantors, filings, restructuring, equity holdings, and getting out positions? How can the private business owner expect to hold his own in the never-never land of business finance? There's only one way, and that's to learn the same terminology and rules used by the money barons. To expect to compete in a baseball game without first knowing how balls and strikes, hits and stolen bases, and outs and homers determine the ultimate winner would be foolish. It's the same with raising capital. Without a formal background in corporate finance, the only chance a private business owner has of winning the money game is to learn the concepts and ground rules of the financiers.

Finance terminology relates to either the form the financing takes or the ability of the borrower to repay. The type of business, the use to which the capital will be put, and the reputation of the business and its owner(s) is the matrix for choosing among the various financing alternatives. The form of the financing and its repayment are then combined to determine where to source the funds.

Putting a financial package together can be confusing and frustrating because there is such a wide variety in the types of financing offered and such a wide choice of sources. Nevertheless, to maintain the financial health of the business, a business owner must understand the difference between short-term and long-term money.

To understand why the distinction between short-term and long-term is so crucial, one must grasp the meaning of the cardinal principle of intelligent financing—*that the use of the money must match the payback period*. This means that the uses to which an owner intends to put the cash determines both the form of the financing, and the source of it. The inability of a business to repay outside funding in the required period almost invariably results from ignoring this matching principle.

Matching funds and uses

Many entrepreneurs make the mistake of incurring short-term debt for long-term uses and long-term debt for short-term uses. An example of the former would be borrowing on a demand note, secured by receivables, to provide cash to buy a piece of production machinery. An example of the latter would be to borrow money on a 30-year mortgage loan to use for working capital. The basic principle in the finance game is to borrow capital to acquire an asset, which in turn, will provide income and cash flow to pay back the money. Income created from a piece of machinery might occur over several years, but short-term debt used to finance the purchase must be repaid out of existing receivables collections. This, in turn, deprives the business of using the cash collected from its sales to meet payrolls and purchase additional inventory—both short-term uses.

Probably the greatest violation of the short/long principle occurs when short-term funds are used to buy a business. The 1980's wave of business acquisitions made with borrowed, short-term debt, has forced more than one acquirer to liquidate company assets to repay the loans. Over a period of time, and we've already seen this in the decade just ended, such destruction of profitable companies by corporate raiders only exacerbates the already enormous social cost of labor turnover and unemployment.

On the flip side, rapid growth companies in high tech industries are the greatest offenders of using long-term funds for short-term uses. This is because commercial banks will seldom lend to a small company without ironclad collateral, and emerging, rapid-growth firms rarely have such a luxury at their disposal. Consequently, these companies have traditionally turned to venture capitalists to raise money for working capital. This form of equity financing is long-term by definition and should only be used for long-term projects, not working capital.

Another example of the misuse of long-term funds occurred in 1989 when Bally's Park Place Casino Hotel in Atlantic City filed a petition with the State of New Jersey seeking permission for the Casino Hotel to float long-term mortgage notes. The plan was to raise $350 million of which $150 million was to be used as a dividend to Bally Manufacturing Corp., the parent corporation. This is clearly a mismatch of long-term funds (mortgage notes) and short-term uses (dividends).

In a sense, the seriousness of the misuse of long-term funds overshadows the misapplication of short-term debt. The use of long-term funds for short-term purposes robs the company of cash required to purchase the long-term assets necessary to generate income for debt repayment. A more simplistic example would be an individual who takes out a five-year loan to buy a moving van with which he will earn an income and then uses the cash to take a vacation. The cash gets spent without buying a truck for which to earn an income and pay back the loan, but the person still retains the obligation to repay the loan from cash raised somewhere else. As the multitude of financing forms and sources unfold throughout this book, it's important to remember the matching principle in determining which form and which source is best for the application you have in mind.

Risk capital and secured capital

Another key concept to keep in mind is the distinction between risk capital and secured capital. Secured capital can be characterized as loans or preferred equity funds supported by a legal right on the part of the lender or investor to seize assets owned by the business, the business owner, or other outside parties in the event of repayment delinquency or other contractual default. The advantage to a lender, or investor, in demanding such security seems obvious (although, as explained further in this chapter, it might not be as beneficial as it appears). If the business defaults, or goes under, the theory is that a secured creditor or investor can liquidate the collateralized asset and recoup some or all of the principal. Because financiers always have this option, their risk diminishes and they are normally willing to charge a lesser amount for the use of the money.

Any capital not secured by some type of convertible asset is considered risk capital. An example would be an equity contribution by a partner or venture capitalist without supporting collateral. The less security offered, and the more questionable the owner's ability to repay the principal, the higher the risk. Throughout the financial community, risk equates with return. The higher the risk of not getting repaid, the higher the interest rate, or other form of return, is demanded by the financier.

Let's examine what the most important financing terms mean to the business owner and how bankers and other lenders often confuse uninformed entrepreneurs into agreeing to a financing scheme that is detrimental to their business.

What is prime rate

Everyone has heard the term *prime rate*, but most are unaware of just what it means. Contrary to popular belief, the prime rate is not controlled by the Federal Reserve Bank or any other government agency. It is a fictitious measurement established by money center banks that acts as a benchmark for measuring interest rates charged on loans. It is a reference rate for commercial bank loans to large corporations. Interest rates charged to other customers are predicated on the prime rate. Mortgage rates are *prime plus X*, installment loans are *prime plus XX*, and working capital loans might be *prime plus XXX*.

Many people in the business world, as well as many consumers, accept this concept without question, believing that the prime rate is somehow based on a bank's analysis of its operating costs, plus a reasonable profit, in the same manner other businesses theoretically set their prices. They feel fortunate to be able to get a loan at, or close to, the prevailing prime rate. But once again the public is fooled. The prime rate is established by a handful of major, money-center banks. It is based on the cost of doing business by these banks, including their cost of money (the interest they pay on deposits), overhead, and a profit factor. That's fine for New York banks with high rent facilities and exorbitant salary structures. But what about the rural bank in Sioux Falls, South Dakota? Certainly overhead costs such as salaries, rent, maintenance, utilities, and so on, must be less than in New York. Yet, their lending rates are based on exactly the same prime rates as Chase and Citicorp. Just think of the profit they must make! Consequently, paying a rate of one or two points over prime really isn't that great. A manufacturing company should be so lucky. This type of noncompetitive environment only exists in the banking industry.

So don't be out-foxed by the money manipulators. You might still have to pay exorbitant interest rates, but at least let the financiers know that you understand their game and can't be fooled by something as blatantly misleading as the prime rate.

Collateral or security

The terms *collateral* and *security* as they relate to borrowed or invested money are used interchangeably. Collateral, or security, as described earlier, represents those assets which the financier can claim and convert to cash if the company defaults on its contractual agreement. Theoretically, this makes sense from the financier's perspective. From a practical viewpoint, however, the insistence on collateral of an equal or greater amount than the loan or investment balance makes little sense except in a bankruptcy action. Realistically, collateral should not be a major consideration in deciding whether or not to put money into a business. The judiciousness of a loan or an investment should be based on the perceived ability of the business to repay the money, with interest, and on the character and reputation of the business owner. But many lenders, and especially commercial bankers, do not like to take any risk. They want to make only risk-free loans, and therefore, demand unreasonable amounts of collateral as support.

On the other hand, smart bankers and other lenders know that the abilities and integrity of the borrower are far more important than any collateral. Collateral can quickly disappear or become worthless. An excellent example occurred during the early eighties in the used equipment market. With the Japanese machine tool industry flooding the U.S. market, the bottom fell out of the used equipment market. A good used machine selling for $100,000 in 1982 dropped to $10,000 in the 1985 market. Yet, commercial bankers and asset based lenders continued to base long-term loan commitments on fictitious, appraised values of this equipment.

By demanding that a company pledge all of its hard assets, they precluded it from borrowing short-term money for exigencies. When defaults occurred, and many did, these secured creditors were faced with the decision to either restructure the payment terms of the loan to allow borrowers extra time for repayment or to foreclose and try to recoup their investment through an auction. Some tried the auction route and lost miserably, but most restructured the loans and are still collecting. Yet, knowing that most hard assets are worth much less on liquidation than the loan balance they secure, bankers, as well as other lenders, continue to insist on inordinate amounts of collateral, stifling the growth prospects of smaller businesses.

Definitions of debt

Corporate finance textbooks describe debt as a liability or obligation of the business to return the principal amount borrowed to the lender at a prescribed time. A lender often includes the total amount of interest payable over the term of the loan as part of the debt, such as with an installment loan. The accounting fraternity also gets into the act, stipulating that businesses must show the outstanding balance of debt obligations as liabilities on their balance sheet. Not to be outdone, the IRS also puts its oar in the financial pond, directing that the profit to the lender (interest) must be included as income on the lender's tax return and allows the debtor business to then deduct such payments as interest expense. Chapter 3 explains the difference in the tax treatment between interest and other forms of repayment for both the recipient and the business taxpayer. To further confuse the uninformed, lenders use different catchphrases to define different types of debt. Let's look at some of the most popular.

Short-term debt

Short-term debt is the favorite of commercial bankers. When a business owner applies for a loan, the banker almost invariably thinks of it in terms of a short-term loan. And for good reason. As discussed in Chapter 1, a commercial bank's main objective in loaning money is to be repaid. Though important, income is secondary in importance to collecting the principal balance.

To the accounting fraternity, a short-term loan means that the principal must be repaid in less than 12 months. To a banker, however, short-term means that he can demand payment of the principal any time he pleases. The financial instrument normally used to evidence a short-term loan is called a demand note. A demand note is a promise to pay back the loan "on demand" from the bank. Without a fixed due date for repayment, the bank can call the loan whenever it chooses. As pointed out in Chapter 1, this subjugates the business owner to potential financial catastrophe unless he keeps the banker happy. This is outright blackmail—though no banker will admit it—and few business owners understand it.

Demand notes from large corporations or favored customers are usually unsecured. This means that if the borrower refuses to repay when the bank issues its demand, the bank's only recourse is to sue for relief in the courts. Most small businesses, however, never get this favored treatment and are forced to secure short-term borrowings with assets readily convertible to cash, such as receivables and certain types of easily salable inventory. By pledging this collateral, many business owners believe that the principal of such short-term loans need not be repaid as long as receivables and inventory remain on its books. But it doesn't work that way. The primary collateral is still the demand note, which allows the bank to demand payment in full at any time, regardless of whether collateral exists. More than one unwary entrepreneur has learned the hard way that unless the banker is kept happy (see Rule #6 in chapter 1), the loss of business, or even bankruptcy, are very real possibilities.

Short-term debt is normally used to provide extra working capital. For example, a growing business often needs to hire additional people to handle the increased work load and working capital debt provides the needed cash to meet this additional payroll—long before any new business materializes; inventory often must be purchased and stocked in anticipation of increased sales, often requiring outside financing; or receivables increase as a result of burgeoning sales, and the working capital loans meet the cash needs until these receivables can be collected. Such uses of short-term debt are common to any growing business and have formed a sound foundation for a growing economy. This is a truly productive use of outside cash. As long as short-term debt is used to provide short-term cash for a growing business, it is productive. When the business levels out or when it begins a decline, such short-term borrowings become nonproductive and detrimental to the well-being of the company.

Because short-term debt creates minimal risk to the lender, the profit he earns—the interest—is usually lower than longer-term loans. Unfortunately, this often leads the business owner to seek short-term financing for any need, regardless of what the funds will be used for, often leading to even further cash shortages.

Loans from a bank or other lender are not the only form of short-term debt. Buying from suppliers on 30, 60, or 90-day terms, customer advance deposits, and progress payments are just some of the more common forms of non-bank, short-term debt. The beauty of borrowing from these sources is that seldom do they charge anything for their money. Occasionally, nominal interest might be assessed, but it is usually less than that charged by a financial institution. The purchased materials or products serve as unattached collateral to this debt, leaving the balance of the business's assets free and clear. Government assistance programs and private foundations are other sources for short-term financing outside of the financial community. Some of these lenders charge very low interest; others determine their rates in the same manner as banks.

Long-term debt

Although business finance textbooks often speak of intermediate term debt, in practice, this term is hardly ever used. Either an obligation must be paid in less than one year—short-term debt—or after one year, in which case it is long-term debt. Probably the most common long-term debt for small businesses is installment debt. When a business buys an automobile, office equipment, or production machinery, it is often done with installment debt. As the name implies, this form of debt allows the borrower to repay the principal and interest in equal amounts—usually monthly—over the term of the loan. Though many variations exist, the most common calculation of the interest on such a loan, and by far the most costly to the borrower, is front-end loaded, compound interest. The calculation of the total interest for the length of the loan is calculated at the beginning, added to the principal amount, and the total divided by the number of payments, as in the following example:

Financed price of car, after down payment	$10,000
Interest rate = 13%	
Term = 5 years	
Total interest on the loan =	
$10,000 × 13% × 5 years	6,500
Total to be paid	$16,500
Number of monthly payments	60
Monthly payment	$275

Without getting involved in present value concepts or discounted cash flow calculations, it's clear to see that a $10,000 car actually costs

$16,500. Compare this to a loan calculated using simple interest and a single payment but allowing for monthly payments similar to typical mortgage loans:

	Installment Loan	Simple Interest Loan
Amount of loan	$10,000	$10,000
Interest rate	13%	13%
Term	60 months	60 months
Total Interest Paid	$6,500	$3,304

Why do lenders like to make installment loans? The answer is obvious. They make **twice** the interest income. But they will never tell the borrower this. How about the borrower? His first monthly payment is exactly the same on a simple interest loan as with an installment loan—$275. By payment number 31, however, halfway through the five years, the monthly payment has decreased to $220 with simple interest; and by payment 48, it is only $190 compared to a level monthly payment of $275 on the installment loan. Most lenders will not readily admit they make loans calculated on simple interest, but most will, if pressed by the customer. If yours won't, then go next door.

Leasing

Leasing has become a popular mode of financing as an alternative to borrowing from a financial institution for the purchase of automobiles or equipment. Chapters 5 and 12 elaborate on leasing as an alternate source of funds. At this point, it is only relevant to mention that leasing is a form of long-term debt. The lease obligation must be paid in its entirety, just like a long-term loan. The lessor earns a profit by renting his money, just like a lender. There are two major differences, however. The tax treatment of lease payments compared with loans (which is explained in the next chapter) and the structure of leases. Leasing companies have mushroomed over the past 20 years and aside from the advantage of not requiring cash down payments, they can be structured individually to the needs of the business owner.

Mezzanine debt

The term mezzanine debt arose with the advent of investment banks as major players in financing business acquisitions. As the name implies, this type of loan acts as a bridge, or mezzanine, between long-term, secured debt and the equity contributions of the business buyer, the investment bank, or both. Because mezzanine debt is typically unsecured, it carries a relatively high rate of interest; generally two points or more over prime.

The funds usually come directly from the investment bank and are repayable when additional equity capital can be arranged; but usually no longer than one to two years. Mezzanine debt can also be used for purposes other than business acquisitions. Actually, whenever a business needs outside capital for long-term applications, but encounters difficulties structuring either long-term debt or an equity package, mezzanine debt can bridge the gap and provide the business owner with enough time to arrange permanent financing. Investment banks remain the principal source of mezzanine debt, although other institutions use the same concept under different names.

Mortgage debt

Mortgages, or mortgage debt, refers to long-term debt secured by real estate—usually land or buildings. The term mortgage defines a specific type of lien placed against the property securing the loan. A mortgage loan normally carries a long-term amortization schedule of 15 to 30 years and a fixed interest rate, negotiated at inception. Lately, however, variable rate loans have become popular in the financial community, fluctuating within a minimum and maximum band depending on the movements of a money-center bank's prime rate. The spread is usually two or three percentage points on either side of the prime. From the perspective of a mortgage banker, the spread affords some protection in the event of skyrocketing market rates. For the borrower, it often provides a means of obtaining a loan otherwise unavailable at a reasonable fixed rate. Variable rate mortgages are usually popular during extreme economic uncertainty and are not prevalent in times of relatively stable conditions. Though many sources offer mortgage loans, including some commercial banks, special financial organizations called mortgage bankers command the market.

Asset based lenders

After World War II, commercial and industrial finance companies emerged as a source of debt funds for individuals and businesses unable to borrow from a commercial bank because of poor credit ratings. Loans were generally for more than one year and carried a higher interest rate than commercial banks. Hard asset collateral was usually required. Over the next three decades, industrial finance companies evolved into what are now called asset based lenders (ABLs).

Though many continue to make loans secured by receivables and inventory, most prefer hard asset collateral—machinery, equipment, or real estate. In the early eighties, before investment bankers became interested in smaller customers, asset based lenders were the prime lenders for smaller leveraged buyouts. The popularity of asset based lenders for LBOs arose principally because these lenders were willing to make five to seven year loans, secured by hard assets, with very little equity contribution from the buyer. In fact, many business acquisitions were made by buyers with no equity contribution at all, financing the deal entirely with funds borrowed from an asset based lender.

This source continues to be popular among business owners either looking for new capital to purchase machinery and equipment or to buy an additional business or product line, mainly because of the low equity requirements. Interest rates are high, however, generally three to five points above prime.

One of the greatest drawbacks in borrowing from an asset based lender other than the high interest cost is that these lenders can be difficult to work with. At the slightest provocation, many will interfere with the operating decisions of a debtor. Because most officers of ABLs have come up through business channels rather than commercial banking, their knowledge of the business world is usually pretty good. Nevertheless, no entrepreneur welcomes an outsider's interference in operating decisions he regards as sacrosanct.

Liquidation pecking order

Though commercial banks are the most worrisome, every lender or investor places heavy emphasis on getting paid back. Consequently, the priority claims, or pecking order, when liquidating a company's assets becomes an important consideration for any financier. Though no entrepreneur ever expects to file bankruptcy or to liquidate his business, the possibility always exists. Should such a catastrophe hit, creditors and investors stand in line with outstretched hands waiting to be paid off. And by law, payments are made based on the seniority of the financing instrument. Because of the frightening increase in business bankruptcies, creditors and investors attempt to structure complex financing instruments with all types of privileges and priorities in the event of liquidation. There is no limit to the concoctions they come up with including warrants, options, priority positions, convertible provisions, guarantees, and warranties. The best advice to a business owner is to be certain he understands all the covenants and provisions in a debt or equity instrument before signing the papers. The following order of claim priorities has been established by the Bankruptcy Code:

1. Short-term, secured creditors, collateralized by receivables, inventory, and other business assets readily convertible to cash.

2. Lease holders secured by the hard asset being leased.
3. Long-term, secured creditors holding liens against hard assets, such as machinery, equipment, and real estate.
4. Employees for wages and commissions earned within 90 days of the filing, up to $2,000 per individual.
5. Claims from an employee benefit plan for services rendered within 180 days of the filing, up to $2,000 per individual.
6. Deposits on customers goods, not exceeding $900 per claim.
7. Most taxes.
8. All other creditors (considered as unsecured).
9. Preferred stock shareholders.
10. Common stock shareholders.

Bonds and stocks

State and municipal revenue bond agreements and covenants are extremely complex and are dealt with in more detail in chapter 8. Corporate bonds are less complicated. Generally, corporate bonds are issued to the public secured by a promise to pay, and in a few cases, specific assets of the business. So-called junk bonds, used for business acquisitions, are an example of high-risk coupon bonds with no collateral securing the instrument; which is why these instruments carry much higher returns.

Debentures are really corporate bonds, but usually the instrument calls for convertible privileges allowing the holder to convert his debenture to common stock under certain conditions. Debentures are hardly ever secured with any type of collateral.

Preferred stock is similar to common stock with two exceptions: (1) it normally does not carry voting rights; and (2) it carries a fixed yield or dividend rate. Preferred stock may also be convertible and the dividends may be cumulative. Some issues also carry callable provisions, which allow the holder to cash in the principal amount under certain conditions or the issuer to retire the shares.

Common stock, of course, is the instrument signifying equity ownership of the corporation. In terms of liquidation rights, common shareholders should not expect any payoff until all other obligations have been satisfied.

Getting out position

Recently, the phrase "getting out position" has been used more and more by investors such as investment bankers and venture capitalists, and in some cases, even by lenders. The phrase refers to a mechanism built into a loan agreement, equity covenant, or other contractual document calling for specific actions to take place that allow the instrument holder to liquidate his holdings under certain conditions. Because investment bankers, venture capitalists, and other investors specializing in equity funding lack the legal protection of secured creditors, "getting out" clauses incorporated in financing instruments are substituted. Business owners also gain because they are not saddled with legally enforceable payback terms, such as due dates or amortization schedules applicable to loans.

In terms of wanting to be assured of getting their principal returned at some point in the future, equity investors are no different than lenders, and therefore, they always strive to structure a deal with a contractual getting out position.

A getting out position might take a variety of forms. Some of the more common include:

1. Conversion rights to a majority share of voting stock.
2. Provisions for board membership and voting control.
3. Second positions behind secured creditors on business assets.
4. Board advisory rights for major policy decisions.
5. Approval rights for major capital expenditures, business acquisitions, or new stock issues.
6. Rights of first refusal on a public stock issue.
7. Predetermined purchase price on such an issue.
8. Restrictions on dividends or other payments to the business owner.
9. Approval rights for outside investments made by the business.

All such agreements provide security to the equity holder against undesirable policy actions by the business owner, but don't really provide for repayment terms. The ultimate getting out position for an equity holder specifies a definitive date by which the owner must come up with sufficient outside capital to repurchase the investors stock holdings. The price to be paid can either be stipulated in the beginning or calculated at the payment date based on the current value of the business.

Regardless of how the agreement might be structured, anyone contemplating financing through investment bankers, venture capitalists, partners, or other equity investors must be prepared not only to give up rights to operating the business in the event of default, but also for a fixed repayment scheme. Most investment bankers and venture capitalists will not invest large sums in a business without being fairly confident that the company can be taken public at some time in the future, which then provides the cash necessary to liquidate their holdings. Chapter 7 looks at the use of an initial public stock offering (IPO) as a mechanism to achieve this payoff, as well as another method for raising long-term equity capital.

Public imaging

Public imaging plays a major role in determining the ease with which a business owner can raise capital. It describes the public perception or reputation of the company looking for financing. Some business owners prefer to maintain a very low, discreet public image. These companies make few waves in the industry, are virtually unknown in their community, and find it difficult to attract outside financing of any magnitude. The wiser entrepreneur understands that the higher the profile his company maintains and the better reputation he has in the industry and community, the more eager major outside lenders or investors are to get into the act. This becomes especially crucial when the owner contemplates a future public stock issue.

There are a number of ways to achieve a good public image, assuming of course, that the company is not in severe financial difficulty or hasn't maintained an antisocial profile in the past. Public imaging has become such an important aspect of progressive business that advertising and public relations firms employed to create a favorable public image now proliferate the business landscape.

Community and industry advertising campaigns eulogizing not only the product or service offered for sale, but also the company profile, is an excellent way to maintain a public image. Visible community consciousness through contributions, participation, and active solicitation of government reforms, brings the company to a favorable light probably more rapidly than any other means. Civic, educational, and social organization membership and support by the CEO, and other company officers, can also help.

Another approach to public imaging employed by a number of companies successful in making an IPO is to encourage board membership by outsiders from the industry or community. If these board members bring a widely known name and favorable reputation with them, the public relations impact on the company can be substantial, and the probability of achieving a successful stock issue escalates. Civic and government leaders, noted attorneys or consultants, university professors, CEOs from other major companies, all qualify as outstanding additions to the board, enhancing a company's public image. Regardless of the means employed, public imaging remains an essential ingredient to attract major amounts of outside capital when, and if, the need ever arises.

Personal guarantees

With very few exceptions, most lenders and investors want some type of personal guarantee from the owner that the loan, or investment, will be repaid as stipulated in the contractual agreement. Although personally guaranteeing anything is usually a bad idea, especially as it relates to the performance of a company, unless valuable collateral can be offered as definitive assurance that repayment will be made, there is really no other acceptable way to raise capital. There are variations that everyone should be aware of, however.

As a fundamental principle, no guarantee is worth the paper it's written on unless the signer owns assets that the holder can access in the event of default and the market value of these assets is equal to, or exceeds, the amount of money being put in. These assets must not be business assets that can be accessed by other creditors. Personal investments such as certificates of deposit, investment securities, pension entitlements, nonresidential real estate, valuable coin, stamp or antique collections, and private automobiles, yachts, or airplanes, might all be viewed as qualifiable assets to support a personal guarantee.

Though local laws vary, most states regard any asset held jointly by husband and wife—including bank accounts, investments, or a residence—as untouchable in the event of personal bankruptcy. Therefore, most creditors or investors will try to get a spouse as a co-guarantor on the personal guarantee agreement. This is foolhardy exposure, and no one should agree to such a condition. No one in his right mind wants to saddle a spouse or family with the risk of losing everything should the business fail. If the lender or investor insists, the only alternative is to look elsewhere for financing.

If a business owner revolts at the insistence of family co-guarantors, some sources of funds will try to get another third party to sign as co-guarantor. A rich uncle or wealthy friend would certainly qualify. But once again, it is always unwise to burden someone else with your own risks, and if a co-guarantor is a prerequisite for getting the money, a person is usually wise to find another source of capital.

One last comment on personal guarantees. If a person should die without fulfilling the guaranteed obligation, the personal guarantee passes to the estate. The beneficiaries—spouse, children, or others—then become liable to satisfy the debt. Clearly, any form of personal guarantee should be avoided, or at least limited, if at all possible.

The impact of macroeconomics

It doesn't take trained economists to understand the impact of regional, national, and global economic fluctuations on a company's ability to raise capital. A handful of specific indicators and a general knowledge of economic trends is enough to provide anyone with an understanding to intelligently judge financial markets.

Of all the economic indicators available through government and trade statistics, media coverage, stock market gurus, and business journals, the most relevant to the private business owner are interest rates, unemployment rates, inflation rates, and current and anticipated industry and national growth curves. As Americans become more attuned to global business conditions, a knowledge of currency exchange rates and economic prognostications for overseas markets should be added to the pot.

Economics impacts financing decisions in a very simple way, contrary to what the banking industry would like us to believe. It's mainly a matter of supply and demand. The more money available in the financial marketplace, the lower the interest rate and the easier it is to raise capital. In a tight money economy, when demand exceeds supply, interest rates go up and raising capital becomes more difficult—at any price. Inflation tends to drive interest rates up, while deflation has the reverse effect. Such pseudo-control mechanisms as the Federal Reserve discount rate to banks and federal budget deficits, have very little real effect on either interest rates or the supply of money, although for psychological reasons the financial community and the government would like us to believe otherwise. With $11 trillion in total American debt and the federal government accounting for less than one-fourth of it, it's hard to visualize how slow moving vacillations in government borrowings has much effect at all. Because the interest rate is controlled primarily by the money center banks, which is theoretically based on their own cost of doing business, the Fed's discount policy has little more than temporary psychological stimulation or retardation effects.

The current and projected tenor of the national economy, however, does play a major role. As the public perceives the economy strengthening, the demand for money increases, along with interest rates. As the economy levels out at a high plateau, public confidence becomes a bit shakier, but still optimistic, and demand for funds remains fairly constant, as do interest rates. If the economy begins a decline, however, or if it stabilizes at a low level with high unemployment and swelling welfare roles, demand for funds decreases markedly, and so do interest rates.

Therefore, the best time to raise outside capital is not in a rapidly growing financial market or at the apex of a cycle, but at the bottom. It is here that rates will be the lowest, and supply the greatest. Many good financing schemes can be put together in such an atmosphere, while the reverse holds true in good times.

Historically, there has been one exception to this rule. If the economy is on a steep slide, many smaller banks will fail because of horrendously mismanaged loan portfolios. While this creates outstanding investment opportunities in foreclosed bank holdings—as in the recent savings and loan fiasco—the willingness of the remaining banks to enter the market with new ventures diminishes. With some foresight and a little effort, however, good financing sources can still be located, even in a down economy.

With all these factors mixing the money market pot, it's important that the business owner recognize what can and can't be done with reasonable efficacy before venturing onto the financial playground. To make the best deal, it is crucial to understand the criteria influencing the willingness of lenders or investors to provide funds.

Summary

The following are the major points that have been covered in this chapter.

1. Use long-term capital—loans or equity—for long-term applications, such as buying machinery, equipment or real estate, buying a company, or establishing a presence overseas.

2. Use short-term capital—customer and vendor advances or loans, government-assisted loans, or a modest amount of commercial bank debt—for short-term applications, such as to pay dividends, build inventory, start an export program, or carry escalating receivables.

3. Avoid personal guarantees as much as possible, and under no circumstances agree to any co-guarantor.

4. When interest rates are high, or money is in short supply, look to leasing as a viable alternative to buying.

5. Given a choice, utilize foundation grants, government-backed loans, investment banks, or even venture capital sources rather than bank debt, even if the cost of capital appears to be higher (in the long run it isn't).

6. Recognize that any lender or investor must have a getting out position, and structure the contractual agreement to provide the minimum risk to both parties.

7. Get on the public imaging bandwagon before looking for substantial outside capital.

8. Most important of all, stay away from commercial banks except for very short-term needs, where the loan can be repaid in less than a year. And then make sure the loan is repaid.

So much for the ground rules of business financing. The next step before beginning the search for low risk, low cost capital is to examine the federal tax laws affecting various financing options.

3

Considering the
basic tax implications

FEDERAL INCOME TAX REGULATIONS HAVE BEEN IN A FLUX FOR THE PAST
40 years. There is no reason to believe that this condition will change in
the foreseeable future. Special interest groups continue to bombard Congress with desired tax law changes to benefit their particular cause. Politicians susceptible to constituency pressure promote variations in specific
features of the tax code to benefit their regions and favorite industries in
an effort to buy votes. Large corporations spend millions of dollars on
political action committees and other lobbying factions to encourage Congress to make tax law changes specifically to improve their bottom line.
The media, state legislatures, big city politicians, and industry trade associations, unhappy with a specific provision in the tax Code, argue for repeal
or change to further their own interests. The federal income tax system in
the United States has always been subject to these pressures and probably
will continue to be in the future. Therefore, the best a private business
owner can hope for in planning financing strategies is to continually seek
the most expert tax advice he can get.

This book is not a treatise on income taxes. It focuses on methods to
raise outside capital and on sound financial management, not the reduction of tax liability. Don't act solely on the basis of tax discussions or recommendations presented here. Consult competent tax advisors before

enacting any financing scheme. This book can only review those facets of the tax laws bearing most heavily on major financing decisions and examine these provisions in light of current tax legislation.

The only certainty about income taxes is that next year some provisions of the Code will change. Nothing remains constant. There are no rules or regulations sacrosanct from congressional, IRS, or tax court changes. But the fact that tax regulations remain fluid does not preclude a general understanding of some of the basics. And that's what this chapter covers.

Many basic features of the Code have remained relatively stable for several years and will probably experience only minor revisions in the foreseeable future. Some are new and confusing and will probably be repealed or materially changed within the next two or three years. Although you should have expert tax advice at your disposal, an examination of the current tax treatment of these basic elements should provide at least a basis for discussion with your tax advisor. This chapter covers only those major elements of the tax code most applicable to the majority of entrepreneurs interested in financing or refinancing a closely held business. These topics fall under six headings:

1. *The tax treatment and the timing of money paid by the corporation to its investors.* The return on investment paid on equity capital and the structure of the equity sale influences raising capital through limited partnerships, partial sales to a partner or employees, and public stock conversions.

2. *The tax advantages and pitfalls in utilizing an S corporation.* Using an S corporation can eliminate potential double taxation of payments to equity holders and permit tax-free stockholder loans. "At risk" rules can invalidate these advantages, however, if the financing is not structured properly.

3. *The tax implications of utilizing a partnership structure.* Raising capital by selling part of the equity to a partner raises tax questions about distributions, losses, and taxable income to the owner.

4. *The hazards of passive activity rules affecting investors.* Passive activity rules can affect the desirability of using limited partnerships, S corporations, and standard partnerships to raise capital.

5. *The impact of foreign taxes and foreign income.* The decision to proceed with an export program, or direct foreign participation, even with financing in hand, will be influenced by the U.S. tax treatment of foreign income. Structuring tiered corporations for financing purposes is also impacted by tax legislation.

6. *The potential tax consequences of the liquidation of assets for financially distressed companies.* Raising capital through the restructuring of a debt-poor company must recognize the tax ramifications of liquidation provisions in the tax reform acts.

Cash payments or withdrawals

In most instances, cash payments from a company to its owner, shareholders, banks, or other investors take on one of two forms for tax purposes: either they are taxable to the recipient or they are tax free and either they are tax deductible to the company or they are not. The key to structuring a tax strategy is to make sure that, at worst, taxes are paid by only one party, not two. Obviously, if a distribution can be made tax free to both recipient and company, so much the better. Double taxation, the same income taxed both to the corporation and the recipient of the distribution, should obviously be avoided whenever possible. Double taxation can be a nightmare as well as grossly unfair. Yet, without lobbying clout, entrepreneurs can do little to change the laws. Instead, they must learn to structure their businesses and distributions to avoid this prejudicial tax treatment as much as possible.

Dividends

Cash distributions treated as dividends under the tax laws are always subject to double taxation. The income creating these dividends is first taxed to the corporation. Then, when dividends are paid, they are taxed again to the recipient.

Distributions are classified as dividends if the payment fails to qualify as either compensation, interest expense, or return of capital (or principal). Under special situations (discussed later), distributions to passive partners in either a limited or standard partnership are always treated as either dividends or return of capital. If the partners' capital accounts are depleted by previous distributions or company losses, the additional payments automatically become dividends. These nonactive partners are considered passive if they are not active in the trade or business of the company or do not make a major contribution to its management. To the extent that distributions are made to passive partners (or investors) during a year in which the company reports a net loss on its return, these payments are treated as a nonreturn of partners' capital. When the capital accounts reach zero, however, or show a negative balance, further distributions are considered dividends, regardless of whether or not the company shows a profit.

There is a real danger to the company of not being allowed to deduct payments made to investment bankers, venture capitalists, limited partner or standard partners. Accordingly, when calculating the cost of using these financing sources, the business owner must recognize the possibility of losing tax deductions.

Interest

Payments to a lender—whether it is a bank, customer, supplier, government agency, individual, or anyone else lending the company money— which are not payments against the principal of the loan, are treated as interest expense to the company. Even if someone loans the company money interest free, such as a relative of the owner, the owner himself, or an outside party, and payments are made against this loan, the IRS automatically assigns part of the payment to interest. The amount assigned will be equal to current rates being paid on U.S. Treasury obligations according to the following:

1. If the debt instrument has a term not in excess of three years—the federal short-term rate.
2. Between three and nine years—the federal mid-term rate.
3. Over nine years—the federal long-term rate.

The interest expense on business loans is deductible by the business and taxed as ordinary income to the recipient. An exception occurs if a lender loans an ESOP (Employee Stock Ownership Plan) money to purchase shares in the company. Half of the interest paid by the ESOP is not included in the income of the lender. On the other hand, principal payments on any type of loan are never deductible to the company and are not income to the recipient, even if paid earlier than required.

Ordinary income or capital gain

Both dividend and interest income are treated as ordinary income under the tax code. This means that the recipient must include this income in his tax return along with all other ordinary income and pay the tax rate applicable to the total. Though the Tax Reform Act of 1986 and the Revenue Act of 1987 substantially reduced both corporate and individual tax rates, the top rates still approximate one-third of taxable income.

Traditionally, long-term capital gains have received preferential tax treatment. Prior to 1986, corporations paid a minimum tax of 28 percent on net, long-term capital gains and individuals paid a maximum rate of 20 percent. The avowed purpose of capital gains preference rates was to encourage investment in long-term capital assets such as real estate and production equipment for businesses, securities, and real property for individuals. Presumably such investment in long-term capital assets furthers economic growth in the country and for years was considered beneficial to everyone. In 1986, however, with the advent of what was purported to be a complete rewrite of the tax system, among many other changes, Congress saw fit to eliminate preferential treatment for long-term investments. Capital gains tax rates disappeared. Gains on the sale of capital assets became taxable at the same rates as those applied to any other income.

Under lobbying pressure from wealthy investors and large, corporate special interest groups, Congress is being pressed to reinstate preferential capital gains rates. Although attempts to pass capital gains legislation in 1989 and 1990 failed, if recent history is an indicator of the future, Congress will probably reduce capital gains rates in 1991 or 1992. There seems to be too much pressure from special interest groups for Congress to leave the rates status quo.

In addition to a potential future tax break for net, long-term capital gains, another advantage in converting ordinary income to capital gains is to use capital losses as offsets, thus reducing the net amount of taxable income. To the extent that an individual has other capital losses, he may net these against capital gains and pay taxes only on the difference. Without the capital gains offset, only $3,000 of such losses are deductible in the current year, although the excess may be carried over to future years. So, from the investor's perspective, the form of income remains an important consideration.

Although creditors gain nothing by the capital gains provisions— interest earned is always ordinary income—equity investors, as well as business owners, must be very conscious of how they structure a financing deal to be certain that as much income as possible is treated as a capital gain. For example, if an investor purchases shares of stock from the corporation and then sells them at a later date at an appreciated value, the income generated is considered capital gains. In the case of initial public offerings or company buy-back provisions, an investor or a partner will pay the lower capital gains rate (if it is then in effect) when he disposes of his holdings. Similarly, a business owner raising capital by selling part of his ownership in the company to partners, a limited partnership, or other investor group, will realize capital gains on the profit. This profit is calculated as the difference between the sale price and the stock's cost basis.

Capital gains also come into play when selling capital assets of the company, such as machinery and equipment, vehicles, furniture and fixtures, patents, or real estate. Although only the gain realized between the sell price of the asset and its original cost will be treated as a capital gain, this is still a tax break. The part of the gain attributable to depreciation taken in prior years is recaptured and treated as ordinary income, however, so the break isn't as great as it might seem. Profits made on the sale of inventory, of course, are always ordinary income.

The reinstatement of capital gains rates will afford the opportunity to reduce the tax burden of both investors and business owners trying to arrange financing schemes through the careful planning and precise timing of financing transactions.

Timing

Proper timing of financing can also have an impact on an entrepreneur's tax bill. Some Code provisions still allow profits on the sale of capital assets to be spread over the years that payments are received from the buyer. This is called an installment sale. The gain reported each year against payments received is calculated by multiplying the payment by the gross profit percentage from the total sale. The gross profit is determined by subtracting the cost basis of the asset from its sell price. The character of income reported on the installment basis remains the same as if the total gain was reported in one year. If the profit is ordinary income, it will be treated as ordinary income each year payments are received. If it qualifies as a capital gain, then it is treated as a capital gain each year.

Benefits of deferred payments accrue to the seller by being allowed to spread his income over a period of years, thus affording at least the possibility of lower tax rates. Of course, a change in the laws could occur and result in a higher rate later on, but that's a normal business risk. Installment sales are especially helpful to a financially troubled company when raising new capital by disposing of some of its assets. For other financing schemes, timing has little impact on the business owner. For the investor, however, the same installment sale rules applied to the disposal of his shareholdings or partnership interest, might be very important and should be recognized when planning a getting out position.

Using an "S" corporation

In spite of congressional efforts to penalize the private business owner, there are still advantages for closely held corporations to being taxed as an S corporation. Nearly every time Congress changes the tax laws, some advantages disappear while others materialize. It's hard to know what they will come up with next. Currently, however, there remains one overwhelming advantage in using the S election: All income or losses of the corporation are passed directly through to shareholders for inclusion in their personal returns. New regulations resulting from the tax legislation in 1986 and 1987 limit the deductibility of corporate losses on personal returns, however. If a shareholder plays a passive role, and does not participate in a material way in the operations of the corporation, such as an outside investor, losses are only deductible to the extent that they offset passive income from other sources. Passive shareholders cannot use S corporation losses to offset other earned income. This stumbling block is referred to as a "passive activity loss" and is explained more completely a little later in this chapter. The disadvantages to nonactive shareholders of investing in an S corporation might force the business owner to convert back to a C corporation if he wants to raise capital through this source. Be aware, however, of the built-in gains provisions.

An S corporation receives the same tax treatment as a partnership. Income or losses pass through the corporation to the shareholders in the same form as they are in the corporation. Interest income to the corporation remains interest income to the shareholders. Capital gains remains capital gains. Ordinary income remains ordinary income. Each shareholder receives the same proportion of each type of income or loss that shares held bear to the total shares outstanding. This pass-through occurs whether cash is distributed or not. If cash is not distributed until later years, it is done so tax free at that time because the tax on earnings has already been paid. Because the corporation pays no tax at all, there can be no double taxation.

Cash can only be distributed in the same proportion as stock holdings, however, whether or not the shareholders are active or passive. For example, if there are several shareholders in your company, but you are the only active participant and own 60 percent of the shares, for every dollar distributed over and above salaries and bonuses, 40 cents must go to other shareholders.

All shareholders must agree to the S election. It is a simple procedure requiring only the filing of Form 2553 with the IRS. Except for very unusual circumstances, permission is always granted. There are three problems to be aware of in making the election, however:

1. The form must be filed within 75 days of the beginning of the tax year to which the election applies.

2. If the corporation reverts back to be taxed as a standard or C corporation at a later time, it must wait a full five years to once again make the S election.

3. If a C corporation converts to an S corporation and the S corporation sells its business assets within 10 years of the election, built-in gains provisions apply.

Making an S election should not be done without a well-thought-out tax plan that anticipates: (1) the amount and type of income the company might generate in the future; (2) the other income or losses you, as an individual, might earn independent of the company; and (3) whether your plans include selling either assets of the company or the entire company in the foreseeable future. It makes no sense to vacillate back and forth between S and C corporations. Once the election is made, it's far more costly and less beneficial to cancel the election than never to make it in the first place.

Another law that penalizes the small businessowner is a built-in gains provision in the Code. To discourage business owners from trying to avoid double taxation by using the S election, these provisions specify that if assets are sold within ten years from the date of conversion from a C corporation to an S corporation, the corporation itself—not its shareholders—will be taxed on any gain realized between the tax basis of the asset and its fair market value at the time of the election. This means two things: (1) the gain is taxed at potentially higher corporate rates; and (2) when the cash realized from the sale is distributed, it is taxed again to the shareholders as a dividend.

For cash basis corporations it is even worse. An S election conversion creates built-in gains to the corporation, and hence is taxed at corporate rates, even if the company is not sold in its entirety. For example, if any asset owned by the corporation is sold within the 10-year period, the corporation pays a tax on the difference between the tax basis and its fair market value at the date of the election. This tax is in addition to that levied on shareholders for the gain on selling the asset.

It should be noted that the built-in gains provisions apply only to the sale of assets—not the sale of the corporation's stock by its shareholders. In spite of these insidious built-in gains provisions, an S election can still be a viable tax savings device, and hopefully, within the near future, enough pressure will be placed on Congress to modify current inequitable provisions.

Getting back to the problem of double taxation; because in an S corporation all income, including gains on selling its assets, are passed through to its shareholders, you'll never need to worry about paying double taxes (except for potential built-in gains). S corporations are especially useful in small retail or personal service businesses when the corporate form of doing business makes sense for legal or other non-tax reasons. The S election provides a way to operate the business as a proprietorship or partnership for tax purposes and still benefit from the protection of the corporate shield.

If you are contemplating a multiple corporation hierarchy, bear in mind that a corporation owning 80 percent or more of the shares of another corporation cannot use the S election. In fact, if the acquiring corporation is currently an S corporation, and acquires 80 percent or more of the stock in another company, it loses its election the day before the deal closes. Therefore, if the parent company is an S corporation, and the decision is made to buy another company, it must be purchased through a different vehicle—the entrepreneur himself, a separate partnership, or a different corporation. On the other hand, the parent S corporation can buy assets rather than stock and still retain its S election.

Income splitting

Although only indirectly related to raising capital, one of the features of an S corporation every entrepreneur should be aware of is the advantage of using the income-splitting mechanism. This reduces the total tax liability of the corporation's income. For example, assume you are the sole shareholder of an S corporation, and report all the profits and losses of the company on your personal return. This level of income results in a personal tax rate of 33 percent. It might be advantageous to spread the company's income among several members of your family and let each person pay taxes on his or her share of the earnings. Conceivably, several members will have less total income than you and the tax rate could be 15 or 28 percent instead of 33 percent. This could be a significant tax savings.

To take advantage of income splitting, all you need to do is issue shares to each of your family members, either from your own holdings or direct from the corporation. If the corporation issues new shares, however, some type of consideration must be given. This could be in the form of a person's time, effort, advice, or actual work. If you use your own shares, you can give the shares away without consideration and without any tax effect. If the corporation has losses, however, care must be taken to avoid the passive activity rules which are reviewed later in this chapter.

Foreign tax credits

If the corporation is involved in international trade, chances are that at some time some foreign country will impose taxes on the company's business conducted in that country. Toward the end of this chapter, we'll take a look at the entire foreign tax issue, but for now we're only concerned with S corporations. Foreign taxes paid by an S corporation pass through as such to the shareholders in the same way as capital gains or interest income. Shareholders can then treat such foreign tax payments as foreign tax credits on individual returns. As with other provisions in the Code, an exception exists here also. An S corporation that is a shareholder in a foreign corporation is not eligible for either a deduction for foreign taxes paid or a foreign tax credit. Therefore, in this case, no pass-through to shareholders is allowed.

Prior to the Tax Reform Act of 1986, foreign losses were allowed; however, now they are not. If a C corporation with foreign losses now becomes an S corporation, or the other way around—going from an S to a C corporation—recapture rules come into play. Deductions taken for foreign losses in the past must now be recaptured and reported as income. For purposes of computing the amount of foreign losses that must be recaptured under these rules, the making or termination of an S election is treated as a disposition of the business and appropriate tax rules apply.

The S corporation has definitely come back into vogue and should be carefully considered as a viable tax saving mechanism. Just remember, the election must be made early in the tax year and you can't go back and forth between an S and a C corporation. Also, you should be aware that using a holding corporation to own more than 80 percent of the stock of an operating company negates the S election.

A business operated as a proprietorship or a partnership, however, need not worry about double taxation. All income from the business is taxed to the business owner on Schedule C of individual Form 1040 or to partners as partnership income on Schedule E. All business cash belongs to the owners and there are no problems with the classification of income or timing.

Using a partnership

A business owner has several options available in structuring a business—corporation, partnership, limited partnership, or proprietorship. Each form encourages different financing alternatives. Company structure and ownership not only play an important financing role, but dictate different options to minimize taxes for a business owner as well as outside investors. We've already seen some of the advantages of using an S corporation under certain circumstances. A partnership can also create flexibility in both ownership and management of diverse product lines or activities in a growth business. Chapter 7 reviews standard partnerships, and chapter 8 covers limited partnerships and explores methods for raising capital through these organization structures. The tax impact on both the business owner and potential partners should be carefully weighed against the benefits of using either of these modes.

A partnership for tax purposes is an organization owned by two or more taxpayers as defined at common law, but also a syndicate, group, pool, joint venture, or other unincorporated organization that carries on a trade or business and which is not, within the meaning of the tax code, a trust, estate, or corporation. A limited partnership that has more corporate than partnership characteristics is treated as a corporation for tax purposes unless it obtains a ruling from the IRS to be treated as a partnership. Such corporate characteristics are defined as:

- The owners are associates with one another.
- The objective of the organization is to carry on a trade or business and divide the profits.
- The organization has continuity of life beyond its individual owners.
- There is a centralization of management.
- The liability for debts of the organization is limited to the property owned by the organization.
- There is free transferability of ownership interests.

If a limited partnership or other organization exhibits a majority of these characteristics (four or more of them), then it is treated as a corporation for tax purposes; otherwise it is treated as a partnership.

Partnership income must be computed in the same way and on the same basis as the taxable income of an individual except that certain items of gain or loss are stated separately, such as:

- short-term capital gains and losses;
- long-term capital gains and losses;
- gains and losses from sales or exchanges of Section 1231 property;
- charitable contributions;
- dividends excluded under Sections 116-247;
- taxes paid or accrued to foreign countries; and
- certain other exclusions.

Moreover, the following items are not allowed as deductions to the partnership:

- personal exemptions
- foreign taxes
- net operating losses
- charitable contributions
- individual's itemized deductions
- capital loss carryovers
- depletion

Distributions to partners

A partnership never pays any income taxes. All income and losses are passed through to the individual partners for inclusion in their personal tax returns. Losses are also passed through, but the "at risk" provisions limit the deductibility of such losses on partners' returns. Profits and losses are reported by each partner regardless of whether or not cash or other property is distributed. When cash or other property is distributed, it is tax free. A partner's tax liability is based on the profit or loss of the partnership, not the amount of cash he receives. The only exception to this rule occurs when the partnership agreement calls for a partner to receive fixed payments regardless of the profit or loss of the partnership. These payments are the same as wages and must be included in the partner's personal return. Because they are guaranteed payable regardless of the profitability of the partnership, they are treated as if they were compensation paid to an outsider. As such, they are deductible to the partnership in arriving at its profit or loss.

The basis for each partner's share of the partnership is accounted for by a partner's capital account. Initially, this capital account will be increased for the amount of cash, or property, that the partner contributes to the partnership in return for his partnership interest. Each year, his share of the partnership profits are charged to his capital account and increase the balance. Losses are credited to the account and reduce the balance. When distributions of cash or other property are made, the partner's capital account is reduced by the amount he receives. Guaranteed fixed payments are the exception to this rule. Because they are treated as salary, they do not affect a partner's capital account. The balance in his capital account at any point in time is called his adjusted basis. A partner can increase his adjusted basis in three ways:

1. by making additional capital contributions to the partnership;
2. by not drawing profits out of the partnership in cash or property; or
3. by an increase in partnership liabilities for which the partner is personally liable.

A partner's adjusted basis comes into play when either of two conditions occur: (1) when the partnership has losses to be reported by the partner on his personal return; and (2) when he sells his partnership interest.

Reporting partnership losses

A partner's share of partnership operating losses, which he can take as deductions on his personal return, are limited by "at risk" provisions in the Code. "At risk" provisions specify that the deductibility of a partner's share of the partnership loss is limited to the amount of money the partner has at risk in the business and could actually lose from a partnership activity. In other words, such losses are only deductible to the extent that they do not exceed the sum of the partner's adjusted basis plus any amounts borrowed for use by the partnership for which the partner has personal liability or has pledged personal assets. This provision was specifically designed to prevent a taxpayer from using partnership tax shelter losses to reduce taxable income from other sources. Although presumably enacted to close a loophole used by wealthy investors, it also penalizes the average business partner by preventing benefits from very legitimate partnership operating losses.

This normally isn't a major hurdle for standard business partnerships, however, because operating partners are seldom free from liability for debts of the company. Also, loans from a partner to his company qualify as an addition to his adjusted basis, so if it appears that the company will have a loss in any one year, and a partner's adjusted basis will not cover his share, a partner can always loan the company money—with interest of course—to cover the discrepancy.

Selling a partnership interest

The second condition impacted by a partner's adjusted basis is when he sells his interest in the business, either to other partners or to an outsider. A partnership interest is a capital asset, therefore, a profit realized on the sale of this interest is a capital gain to the partner excluding that which is allocable to inventory, receivables, or other noncapital assets of the partnership. The proportionate gain assignable to a partner's interest in these assets is treated as ordinary income.

The amount of gain on the sale is calculated as the difference between the adjusted basis and the selling price of the interest. If the adjusted basis is zero, the entire price paid is a gain. If, however, the adjusted basis is negative—less than zero—then the gain becomes the entire selling price of the interest, plus the amount that the partner's adjusted basis is less than zero. If the partner has loaned the company money, or if he or she is personally liable for company debts, then these amounts must be added to the partner's capital account in determining the adjusted basis for calculating the gain on the sale just as with the reporting of partnership losses. As a footnote, even if a partner does not sell an interest, if money is distributed above the adjusted basis, this excess will be treated as if the interest was sold and the appropriate form of gain must be reported on the partner's personal return.

New rules for passive activity losses

Prior to the Tax Reform Act of 1986, millions of taxpayers were taking advantage of losses from partnership, limited partnership, and S corporation tax shelters to offset other earned income. In fact, the major selling point in marketing units in limited partnerships was that losses could be used to offset other income of the investor, and in this way get Uncle Sam, in essence, to pay for the investment with tax savings. Now, the Code clearly differentiates between a person who is an active participant in a business and one who is merely a passive investor.

An active participant in a limited partnership has no difficulty deducting partnership losses against other earned income under the same provisions a shareholder would follow as a shareholder in an S corporation. The passive investor does have a problem, however. Section 469 of the Code classifies the losses sustained by a passive investor as passive activity losses or PALs.

The idea behind Section 469 made sense at the time it was written. It was an attempt to close a very costly loophole in the Code as part of the justification for the overall reduction in tax rates. Taxpayers could continue to invest in tax shelters through limited partnerships or other structures but could not deduct losses against other earned income. The argument went that without a limitation on tax shelters, the revenue to generate rate reductions could not be realized. As with many features of the Code, however, the IRS has interpreted Section 469 just the reverse of what Congress intended. With a myriad of statutory rules and administrative regulations, the IRS, with its zeal to limit the creation of passive income available to offset PALs, has enacted interpretive rules so complex and so difficult to administer that the reverse effect has occurred. Namely, that regulations defining active participation are now far easier to comply with than Congress ever imagined.

The rules governing PALs fall under three broad categories: a definition of the activity as passive or active, recharacterization rules, and material participation rules. Interestingly, the first two restrict passive income—not passive losses—which wasn't the intent of Congress at all. Generally, a passive activity is either a rental activity or a trade or business activity in which the taxpayer does not actively participate.

Definitions of material participation are so complex that it cannot be said that all nonactive limited partners are passive investors. One definition, for example, indicates that if a taxpayer spends 100 hours a year actively doing something in the business, he or she qualifies as an active participant. This amounts to 2 hours a week and can be fulfilled by board of directors policy sessions, answering a telephone, writing letters, making bank deposits, or general consultation, among any number of other activities.

Even definitions of rental activities as passive are not clear-cut. The regulations list six conditions exempting a rental activity from the passive activity rules. One example deals with tangible property owned by the company, such as a condo in the Caribbean, which is rented to customers or clients during the year. The income from this rental is not considered passive rental income if it is incidental to a nonrental activity involving property held for investment or property used in a trade or business. Recharacterization rules are even worse, as the following two examples illustrate.

1. *Significant participation rule.* Net income from a significant participation activity is treated as nonpassive income even though a loss from such activity would be a passive loss.

2. *Self-enhanced rental property rule.* Net rental income, including any gain from the disposition of rental property, is nonpassive if (a) the gain on disposition occurs during the taxable year; (b) the use of the property in the rental activity commences less than 12 months prior to the date of disposition; and (c) the taxpayer materially or significantly participates in an activity that involves the performance of services for the purpose of enhancing the value of such property.

The calculation of PAL offsets, appropriate planning to avoid PALs, or further explanation of additional special rules affecting the handling and definitions of PALs are far too complex to be included in a book of this scope. Just knowing that Section 469 and passive activity losses exist, however, puts the business owner on the alert when contemplating a limited partnership to raise capital. By staying alert to major changes in the regulations, and in the Code itself, the business owner might be able to take advantage of changes affecting PALs that are bound to occur in the next year or two. The PAL has professional tax advisors so confused and upset with the IRS that it appears to be just a matter of time before further changes are enacted to at least clarify the law.

Foreign taxes

Increasingly, American companies, large and small, are finding that burgeoning foreign markets offer opportunities far in excess of those found domestically. Methods for financing export programs and overseas business facilities are discussed in chapters 12 and 13. Before entering the global market, however, it's important to be certain the company is structured properly to minimize the tax impact of foreign income as well as to gain the greatest benefits from financing programs. There are five broad categories in the tax laws relevant to an American company doing business overseas:

1. U.S. taxes imposed on worldwide income of American companies.
2. Foreign tax credits.
3. Foreign sales corporations.
4. Controlled foreign corporations.
5. Foreign personal holding companies.

As a general rule, a U.S. company must report income from all sources—domestic and foreign. Taxes are paid on this total income regardless of the tax laws in, or taxes paid to, foreign countries. Most developed countries, and many developing nations, have negotiated tax treaties with the United States. A negative fallout of these treaties is that a foreign government agrees to provide the IRS information about a company's business in their country so that the IRS can perform complete audits of American taxpayers. In other words, with tax treaties in place, it is difficult for an American corporation to hide foreign income from the IRS. On the other side of the coin, however, U.S. tax laws allow either a deduction on the corporation's return or a credit against the corporation's tax for income taxes paid or accrued to a foreign government with whom there is a tax treaty. The only real restriction is that the foreign tax must be an income tax or substantially equivalent to an income tax. If it is not, then no deduction or credit is allowed.

Foreign Sales Corporations (FSCs) replace the old Domestic International Sales Corporation (DISC) as a means of reducing tax liabilities on export sales. As long as the FSC is established in a qualifying country and both the FSC and the domestic parent corporation comply with the rigid requirements for documentation imposed by the Code, using an FSC can save up to 15 percent of taxes on income generated through export sales. Chapter 12 explores the ramifications of FSCs in greater depth.

Controlled Foreign Corporation and Foreign Personal Holding Company regulations apply to the establishment of subsidiaries of domestic corporations in foreign locations. The applicable regulations attempt to restrict American companies from hiding income in foreign locations or otherwise skirting U.S. tax laws. Chapter 13, which deals with raising capital to finance an expansion overseas, provides further information on the tax ramifications of these two subjects. Any entrepreneur seriously considering establishing an overseas presence should read *Tap the Hidden Wealth in Your Business*, which explains how to set up and manage foreign corporations to avoid, or at the least, minimize the stringent, inequitable provisions of the U.S. tax laws applicable to foreign income.

Liquidations

Many financially distressed companies find that the best way to restructure their company to raise capital is to first complete a partial liquidation. Prior to 1986, the owner of a privately held corporation could liquidate the assets of his company under Sections 334(b) and 337 of the Code tax free and distribute the liquidation proceeds to the shareholders. This was used effectively to rid the prior company of stranglehold liens and allow the business owner to use extra assets for additional collateral. Now, however, with the repeal of this "General Utilities Doctrine," conditions have changed. In a complete corporate liquidation, all assets of the company will be deemed to have been sold at the assets' fair market value, and any gain over this amount will be taxable income. No gain or loss will be recognized, however, to the extent that there is nonrecognition of gain or loss under tax-free reorganization provisions. There are exclusions: (1) no gain or loss is recognized when property of a subsidiary is distributed 100 percent to its parent; and (2) a corporate buyer and a seller of a controlled subsidiary will be entitled to treat the sale of the subsidiary's stock as a sale of its underlying assets.

The sale of a product line, major production assets, a division, or a subsidiary of a company, such as might occur when raising capital for a financially distressed company, do not fall under the corporate liquidation provisions. These sales are treated the same as the sale of any business asset and reflect appropriate capital gain, or ordinary income, treatment. A financially distressed corporation can, however, go one step further and actually dismantle part of its business to raise capital. This is treated as a "partial liquidation" under the Code. Generally, there must be a partial liquidation plan in existence, and the partial liquidation must occur in the same year as the plan date.

Although there is no general definition of partial liquidation in the Code, the law does provide a sort of "safe harbor" rule. Under this rule, distribution will qualify as a partial liquidation if it is attributable to the corporation's ceasing to conduct a business that it actively conducted for at least five years ending with the date of distribution and if the corporation continues to conduct at least one other trade or business immediately after the distribution. Gains on partial liquidations are not recognized by the corporation. Special rules relating to depreciable property may or may not apply depending on the circumstances. The rules are very complicated and a business owner contemplating a partial liquidation to raise capital should understand the tax implications of his actions before entering into the transaction.

Summary

To sum up the special tax considerations we've looked at in this chapter: the most important aspect of tax planning, whether for raising capital or for any other business transaction, is to engage and continually consult a competent tax advisor who is well versed in corporate tax transactions. Don't rely on someone who prepares your individual tax return to be up to speed on corporate matters. Find a qualified tax attorney, or CPA, who can demonstrate that he specializes in corporate tax matters and does not handle taxes as a part-time endeavor. Many entrepreneurs have been fooled into believing that just because a person prepares individual tax returns he is an expert in all tax matters. Nothing could be further from the truth. You're far better off spending the money to get qualified, experienced tax counsel than to skimp and end up making costly errors in your tax planning.

This chapter has covered the following topics relating to tax ramifications of financing alternatives:

1. The character and tax consequences of cash payments or withdrawals from the company have been examined including dividends, interest payments on loans to the business, and a return of capital.

2. The characterization of income as ordinary income or capital gains has been discussed. Although currently, there is no difference in tax rates, it seems inevitable that Congress will once again change its mind and enact legislation that favors capital gains.

3. Timing the transaction is an important consideration to investors. The chapter looked at the benefit of spreading income over a period of years by the use of installment sales techniques.

4. The S corporation can be an effective way to spread income and reduce tax rates, however, built-in gains provisions tend to modify these advantages.

5. Structuring the business as a partnership rather than a corporation can be both beneficial and risky. The tax treatment of partnership profits and losses and of selling a partnership interest was examined.

6. Passive activity losses under the current laws have tended to reduce the effectiveness of selling limited partnership units as a tax shelter to wealthy individuals and some examples of excludable conditions were explored.

7. For any business owner seriously considering an export program, or establishing a presence overseas, the tax impact of generating foreign income, and the taxes paid to foreign governments, must be carefully entered into any expansion equation.

8. For a financially distressed company, a partial liquidation of assets might be the only way to recapitalize the entity and the tax ramifications of doing this were explored.

Federal income taxes, especially as applied to business transactions, are many and complex. A complete examination is far beyond the scope of this book. Although there are many less important rules and regulations that have not been covered, these eight areas seem to be the most bothersome for entrepreneurs as they begin the process of refinancing, or otherwise raising outside capital for their business. Once a competent tax advisor has been consulted, the next step in raising new capital is to construct a financing plan, which is covered in chapter 4.

4

Preparing
a financing plan

TIM HOLGREN AND SUE SCHNELL JOINED FORCES IN THE EARLY SEVENTIES TO
start an automobile dealership near Cincinnati. In the beginning, they sold
Volkswagens, but later, as the market for VWs declined, they changed to
Oldsmobiles and Saabs. By the mid-eighties, business was booming and
the partners realized it was time to expand. Always optimistic, they opted
for two additional dealerships: one near Dayton and the other in Louisville. Initial estimates revealed that $5 million would be needed to get both
businesses off the ground. Armed with a three-page description of how
the money would be spent, Tim approached the Cincinnati office of the
SBA for a loan. Four weeks, several interviews, and what seemed like a
ream of applications, verifications, and justifications later, the partners ran
into a stone wall.

Several years earlier, Tim and I had belonged to the same golf club.
Knowing I had worked with mutual business acquaintances to raise capital, Tim asked for help. Following my recommendation, Tim and Sue hired
a local CPA to assist in preparing a financing plan before resubmission of
their application. In another 30 days, armed with a complete, fully documented and professionally prepared financing plan, the partners succeeded in landing a direct loan from the SBA plus investor financing for

54

both the Louisville and the Dayton locations. Within six months, the new dealerships were opened.

Probably the greatest mistake a business owner can make when trying to raise outside capital is to conduct the search without a well-thought-out, fully documented, professionally prepared financing plan. Few marketing or production-oriented entrepreneurs take kindly to the task of laboriously thinking through and then committing to paper, precisely how they expect to apply the financing; and then how and when they plan to pay it back. It's much easier to talk about broad generalizations, such as the need for working capital, a new facility, or competitive advantages they could gain by starting an export program. With characteristic optimism, most business owners genuinely believe that they will be able to pay back all borrowed or invested funds when due. Their managerial abilities preclude the possibility of anything going wrong, and they have difficulty understanding why the lender or investor doesn't believe them when told of the obvious opportunities to earn income.

On the other hand, lenders and investors are a cautious lot. From their perspective, it makes no sense to loan or invest funds on the whim of an entrepreneur. Too many times, optimistic expectations have a way of becoming financial disasters. The one constant in the business world is that if anything can go wrong, it will. Additionally, once funds are received, the recipient often forgets the optimism his verbalizations produced in the beginning. Without something concrete to prove initial promises, a lender or investor has nothing to fall back on for leverage in encouraging the entrepreneur to perform as promised.

For these reasons, few lenders or investors will commit funds without a fully documented plan describing in detail how the capital will be used and what business conditions can be expected to exist in the future allowing repayment. In the parlance of the financial community, such a document is referred to as a financing plan.

Business plans, strategic plans, operating plans, prospectuses, and many other types of forecasts and documented expectations permeate the business community. Every time the business owner turns around someone seems to be asking for another plan of one type or another. While all contribute to the efficacy of business management, the financing plan assumes slightly different connotations than the others. It is a commitment by the owner to use someone else's money to take a specific action and serves as his commitment, or promise, to repay. As such, the financing plan must be prepared in the format and language of financiers and be conservative enough to ensure a high probability of being achieved. It's the same as the owner signing a legally binding contract to perform. Furthermore, it is a definitive requirement for obtaining outside financing from any source.

Although a financing plan is similar to a business plan, there are several important differences. The commitment to repay and the use of language familiar to financiers are two critical differences. In addition, a financing plan is much shorter than a business plan. It is not as inclusive and concentrates on the financial aspects of the business rather than the company's marketing, production, engineering, or personnel activities. A financing plan emphasizes the cash flow history and the potential for the future generation of cash rather than market or sales growth. Another important difference is that although a typical business plan includes personal profiles of key managers, they are brief and explanatory. In a financing plan, however, one of the most crucial elements is proof that the business owner has the financial responsibility, managerial expertise, and strength of character to convince the lender or investor that he will be personally responsible for the repayment of the loan or investment—regardless of personal guarantees.

Some financing sources require slight variations in both format and content of the financing plan. An offering prospectus must meet the requirements of the Securities and Exchange Commission for a public stock offering. Applications for industrial revenue bonds must follow the special format defined by the specific issuing body and they are all slightly different. Investment bankers and venture capitalists want to see calculations of what cash a public stock offering might bring in the future. Offerings for limited partnerships, except for private issues, must follow regulations specified by the state of business residency, and they all have small variations in format. Bid packages for government contract work take on a completely different profile. Explanations and examples of the types of plans for submission to each of these sources are included in the appropriate chapters that follow.

Although it is impossible to review the precise format requirements of a financing plan for every conceivable source of funds, there are common elements each require, and fortunately, these vary only slightly between sources. Later in this chapter, examples illustrate how to construct a typical plan, which can be used for either debt or equity financing.

The key elements

A financing plan consists of five sections:

1. Description of ownership and capitalization
2. Description of product, service, markets, and competition
3. Historical financial statements
4. Pro forma financial statements
5. Evidence of owner's managerial ability to perform

Though no prescribed length prevails, usually 25 to 50 typed pages are necessary to fully ensure a comprehensive presentation.

Every financial plan should begin with a preamble—a brief, one or two paragraph explanation of how much capital is requested and how the funds will be used. This should be a quick look only and not an in-depth explanation. Following the preamble, the first section in the body of the plan should include a complete description of the structure of the owner-ship and management of the company. The following questions must be answered truthfully and completely:

1. Is the company owned and managed by a single individual?
2. Are other managers available with specific expertise?
3. How does the company manage its cash—what internal controls exist?
4. If there are two or more partners, how are responsibilities split?
5. Has there been a change in ownership or management during the past five years?
6. If so, why, and what changes?
7. Are family members employed? In what positions?
8. Is there an outside board of directors? What are the members' personal credentials?
9. Are there any minority shareholders? What are their roles in the company?
10. Has the company ever been in severe financial trouble such as a Chapter 11 bankruptcy?
11. Have the owners ever filed personal bankruptcy?
12. What references can be offered to prove financial viability and integrity of the owner(s)?
13. What is the business structure—corporation, partnership, proprietorship, or other?
14. What are the respective ownership shares?
15. What are the owners willing to pledge as personal collateral outside of the business as evidenced by personal financial statements?

This introductory section provides the financier with a detailed picture of how the company is structured, and the financial viability of its owners. If a business can't pass the muster at this stage, there is no need to go further. No lender or investor will provide funding to a business owned by individuals who cannot provide concrete evidence of personal financial responsibility. Although unfortunate, and certainly unfair in many cases, if either an individual owner, or his business, have been through the bankruptcy courts, most lenders or investors frown on taking a risk with their money. Of course, exceptions exist. Perhaps the bankruptcy was intentional and short-lived. Maybe extenuating circumstances forced such a drastic measure. In some cases, force majeure events such as a flood, fire, riot, hurricane, or tornado mandated a bankruptcy action to forestall collapse. These conditions will normally be accepted as beyond the control of the owner(s) and unlikely to happen again. Generally, however, a lender or investor will insist that certain safeguards be built into the financing agreement, which they would not otherwise require, such as a more stringent personal guarantee or outside co-guarantors.

Although it can be unfair, a history of financial difficulty always raises doubts about the owner or business being able to perform as promised in the future. More than one entrepreneur, faced with such barricades to raising capital, must resort to the techniques described in chapter 14 for restructuring financially troubled companies.

The second topic covered in the introductory section deals with the current capitalization of the company. Capitalization refers to the structure of debt and equity forming the current foundation for operating the business. Just as with a house or other building, the foundation provides support for everything built on top of it. The same holds true in a business. Equity contributed and debt borrowed provide the money to support the inventory, machinery, equipment, real estate, and other assets. Capital reserves also provide cash to operate the business while waiting to collect receivables. A lender or investor wants to know right up front, what existing debt and outside equity the business is obligated to repay—as well as any repayment terms already contracted for—and how much of the equity came from the owner. Answers to the following questions must be included in this section:

Regarding current loans outstanding

1. What loans are currently on the balance sheet?
2. To whom are they payable and what are the interest rates and repayment terms?
3. What business or personal assets have been used as collateral to these loans?
4. Are there early repayment penalties?
5. What are the relationships between the owner and these lenders? Amicable, adversarial, indifferent?
6. How well does the owner know the loan officers handling his account?
7. Has there ever been any problem in complying with the lenders' reporting requirements or other covenants?

8. Is the business currently in default on any loans?

9. Has the owner sought to fulfill his new capital needs through these lenders?

10. If yes, what was their response and why was the request turned down? If not, why not?

Regarding equity

1. Who are the passive investors, if any?

2. What assets have they taken as collateral, if any?

3. What are the terms of any equity agreements?

4. Can the equity holders call their investment?

5. What instruments are used, and what provisions do they carry: voting or nonvoting common stock, preferred stock (callable or convertible), dividend provisions (fixed yield, cumulative, or other), warrants, options, convertibles, and so on?

6. Are there any dividends in arrears?

7. Any restrictive covenants?

8. Was the placement of this equity private or public?

9. Why hasn't additional capital been requested from these sources?

Product/service, markets, competition

The next section of the plan should fully describe major products or services offered for sale, the markets into which they are sold, and the competition. Although at first glance this section appears to be the easiest for most business owners to handle, the presentation should be substantially different from either a business plan, strategic plan, or offering prospectus. It's important to remember that the reader of a financing plan might be a lender or investor with virtually no background in the type of markets or products of the company. On the other hand, he might be a sophisticated investment banker or a potential partner who has substantial familiarity with the business. Therefore, the owner must be careful to couch his descriptive narrative in terms readily identifiable to the uninitiated and still comprehensive enough to interest those well versed in his industry.

The trickiest part usually covers the products or services offered for sale. While describing an accounting software program sold through mail order channels might be relatively easy, explaining a line of new high technology silicone chips to a lender without a computer background could be a herculean task. Nevertheless, the success in selling a financing plan often hinges on how clearly the financier can visualize the company's products.

When elaborating on the structure, size, and share of a company's market, it's important to keep the dialogue simple. Most business owners are so familiar with the intricacies and characteristics of their market that they forget that, to an outsider, learning the vernacular is a new experience. A 22.7 percent market share might be relevant to the owner, but to a lender, 20 percent or 25 percent is just as meaningful. Market fluctuations influenced by fractional changes in nonresidential construction indicators might help a sales manager gauge market acceptance of a new product line, but to a lender or investor unversed in market economics, this might be merely an added paragraph to wade through.

On the other hand, every lender or investor wants to know about competition. Especially if competitors are known entities, such as General Motors, AT&T, or IBM. For lesser known competitors, brief descriptions of the companies, their locations, ownership, and size often prove helpful to understanding the applicant's market strength. Regardless of the tact employed, market competition can be a crucial determinant in the financier's mind when judging whether or not the applicant can perform as promised. The prevalent perception in the financial community is that if a business owner does not understand his company's competition, in-depth, or cannot describe competitors clearly, he or she probably isn't a very good manager, and therefore, a bad risk.

Historical financial statements

Many private business owners, especially small businesses, hate to keep financial records. There's something mysterious, dull, and unproductive about income and expenses, assets and liabilities, cash flow, and general ledgers. It's much more fun supervising the shop, talking to customers, or being in the field selling a product. "I'll worry about financial records when it's time to do the tax return, but that's all," is as common in the world of closely held companies as beer and popcorn is at baseball games. Many entrepreneurs get by for years without worrying about financial statements or audit reports. But when it comes time to go after outside financing, it's a different story.

Regardless of how long the company has been in existence—one month to several years—any lender or investor will insist on historical financial statements as part of the financing plan. The source of outside capital is immaterial. Whether you borrow from a bank, the SBA, or other government agencies; whether you sell stock to the public or a share of the business to a partner; whether you apply for a foundation grant or structure a limited partnership, nothing can be done without historical financial statements.

Historical financial statements included in a financing plan must consist of balance sheets, income statements, and statements of cash flow.

These statements can only be prepared if you have a set of accounting records maintained according to what the accounting fraternity calls generally accepted accounting principles (GAAP). Most private business owners do not have an accounting background, and even if they do, they are not interested in spending their own time and effort compiling volumes of numbers. The best solution might be to hire an outside bookkeeper to keep the records on a daily basis and then bring in an outside public accountant—CPA or otherwise—to prepare monthly, quarterly, or annual financial statements. Some fund-raising activities, such as public stock issues, stipulate that annual financial statements for at least two years prior to the issue must be audited by a CPA. If this seems to be a viable source of capital for you, hiring a CPA early in the game might save a bundle of money and grief later on. If formal accounting records are not maintained on a regular basis, hire the appropriate personnel to start the process right now. Without financial statements, raising outside capital is impossible.

Pro forma financial statements

Probably the most difficult section of the financing plan for most business owners—pro forma financial statements—is also the most important. This section is the owner's one and only chance to show how much cash flow will be generated, and therefore, how and when the money will be repaid to the lender or investor. The term pro forma as used in financial circles means a forecast of what the financial statements will look like in the future after receiving the proposed financing. In other words, what effect will the additional cash have on the financial performance of the business. As with historical financial statements, if you have any reservation about your capability or technical competence to prepare such pro forma statements, engage a qualified CPA to do the job. It's well worth the money and could be the deciding factor in raising the capital. Later on in this chapter, we'll take a look at how and where to locate qualified accounting, legal, and consulting professionals to assist in preparing not only pro forma statements, but the entire financing plan.

A typical set of pro forma statements contains balance sheets, income statements, and statements of cash flow. They are normally prepared for five years into the future and include comparisons with actual historical statements for the past three years. Ideally, they are prepared in the same format as your internal statements; but if the application of the new capital results in identifiable changes such as the addition of a new building or an increase in sales from an export program, these elements should be stated separately for ease of understanding. The format of pro forma statements will vary with each specific business and no universal presentation exists. A little later in this chapter, however, we'll take a look at one format that is adaptable to many types of businesses and acceptable to many lenders and investors.

Owner's managerial ability

Smart investors, and most lenders, regard an owner's ability to manage his or her company profitably as the most important criterion in granting funds. The reason is obvious. If money is loaned or invested based on pro forma projections, and if the owner can't provide evidence of his ability to manage the company profitably, the credibility of these projections becomes tainted. It goes without saying that if an investor, lender, or other source of funding doesn't believe you can perform as you say you will in the pro forma forecasts, he certainly won't put money into the company. Yet, time and again, business owners try to convince the financial community of their business acumen with generalization and bravado and very little concrete proof.

What type of proof should be offered? It can come in many forms: What has been the profitability and cash flow of the business? What does the company's current commercial banker think of the owner's abilities? Do the company and the owner have a good public image in the industry? How about community reputation; is the owner known as a shaker and mover or is his or her presence invisible? Has the customer relations and customer service record been exemplary, or do customers buy from the company only because prices are low or because no other convenient source for the product exists?

The perceived abilities of the owner by employees, customers, the community, and the industry to run a successful company might be misleading and not tell the whole story but lenders and investors depend on such public imaging to support their own intuitive judgment. Long before applying for outside capital, a smart business owner will make a concerted effort toward developing a public image at least consistent with community and industry standards, and hopefully, better. So much for the content of the plan. Now it's time to move ahead and look at how a typical plan is formatted and some examples of how to write each section so that it will meet the requirements of the financial community.

A sample financing plan

The Cleanwell Carpet Company (CLECO), produced sales of $5 million and profits of close to 12 percent before taxes. The owner, Jerry Atwell, was proud of the company's expansion over the past seven years from one store to four stores and a warehouse serving two states. With sales continuing to grow, but competition forcing increasing discounts, especially to large-volume customers, Jerry thought it was time to achieve some vertical integration by expanding into the delivery business with his own fleet of trucks. This would enable the company to move the carpets from three suppliers' factory locations to his warehouse, and then to his four stores—

at greatly reduced shipping costs. In fact, he calculated that the company could save over 75 percent of current shipping costs, which should more than offset discounted prices forced by competition. Completing a lease/buy analysis, he determined that purchasing the trucks would be the most economical way to go and he estimated that about $1 million would do the trick.

His CPA, who had prepared his company's annual financial statements for the past four years agreed to help Jerry write the financing plan and prepare the pro forma statements. CLECO's actual financial statements for the past three years should be placed in the exhibits to the financing plan. Now, let's take a look at segments of the financing plan that Jerry and his CPA prepared for raising $1 million in long-term capital. The following was the information in his preamble:

> Cleanwell Carpet Company plans to expand its current business base by initiating its own carpet pick up and delivery service, thus benefiting from substantially reduced outside shipping and delivery costs. To accomplish this task, the company plans to acquire a fleet of trucks for a total cost of $1 million, which is the amount requested in this financing plan.

Section I—Ownership and Current Capitalization

A. In 1978, Cleanwell Carpet Company (CLECO) was incorporated by Jerry Atwell, who started the business in a leased showroom in Devon, Pennsylvania, a suburb of Philadelphia. The company sold a limited selection of high quality carpets and tile, principally to residential customers. Over the years, the company grew and currently is doing slightly over $5 million in annual sales.

Jerry Atwell continues as the principal shareholder, holding 75 percent of the outstanding voting capital shares, categorized as Class A common stock (outstanding shares total 1,500, no par value). His wife, Martha, holds the position of vice president and secretary of the corporation, supervises the accounting and administrative office, and owns 15 percent of the Class A shares. Jerry Atwell's brother-in-law, Richard Jones, vice president and sales manager, owns the other 10 percent. Two years ago, the company required additional capital to open its fourth store and a new Class B, nonvoting common stock (1,000 shares, no par value) was sold to three employees. The combined equity from both classes of common shares currently equals $200,000—$150,000 for Class A and $50,000 for Class B.

Neither class of stock carries any restrictive covenants and no dividends are required. In fact, dividends have never paid on either class. Class B shares are callable at any time by CLECO at current book value, plus a 25 percent premium. Class A shares are not callable. Additional shares are not available for issuance at this time, and Class A and B shareholders have indicated they are not willing to consider a new issue.

No collateral secures either class of common stock.

At this point, Jerry could include a brief description of the backgrounds of his wife and brother-in-law, but because their managerial responsibilities were minor compared to his, he decided this was unnecessary.

> B. CLECO has, from time to time, borrowed short-term funds on demand notes from Fidelity Bank of Philadelphia to handle fluctuating working capital needs. Currently, this operating line shows an outstanding balance of $25,000 secured by a first position on all accounts receivable, which totalled $150,000 on December 31. Interest is charged at prime plus one point. There are no personal guarantees outstanding against these demand notes and no assets are encumbered other than receivables.

> Relations with Fidelity Bank have been amicable; however, CLECO has intentionally kept borrowings to a minimum, utilizing the line only during peak business periods. The bank has indicated a willingness to consider executing a long-term note secured by the fleet of new trucks to be purchased but for diversification purposes the company is seeking these funds elsewhere.

Lenders of all types are usually very touchy about this last point. While many commercial bankers get greedy and prefer to keep a customer under their control by stating a willingness to handle all borrowing needs, a few smart bankers recognize the increased risk to both parties in doing this and encourage spreading the risk to other lenders. From the perspective of a business owner, lumping short-term and long-term borrowings with one source—whether a commercial bank or another source—increases a bank's power over his or her business and diminishes the owner's control. If both short-term and long-term borrowings are necessary, a person is almost always better off to spread the loans between two or more sources, even if it does take more time and effort to locate appropriate ones.

Section II—Services, Markets, and Competition
A. CLECO sells high quality carpets from four retail locations in Devon, Coatesville, and Chadds Ford, Pennsylvania and Wilmington, Delaware. Additionally, the company stocks approximately six months of backup inventory for the four stores at its own warehouse in West Chester, Pennsylvania. Currently, CLECO contracts with a local delivery service to transport carpets from the warehouse to its retail locations and from

these stores to customers. Because carpets are sold f.o.b. the factory, the company pays standard tariff rates for transporting carpet rolls from each of its suppliers' factories to West Chester. By acquiring its own fleet of trucks, the company believes the cost of transporting carpets from, and to, the various locations will be reduced by more than 75 percent.

Though customarily such a description of the use of new funds would be found in the introductory preamble, CLECO's additional inclusion of such an explanation in this section emphasizes and clarifies the company's plans. At times, such a reiteration adds clarity to the plan. Usually, however, such an inclusion here only detracts from a succinct description of the product or service. Most financiers and government agencies prefer to limit explanations of the use of funds to the preamble with the financial results of such additional capital reflected in the pro forma statements.

B. The company's markets are divided into three segments: residential homeowners, builders and developers, and commercial and industrial replacement markets. Annual volume to each segment is approximately as follows:

	Percent of Total Sales
Residential homeowners	15
Builders and developers	45
Commercial/industrial replacement	40

Over the past three years, sales to builders and developers have been increasing by approximately 18 percent per year while commercial/industrial replacement sales have decreased slightly. The residential homeowners market has remained about constant. Pricing continues soft in all except the residential segment, reflecting increased competition from foreign manufacturers' discount pricing to distributors.

At this point, Jerry should disclose the economic reasons for the fluctuations in segment sales and an explanation of pricing strategy both within CLECO and throughout the industry. He should also give a fairly comprehensive analysis of the projected impact of foreign imports on future sales and disclose any industry plans to counteract such competition.

C. Regional competition has been increasing lately because of two new carpet chains entering the local market. Though financially backed by a West Coast consortium and concentrating on carpets made with Taiwanese and other Asian yarns, carpets from these two chains appeal to the price-conscious developer who is unconcerned with product durability. The company expects a reversal of the success of these chains within three years when carpets begin to wear out and replacements are needed in one-half the time of CLECO's products. Other than the two chains, competitors are mostly small outlet stores without substantial ties to manufacturers. With the addition of its new trucking fleet, CLECO expects to become the dominant supplier in the Delaware Valley for all three market segments.

Atwell goes on to explain in detail how CLECO's market share in each of the segments has grown over the years and what he projects as future market share over the ensuing five years. He also elaborates on the company's anticipated pricing policies once shipping costs are reduced with the truck fleet.

Section III—Historical Financial Statements

CLECO retains an outside accountant to prepare monthly financial statements and cash reports. Annual financial statements are audited by Row and Walk, certified public accountants. Exhibit A includes audited financial statements for the past three years, together with the auditor's certificates. A summary of key financial statistics for the past three years follows:

| | ($ 000) | | |
	19X1	19X2	19X3
Sales	$2,500	$3,800	$5,100
Pre-tax profits	250	400	600
Net cash flow before officers compensation	385	389	385
Total assets	2,037	2,116	2,432
Officers compensation	250	360	380

Although this type of summary is not always required, it doesn't hurt to give the reader a quick glance at how the company has done in prior years. Usually, if performance has been stellar, such a summary is included in this section. If not, its omission leads the financier directly to the Exhibits to see the full financial statements.

The next section is the pro forma financial statements. This is really the key section. Some lenders and investors prefer to see this section first, and might request the business owner to give them a quick synopsis of the pro forma statements prior to submitting a financing plan. Others prefer to get the presentation all at one time. The format of pro forma statements varies with the specific business and the type of financial records available. The line headings that follow, however, are generally acceptable to both lenders and investors:

Balance sheet line items

ASSETS

Cash

Accounts receivable

Inventory

Prepaid expenses

    Total current assets

Land and buildings

Machinery and equipment

Other depreciable property

    Total

Less: Accumulated depreciation

    Net book value

Other assets

    Total assets

LIABILITIES

Notes payable to banks

Notes payable to others

Accounts payable

Accrued expenses and taxes

Current portion of long term debt

    Total current liabilities

    Long-term debt:

Notes

Leases

Mortgages

Other (including bonds and debentures)

    Total

Less: Current portion included above

    Net long term debt

Total liabilities

EQUITY

Preferred stock outstanding

Common stock outstanding

Retained earnings beginning of period

After-tax profit for the period

Retained earnings end of period

    Total equity

    Total liabilities and equity

Statement of income items:

Sales
Cost of sales
    Gross profit
Operating expenses
    Selling
    Research and development
    General and administrative
    Other expenses
    Total operating expenses
Profit before interest and taxes
Interest expense
Profit before taxes
Income taxes
Net profit
    Percent to sales

Statement of cash flow items:

CASH RECEIPTS
    From net profit
    Add back noncash items:
    Depreciation
    Amortization
    Other
        Cash receipts from operations
    New loans
    New equity contribution
    Sale of assets
    Other cash receipts
    Decrease in working capital items
        Total cash receipts

CASH DISBURSEMENTS
    Purchase of machinery, equipment, and real estate
    Principal payments on long-term debt
    Dividend payments
    Purchase of treasury stock
    Other long-term asset purchases
    Other long-term liability payments
    Increase in working capital items
        Total cash disbursements
    Net cash increase (decrease)

Beginning cash balance
Ending cash balance

Normally, the pro forma statements are prepared in columnar form for five years into the future and compared to historical statements for the past three years. In other words, each pro forma statement would show eight columns of figures. The pro forma statement of income submitted by Jerry Atwell is included in the exhibits of his financing plan.

It is also important to include a page or two of economic and business assumptions used in preparing the projections. For example, the business owner's estimate of interest rate and inflation rate fluctuations, industry curves, and other economic indicators affecting his business; additions or deletions to personnel over the period; acquisition of new facilities or equipment; other factors causing projected increases or decreases in annual sales; projected tax changes, and so on. Any assumption causing a major impact on future performance should be listed. This way, should actual performance not match the forecast, the business owner can later assuage concerns by pointing to inaccuracies in forecasted assumptions—which nobody can be blamed for.

The final section of the plan—management—must present evidence that the owner and other key managers have the credentials to reasonably assure a banker or investor that they can perform as indicated in the pro forma statements. Evidence will vary with each situation; the following was offered by Jerry Atwell:

Section V—Management
The principal shareholder of CLECO, Jerry Atwell, was with Burlington Mills for 12 years in various marketing capacities before leaving to form CLECO. In seven years, he has managed the company through several growth stages, expanding to four retail outlets and a stocking warehouse. The company now has 30 employees and remains poised to take the next big jump toward integration. Atwell has led the company continuously during this period and has been the driving force behind this rapid sales growth. The reference letters included as Exhibits to this plan present proof of this entrepreneur's involvement in community and civic affairs and his leadership in regional industry groups.

Atwell went on to describe the credentials of each of his managers and his brother-in-law and concluded with a list of industry achievements by both Atwell and CLECO. Two important references were omitted, however. A letter from his present commercial bank loan officer and commendation letters from customers. Lenders and investors look for this type of managerial evidence, and references and letters of commendation should always be included.

That finishes the financial plan. The only other feature adding to the integrity of the plan would be some photos of the facilities or the products, but this window dressing only helps if there is something glamorous to show.

Packaging the plan

Once the financial plan is completed, it should be packaged in the most professional way possible to attract the attention of a lender or investor. As in any other business endeavor, the "look right" is often as important—or even more important—than the "be right." Showmanship forms the foundation for any successful sales campaign, and that's exactly what presenting a financing plan is—a sales campaign. No one wants to buy from a sloppy looking salesman or from a company with a messy office, chaotic production facility, or threadbare, worn out equipment. It's the same with selling a financing plan. No one wants to look at a request for funds if either the presenter or the plan looks like he or she, or it, has been through the wars.

The financing plan should always be presented personally by the business owner. Don't delegate this task to a subordinate. It's too important. The financier wants to know you, what you look like, how you carry yourself, and whether or not you can articulate what you want. They don't want to hear the story from an employee. Sometimes you'll be requested to mail the plan rather than present it in person. Try to avoid this approach, but if necessary, at least use Federal Express or some other private courier service. It looks more professional than sending it through the mail. But try to get a personal appointment, if not for the submission, at least as soon as possible thereafter. It's really that important. Whether the plan is presented in person or incognito, if it doesn't portray a professional approach, the odds are high that it will quickly find its way to the trash barrel.

If the plan is voluminous, say more than 100 pages, then the best packaging can be done with a professionally bound book rather than any type of loose-leaf cover and holder. Nearly any small book bindery will do the job for $100 to $200. A cheap price to pay for a professional job. Most financing plans are short enough to be packaged loose-leaf, however. The best and most convenient way is to use the plastic spiral bindings popular for internal reports. Of course, in either case, the pages should be numbered, with a table of contents and section dividers. Also, it's helpful to use a hard cover with appropriate full-color artwork. Most small ad agencies can do the work for you. If you can't find an ad agency, use one of the top quick-print facilities that have desktop publishing with laser or post-script printers. Be certain the cover is hard paper stock, not merely 40-pound paper. Use plenty of colors—tastefully mixed of course—and laminate both the front and back covers. Again, a top-notch, quick-print shop with laminating capabilities can do this for you.

Just to be on the safe side, because you'll probably present the plan to several potential sources, get about a dozen or so copies right in the beginning. It's a lot cheaper than going back for more later. Regardless of the technique used, if the financing plan looks professional, it will be regarded with professional interest. Time and again, I have seen both lenders and investors peruse a professionally prepared plan cover to cover, whereas, had it been sloppily prepared or presented, the reader would have tossed it.

Another rule of thumb in the financing game is: The higher the amount of capital requested, the easier it is to get—from any source. Of course, there are exceptions. The SBA, for example, has definite maximum limits and, of course, the value of any collateral must be sufficient to cover the amount of the loan. Experience has proven, however, that given the proper collateral, it's much easier to raise $10 or $20 million than $500,000. So if you have an option, go for the higher amount. The amount requested has nothing to do with the criteria for a professional package, however. Professionalism sells at any level.

Professional advisors

Few private business owners should attempt to prepare a financing plan by themselves. Most don't have the ability to do it right nor the time to spend on it. It is almost always worth the cost to have a professional advisor, such as a CPA, a consultant, or in some cases, a lawyer, to either assist in the endeavor or compose a draft of the plan on his own (with input from the owner, of course).

At times, it's difficult to know where to find this level of competence. Hiring the wrong professional advisor is worse than having none at all. Rather than arbitrarily selecting an advisor from the phone book or through friends or business acquaintances, it makes more sense to interview two or more candidates to be certain they know what they are doing. Just because a practitioner calls himself a CPA, consultant, or lawyer doesn't mean he knows how to construct a financing plan. After a number of hit and miss attempts at choosing professional advisors, I devised the following short questionnaire to assist in evaluating the competence of professionals being interviewed:

Questionnaire for Choosing
a Professional Advisor
for a Financing Plan

1. Have you ever prepared a financing plan before?

2. Do you know the difference between a financing plan and a business plan or strategic plan?

3. Have you had experience in the business world outside of your professional status? Owned a company?

4. Have you ever arranged financing for a client or for yourself? Through a commercial bank? Through investors? From other sources?

5. Once started, how much time will you devote to my plan?

6. What are your hourly rates?

7. Will you contract for the entire job at a fixed fee?

8. What references can you present from lenders or investors you have worked with before?

9. Can I contact any of your clients with whom you have worked to arrange financing?

10. Can you present any professional references I can talk to?

11. Can you provide assistance in sourcing financing?

The final question is not crucial, because professionals capable of doing this are generally not capable of giving much assistance in preparing the plan. Occasionally, one will have capabilities in both, and it doesn't hurt to ask. The two most important matters to get resolved at the interview are the professional's specific experience in preparing financing plans and how much the job will cost. Obviously, you'll want to check as many references as possible if your choice looks like a viable prospect.

That finishes the preparation of the financing plan. So far, we've looked at some of the concepts, rules, and terms used by the financial community, the pertinent federal tax considerations affecting various financing structures, a method for preparing a financing plan, and guidelines for selecting competent professional advisors to assist in its preparation. We've also seen why a business owner should not borrow from a commercial bank except for very short-term funds needed for working capital peaks. If not a commercial banker, then what other options are available? The next chapter explains how to go about sourcing outside financing beyond the commercial banker. We'll take a look at the role money brokers play in the financing game, as well as how, and where, to get help from practicing lawyers, accountants, and consultants. Finally, we'll see how investment bankers play a prominent role in sourcing funds.

5

Using professionals

ANNE COGNOWSKI WAS THE CEO AND PRINCIPAL SHAREHOLDER OF A $7 million manufacturer of electronic devices for testing impurities in residential water wells. Starting the business in 1977 with $10,000 of her own money and another $15,000 from investor friends, Anne had been successful during the ensuing 10 years in growing the company beyond her wildest dreams. But now she was at a threshold. Competition had mushroomed and Anne realized that to maintain her share of the burgeoning market, major expansion moves must be implemented. But where would the capital come from? Though her company was highly profitable, most excess cash had been plowed back into working capital to sustain the rapid sales growth. Much to her chagrin, Anne realized that to survive, she must go to the outside to raise enough capital for her expansion plans. But never having tapped the financial markets before, she had no idea where to begin.

Through the recommendation of a mutual friend, Anne engaged me to act as her financial advisor in locating $6.6 million in expansion financing. Through personal contacts in the financial community, I put together a consortium of a small investment bank, two private individuals looking for investment opportunities, and a leasing company willing to handle 10-year equipment leases. With the long-term debt and equity from the consortium, Anne completed her expansion. Today, she runs a company approaching $15 million in annual sales—and still highly profitable.

The two primary reasons business owners seek to fulfill financing needs through commercial banks are: (1) they believe bank advertisements about friendly bankers wanting to help small businesses; and (2) they don't know where, or how, to locate other sources of funds. Chapter 1 exploded the first myth by showing that media advertising is one thing, but actually helping is quite another. Little evidence remains that commercial banks are the white knights they would like us to believe. Now, let's take a look at solving the second riddle.

For business owners inexperienced in the ways of the financial community, locating sources of capital for specific purposes can be, and often is, the worst nightmare they'll encounter in growing or trying to save a company. Advertisements from individuals and companies claiming they have money to invest proliferate the Wall Street Journal, major city newspapers, and business magazines. Ninety-nine percent of these are shylocks out for the quick buck from gullible and desperate business owners. The ads look appealing but once investigated, turn out to be nothing more than come-ons. Collateral requirements are excessive, interest rates exorbitant, and loan or investment documentation inordinately restrictive. Most of these charlatans don't even have the money they advertise. When an unwary entrepreneur solicits a response, many will source the money from illegal or questionable parties. Some, however, are very legitimate money brokers, whose sole occupation is locating debt and investment funds for businesses.

The money brokers

Money brokerage houses come in many forms. Some are set up with one person, a desk, and a telephone. Others are full-fledged operating companies employing sales, clerical, and financial staffs. Although money brokers usually operate regionally and are listed in the Yellow Pages of city telephone directories, a few maintain active contacts throughout the country and overseas. These broad-based brokers are normally contacted through references. Ask your accountant or lawyer for leads. You can also use the Yellow Pages to locate a regional broker and, invariably, if you need a large amount of capital, say over $100 million, he will put you in touch with the appropriate contact. A word of warning, however. Just as in any business, there are frauds and crooks in the money brokerage game. Be sure to check references with a local banker, the chamber of commerce, or the Better Business Bureau.

Management consultants, especially those engaged in mergers and acquisitions (M&A) consulting, often have good contacts with reputable money brokers and can provide money sourcing services along with their normal consulting activities. A competent, well-connected, M&A consultant can often be a fast and inexpensive way to locate the right broker.

Next to M&A consultants, public accounting firms probably offer the best opportunity in the professions for making appropriate financing contacts. Large CPA firms frequently know of lenders or investors, individuals, or companies eager to find a home for excess funds. Smaller public accounting firms might also have one or two contacts, and it certainly can't hurt to give them a call. Without personal contacts in the money markets, advice from your company's accountant, auditor, or tax advisor is probably the safest way to get started. These professionals are usually willing to provide a contact or two as a first step. Many smaller CPA firms with principals originally from the Big 5 usually maintain old contacts in the larger firm.

Some lawyers can also help in providing leads to reputable lending or investing agencies. Though it's difficult to locate such legal expertise at random, your company's legal counsel should be able to provide at least the first contact. From there, references should flow to other qualified lawyers or law firms. Large, big-city firms nearly always have several clients or contacts in the financing markets. Often, one partner specializes in the field, but usually it's not a good idea to call one of these large law firms cold. Lawyers are especially careful about giving out information of any kind to strangers. It's much better to get a reference from your company counsel to bridge the gap.

Before making contact with any of these middlemen, however, be sure to have your financing plan completed and ready for delivery. In the financing game, after the initial contact and appointment, matters move very rapidly. Deals have been lost simply because the business owner was not completely prepared when the source wanted to move. Additionally, it's entirely possible the broker or middleman will want to review the financing plan before providing definitive leads. Remember, it's crucial to strike when the iron's hot. Don't make either a middleman or a financing source wait. Once an appointment is arranged, go at it, hook, line, and sinker. Before contacting one of these middlemen, however, it's helpful to understand some of the basic criteria influencing when, and where, they conduct the search and manage the process.

The borrower's matrix

Whether you're looking for debt financing or equity, keep in mind that you are still a borrower. Maybe not technically in the strict sense of the law, but certainly in the eyes of the financier. His willingness to provide funds is predicated on first earning income on the money and then getting the principal repaid in the future. This makes the recipient a borrower. So when I use the term *borrower*, the reference is to a business owner receiving outside funds of any type and from any source.

To understand how a lender or investor looks at an opportunity, it's necessary to think in terms of a matrix of options and relative risks and rewards for each. Though the matrix is multidimensional and therefore impossible to portray on two-dimensional paper, this doesn't make it any less relevant. The three parameters of the borrower's matrix are:

1. The type of business—lumberyard, computer store, furniture manufacturer, design and consulting, engineering firm, art gallery, and so on.

2. The size of the business—defined as a combination of net worth, total assets, sales, and profitability.

3. The application of the funds.

A middleman sourcing funds for a client has a reputation to uphold. A potential lender or investor knows he won't be bothered with an unsuitable deal. Therefore, before making any contacts or even reviewing the financing plan, a middleman will want a verbal description of the borrower's matrix.

Type of business

The type of business the borrower has, has a bearing on who should be approached. A boutique investment banker specializing in the publishing industry, for example, will have little interest in a lumberyard or computer store, but might be interested in a printing company, sales promotion business, or design and copy editing firm. It would be useless to approach an asset based lender looking for deals involving hard-asset collateral with an art gallery client; but they might jump at an opportunity to finance a machine tool manufacturer. Because the type of business is so important to finding the right source, you should be prepared to offer a succinct verbal definition of your business right in the beginning.

Size of company

Knowing the size of the business is also important to the middleman. A computer repair service with sales of $500,000 might be a perfect match for an SBA guaranteed loan or, if it is minority owned (by SBA definitions), it might qualify for a direct SBA loan. A $30 million manufacturer of ball bearings, however, wouldn't stand a chance with the SBA. Similarly, a company with low margins or a history of fluctuating profits would have a hard time getting funds through the esoteric world of venture capital; but with appropriate hard assets, the deal could be extremely attractive to an asset based lender. A strong financial history with a significant upward trend in profit projections would probably interest an investment banker.

Use of funds

The use of funds becomes the third leg of the borrower's matrix. Internal expansion requirements for new equipment or buildings attract different financing sources than a new export program. Buying a business mandates a different type of lender or investor—or both—than developing a new product or other R&D project. New product development might be very attractive to a venture capitalist who disdains modest growth companies in mature industries.

Such a multidimensional matrix yields an unlimited number of possibilities for both the business owner and the financing middleman to grapple with. Fortunately, there are some common questions usually asked at the first contact that can funnel the search in the right direction. Carefully responding to the following questionnaire can assist in discussing the project with the appropriate financing middlemen and provide enough information for one of them to either accept or reject the assignment.

Borrower's Matrix Questionnaire

Type of business

1. Does the company have machinery or equipment?
2. If yes, what is the approximate current resale value?
3. Does the company own real estate?
4. If so, where, in what condition, and what is its approximate market value?
5. What is the inventory value?
6. What is the balance of receivables?
7. Does the company have substantial repeat customer business?
8. Is there a backlog of customer orders? How much?
9. What are the names and titles of managers?
10. How long has the company been in business?
11. What is the structure of the company? Proprietorship, partnership, corporation?
12. How broad is its market?
13. Who are the major competitors?
14. Is it minority owned or managed?

15. Is the company involved in urban restoration or any other socially beneficial activity?

Size of the company

1. What are annual sales?
2. What are annual profits?
3. What is net worth?
4. What is the total asset value?
5. Has the company been profitable for the past three years?
6. What is the projected growth in sales (in percent) over the next five years?
7. How will profits fare over this period?
8. Are there industry statistics available for sales growth or profitability?
9. If yes, how does the company compare?
10. How many employees are there?
11. What percentage are minorities?

How will the funds be used

1. To buy equipment or real estate?
2. To buy a company?
3. To fund a product development project?
4. To recapitalize the company or restructure debt?
5. To provide additional working capital?
6. To pay dividends?
7. To establish or expand an export program?
8. To establish a presence overseas?
9. To pay taxes?
10. Other purposes? What are they?

It's a good idea to have the answers to these questions available when making the first phone call or attending the first meeting with a money broker or other advisor. That way, they'll know you've done your homework and won't be wasting their time.

Sourcing fees

Sourcing fees charged by money brokers or professional practitioners vary widely. Often, the fee structure depends on the amount being raised. It might also be influenced by the size of the borrower (what the traffic will bear). In some cases, by using your own public accountant or lawyer, there might be no fee at all. An outside professional such as a public accountant, lawyer, or consultant will normally charge a flat fee for amounts below $500,000. This runs between $10,000 and $20,000. For amounts up to $100 million, fees are usually a percentage of the loan or investment and range from 1/2 percent to 2 percent. For amounts over $100 million, the fee is always negotiable and can be as high as 3 percent or as low as 1/4 percent.

Money brokers generally follow the same pattern, although in most cases, they will be on the high end of the spectrum. Because arranging financing is usually their sole source of income, and because they are usually called in when other sources have failed, higher fees can be justified. If a borrower wants the capital bad enough and can't get it any other way, a money broker is in the driver's seat.

One final comment on fees: for a financially troubled company trying to arrange a restructuring plan, financing fees can be a major cost. It can also be extremely difficult to locate appropriate sources. For these reasons, a business owner is often better off hiring a competent consultant with contacts in the financing marketplace, not only to source the financing, but also to assist in preparing the financing plan and devising alternate possibilities for restructuring. It's usually well worth the cost, and a potential lender or investor looks favorably on a customer seeking competent professional advice.

If a borrower doesn't want to engage a money broker or professional middleman to source the financing and meets certain type of business, size, and application of funds criteria, direct sourcing through investment bankers might be the answer.

Using investment banks

During the past 20 years, investment bankers have emerged from the pack of money manipulators as the prime mover in the merger and acquisition game. A cross between venture capital firms and securities brokerage companies, investment banks evolved as a major source of financing for individuals and companies eager to take part in the merger and acquisition (M&A) mania. It was an almost perfect fit. Small and large acquirers alike needed contacts in the money markets, both through the banking fraternity and on Wall Street, to structure financing packages now commonly called leveraged buyouts, or LBOs.

Making their mark in the M&A game, many investment banks branched out, offering both financial advisory services and actual financing sources. In the financial advisory services market, investment banks compete directly with money brokers and professional practitioners offering services for financing and financial management. They have a leg up on their competition, however, by being perfectly positioned in the middle of the financial markets. Many investment bankers originated in securities brokerage firms of one type or another. This background provided access to wealthy individuals, eager to place their funds in good investments and companies trying to raise capital by issuing stock through publicly traded markets. With this repertoire of personal contacts, when the investment banker set out to make financing deals, he already had an active list of interested parties on both sides of the fence.

Other investment bankers grew up in the venture capital arena. Arranging both debt and equity financing for new, high tech start-up ventures placed this advisor in the unique position of compiling company intelligence and financing options usually unavailable to the commercial banker, asset based lender, money broker, or professional practitioner.

The success of investment bankers with financial advisory services brought enormous funds to their coffers. The natural next step was to reinvest these funds in companies and deals they already knew about from their vast network of contacts. As M&A mania escalated, more and more investment bankers ended up with significant stakes in growing, closely held companies. During the eighties, as the stock market progressed through ever higher values and prices of even the most pedestrian companies sold for as much as 20 times earnings, investment bankers coaxed their clients to go public—to issue stock on the open market. As these issues caught on, investment banks continued to expand, and the wealth controlled by these new bankers accumulated to astronomical proportions.

The next logical step was to put together financing packages not only with money from their own accounts and those of friends and associates, but to market this packaging service to small and midsized companies. Thus, they created a second major market; that of providing financing sources for all types of projects and uses not limited to LBOs.

Today, the investment banking industry prides itself on its capability of acting either as a middleman in arranging financing for any purpose or as an equity partner in growth companies. The term *investment banking* is often a misnomer and, at best, is a confusing description of services offered by these firms. Selling financial advisory services is a prime example.

Investment bankers as financial advisors

Financial advisory services are really consulting services and in this sense compete directly with the management consulting profession. Smaller, growth-oriented companies and midsized businesses with expansion motives usually form the nucleus of advisory services clients. These smaller firms normally do not have the financial specialists on their management staffs to intelligently evaluate needs and structure options for financing packages, nor do they usually maintain current intelligence and contacts in the financial markets to weigh alternative possibilities for raising funds. Many companies are denied traditional financing alternatives because they lack hard assets, have been unprofitable, or are in mundane, mature industries. Most are not familiar with the more esoteric sources of capital, such as special government funding, private foundations, international investment sources, or with the mechanics of making an initial stock issue. Thus, they become a ready market for the investment banker's capabilities and expertise.

The investment banker, eager to sell these advisory services at substantial fees—often far in excess of normal management consulting fees—welcomes the opportunity to participate in a smaller company's growth plans. Typically, an investment banker will spend several days meeting with the business owner and key management staff. He performs an evaluation of the managers' capabilities and the company's potential growth opportunities. Calculations, appraisals, interviews, and balance sheet analyses all lead to recommendations for specific alternatives most likely to fit the owner's particular circumstances. Once the owner chooses one with the most appeal—weighing risk, cost, control, payback period, and a myriad of other factors—the investment banker can then, at the owner's option, go on to structure a specific financing package. As an advisor, he can also help prepare a financial plan and even assist in presenting it to financing sources.

After several false starts in the capital markets, Abe Greene finally resorted to an investment banker, and now unflinchingly recommends this step to other business owners. AstaForm Molding, Inc., produced low-cost, throw-away molds for a segment of the plastic injection molding industry. Its largest customers manufactured plastic toys fashioned after cartoon characters. Abe inherited the business from his father-in-law three years earlier and now needed to raise approximately $1.2 million for some new equipment and working funds for an innovative product development program. Stumbling through three commercial banks and even a finance company, only to learn that his collateral wasn't sufficient, Abe eventually contacted a small investment bank in northern New Jersey to help locate the capital. Not wishing to pay fees of $125,000, Abe agreed to give the investment banker 10 percent of his equity in exchange for sourcing, negotiating, and closing the $1.2 million deal.

It took about six months, but in the end, the investment banker succeeded in arranging not $1.2 million, but $2 million. He placed $700,000 in long-term debt with an Israeli bank and $1 million in convertible debentures with a limited partnership. The balance of $300,000 was raised from two private investors in exchange for 8 percent noncumulative, convertible preferred stock. Abe was exuberant, not only to get the financing, but to have the investment banker as a permanent member of his board. Three years later, this relationship gave Abe enough clout in the financial markets to coerce a local mortgage company into a 20 year, 10.25 percent mortgage on a new plant—with only a 10 percent down payment!

Investment bankers as a financing source

Some investment bankers are equipped to participate in a financing program and either contribute part of the equity financing in exchange for a share in the company or provide mezzanine debt to bridge the gap until long-term financing can be secured. In some cases, the investment banker will also participate in long-term loans or fund the debt all by himself. Usually, however, he prefers to take a lead role in the whole financing package, bringing together other sources for the short- or long-term debt portions and reserve equity participation for himself.

Most investment banks are able to perform this function because of their vast network of investors and banks that are more than willing to participate with an investment bank in the lead. The attitude in the financial community seems to be that if an investment banker knows the company well enough and has enough confidence in its management to invest its own money as an equity player, the risk to other secured parties lessens considerably.

A common vehicle currently in vogue for structuring expansion or acquisition financing packages is a limited partnership, with an investment banker taking the lead in putting the deal together. Chapter 8 covers the normal structuring and use of limited partnerships and, at this point, it is sufficient to note that such structuring has become enormously popular in the investing field.

Another popular method the financial community uses is to finance the existing corporate entity with a combination of short-term working capital loans from a commercial bank, long-term debt funds from an asset based lender, and equity funding from an investment bank. Normally, this type of package provides all the money a closely held corporation needs to meet its expansion goals. In the event special funding is required, say for an export program or to restructure a financially troubled company, an investment bank might stop its advisory services and recommend other sources as lead packagers. This is especially true when restructuring is required. Investment bankers looking for large increments in investment appreciation over a relatively short period of time (five to seven years) are not usually interested in participating in restructurings.

How investment banks are structured

Investment banks come in all forms, sizes, and ownership structures. There are as many variations as there are means of structuring a financing package. Even though they all provide more or less the same activities, the structure of any given firm influences whether it will fit your criteria. Criteria may vary, but if an investment bank is used either as a financial advisor or to actually raise capital, it's important to understand the different structures and ownership because:

- The size of the financing package determines what size of investment bank to engage.
- Investment banks affiliated with large commercial banks can easily package long-term debt and an operating line in one source.
- Investment banks affiliated with brokerage houses work best for underwriting an IPO.
- Private firms usually interfere the least with management prerogatives.
- Small houses are best for overall financial advisory services because it's easier to work with the principals, not staff people.
- Small to midsized private firms tend to concentrate on industry specialization.

Investment banks can be structured in any of the following 10 arrangements. This breakdown first appeared in *Buying In: A Complete Guide to Buying a Business or Professional Practice*, and remains an up-to-date description of investment bank structures:

1. A small group of ex-security analysts who have formed their own company to offer financial consulting and packaging for small deals with equity requirements under $500,000. (TDH Capital, Wissahickon Partners.)

2. A division or subsidiary within a large brokerage house. (Bear Sterns, Merrill Lynch.)

3. A midsized house, either privately owned or the subsidiary of a brokerage house, offering a complete range of services for deals in the $10 to $20 million range. (Golder Thoma & Cressey, Howard Lawson & Co.)

4. Larger private firms or the subsidiaries of brokerage houses doing deals over $20 million but less than $100 million. (James River Capital, Narragansett Capital, Sprout Capital Group.)

5. Giant firms handling deals above $100 million mainly for very large corporate clients. (Goldman Sachs, Salomon Bros.)

6. Divisions of commercial banks offering a complete range of services and handling deals up to $50 million. (Fleet Growth Industries, BNE Associates, Connecticut National Bank.)

7. Divisions or subsidiaries of large insurance companies handling deals on their own account up to $1 billion. (Allstate Insurance, Pru Capital—part of Prudential Insurance.)

8. Wealthy family private trusts. (Rothschild, Inc.).

9. Subsidiaries of large foreign banks or trusts offering special industry deals of any size but mainly over $100 million. (Charterhouse Group International, Midland Capital.)

10. Spin-offs or divisions of pure venture capital firms concentrating in early stage development companies.

The criteria of specific investment banks relating to the size of a financing package keeps changing, depending on portfolios, reputation of client, market conditions, and available cash at the moment; but most firms like to work within given ranges. Weighing the type of industry, stage of development, growth prospects, and management talent also fluctuates continually. As economic, environmental, and financial conditions change, so does investment criteria. Investment banks leaning toward the venture capital side of the industry are especially fluid, moving rapidly from start-up financing to first, second, and third-stage packages. To choose an investment banking house for a specific deal requires a fair amount of research. No contractual arrangement should be executed without a thorough understanding of the capabilities of the principals or management of the firm and judicious checking of references from prior clients. Additional investment banks and venture capital firms with a good reputation in the industry are listed in Appendix B. Be careful to choose one that meets your criteria and you should be off to a good start.

One word of caution relating to locating a competent investment bank or any qualified financing middleman, including money brokers and professional practitioners: Most really good contacts in the financing game are made through reputation or by word of mouth, so ask around. Follow leads from other business owners, public accountants, consultants, or lawyers. Interview any reasonable prospect and be certain your personalities mesh. As in all business endeavors, the more you know about a specific discipline and the more frequently you ask for advice and recommendations, the more contacts and knowledge you will gain. Don't be afraid to open the door to suggestions and recommendations from anyone. Then follow up the leads and use your own judgment about whom to engage. The best of all worlds occurs when you have selected two or three reputable investment bankers who can do the job and then have the option of choosing the best of the lot.

Two sisters, Rosemary and Janice, started a computer consulting business in 1982 and successfully expanded the business to more than 60 clients in four years. Late in 1986, the sisters jumped at an opportunity that arose to acquire a small software distributor in the next town for $2 million, but they had no idea where or how to raise the financing. As a friend, I recommended a small investment bank specializing in the computer software industry as a potential source. We prepared a financing plan, and Rosemary presented it to the banker. Enthusiastic, but conservative, he told Rosemary he would try, but couldn't guarantee to raise the funds. Six months later, the software distributor was ready to back out of the deal if the sisters couldn't raise the cash in a hurry. All my efforts to budge the investment banker failed, and the deal finally collapsed.

Never again, I told Rosemary and Janice, as well as myself, would I recommend only one source of capital, and never again have I suggested hiring an investment banker without insisting on a thorough interview process. The following questionnaire evolved as a tool to conduct such interviews:

Questionnaire for Choosing an Investment Banker

1. What size deals do you specialize in?
2. What industries do you prefer?
3. Are there any geographic limitations or preferences?
4. What stages of financing are you interested in—seed capital, first stage, second stage, refinancing, recapitalizing?
5. What historic and future growth curves do you look for?
6. What level of profitability do you want?
7. How do you feel about additional company or product line acquisitions?
8. Do you handle the restructuring of financially troubled companies?
9. What role do you prefer—advisor, packager, investor?
10. If a packager, what type of sources do you usually go after—pensions, foundations, individuals, commercial banks, asset based lenders, or other?
11. If an investor, what standards do you follow for return on your investment—20%, 30%, 40%?

12. What payback term do you prefer—three years, five years, eight years, other?

13. Where does your own capital come from—private investors, trust funds, overseas capital?

14. What is the ownership structure of your firm?

15. Do you publish financial statements?

16. Do you insist on personal guarantees?

17. Do you want a seat on the board or a board advisor position?

18. What percentage of ownership do you normally take?

19. Are you experienced in international trade?

20. Do you handle export financing or international expansion?

21. Who would be the liaison contact in your firm—a principal, officer, staff person, or other?

22. What deals have you handled in the past three years?

23. What are the sizes of these deals?

24. Can I contact the CEOs of these clients for references?

25. Do you have bank references you can give me?

26. Will you send me a sample of the type of contractual agreement you normally use?

27. When and where can we meet for the first interview?

Locating appropriate financial advisors prior to embarking on an IPO requires a slightly different twist. Although the same investment banker chosen to assist in raising other financing might have the qualifications to also assist in a public stock offering, the reverse could also be true. The key to a public offering is frequently the caliber of underwriter chosen to market the issue, which may or may not be an investment banker. Chapter 7 covers this entire issue in-depth.

Using venture capital firms

Currently, the distinction between investment banks and venture capital firms is blurred. At one time, venture capitalists clearly handled only high growth, relatively new companies who needed equity capital to develop and market new products. Supported by the SBA, Small Business Investment Corporations (SBICs) blossomed to fill this entrepreneurial need. As the amount of required capital increased beyond SBIC limits, better funded venture capital firms sprang up. These new high risk-takers demanded, and received, significant equity interests in companies they financed. In many cases, they took a majority equity position to be certain of protecting their investment. It was not uncommon for the entrepreneur who founded a company to end up with only a minority ownership. The gambles worked well, however, and many electronic, computer, and medical technology companies thriving in the marketplace today could not have made it without capital from the venture markets.

Although venture capital firms continue to finance smaller, high tech companies (chapter 10 covers the use of this source for raising capital for R&D projects), most of the larger financing schemes have been usurped by investment banks. Again, however, it's hard to tell the difference. Larger venture capital firms perform investment banking functions and several investment banks get involved in venture activities.

Generally, a venture capital firm is in business to provide equity, mezzanine, and sometimes, secured financing for start-up or first or second-stage developing companies. The emergence of entrepreneurial start-up companies in such esoteric markets as computer software and peripherals, medical diagnostic equipment, satellite communications technology, and electronic instrumentation, owe their existence to initial funding from venture capital firms. By investing equity in these start-up companies and then taking them public in five to seven years, venture capital firms doubled, tripled, even quadrupled their investments in short order. The same philosophy exists today. They're not especially interested in earning straight income on their investments—such as interest or dividends—but look primarily for sure-bet opportunities to reap enormous capital gains through public issues. Venture capital firms tend to stay away from financial consulting. They like to invest their own funds or be a lead investor for a group of equity participants in early stage development deals. For this reason, most investments are in very small developing companies.

Venture capital firms normally insist on a controlling share of the company. Although many firms will never exert control over the operations of the company—restricting their activity to a board seat and participation in major policy decisions—some do, in fact, interfere with operating decisions. To get a reputable venture capitalist to admit to such a sacrilege, however, would be difficult.

These firms serve a special need in the financing marketplace. With little or no collateral to secure a loan and earnings records that won't support substantial cash flow projections, many small companies cannot raise funds anywhere else. From a financing viewpoint, this type of deal provides the greatest risk for the financier. Therefore, his reward must be substantial. If a venture capital firm seems to be the best way to go, try to find one whose management has some operating experience that fits your industry. In this case, at least their advice should be helpful.

Sourcing funds without a middleman

In some cases, it just doesn't make sense to use a middleman in arranging financing, and there is no hard and fast rule saying you must. Many people prefer to source capital needs themselves. It's definitely less expensive to do it that way and it might be faster under certain circumstances. A business owner obviously knows his business and its needs better than an outsider and, therefore, might be able to focus his capital search more directly. In some cases, such as becoming active in government contracting, which provides progress payments, a middleman would only get in the way. Private foundations are another source that the business owner can research himself—assuming he has the time.

The next chapter introduces the benefits and risks of using either government progress payments or private foundations as viable sources of outside capital. Although these sources are not applicable to everyone, it's surprising how many entrepreneurs overlook these low cost, often free, sources to finance expansion, development projects, and even working capital needs.

6

Government and foundation funding

IT'S SURPRISING HOW MANY BUSINESS OWNERS DISREGARD GOVERNMENT contracting as a viable source of outside financing. Large corporations use this source consistently, yet small and midsized companies seldom view this means as a potential alternative for raising capital.

In addition to government contracting, the Small Business Administration (SBA) is often a viable and convenient source of funding. This chapter looks at both of these sources as well as several, lesser-known government agencies providing financial assistance. Toward the end of the chapter, private foundations are also examined as a potential source for financing specific projects that have socially beneficial results.

Government contract progress payments

Defense contractors have used progress payments for decades as a way to finance research, design, and production costs of products sold to the U.S. government. Like any massive customer, the federal government, with its myriad of agencies and programs, purchases literally hundreds of thousands of different products from the private sector every year. From paper clips and rubber bands to complex state-of-the-art military electronics, the government must stock thousands of warehouses with goods and supply millions of people with all types of materiel. And all of these products originate with the private sector.

Many products purchased by the government are done so under contract and funded with progress payments, payments made to a supplier in advance of shipping the merchandise. Advance payments eliminate the need to carry excessive inventory or risk uncollectible receivables. Relieved of this costly exercise, a company can divert its working capital funds to other, non-government products. The following example illustrates how the process works. Even though Mark's company produces military hardware components, the same procedures apply to many other products.

Mark Johnson was the CEO of Accurate Technology Machining Corp. (ATMAC). Although several machined products were sold to office equipment companies and to sporting goods manufacturers, ATMAC's primary product line was a large, complex four-wheeled robot used to automatically place highly combustible missiles and bombs in storage holders. These robots were all sold to the U.S. Navy and Air Force under three-year, renewable contracts.

Many of the robot components required a special, very expensive, titanium alloy that was difficult to obtain domestically. Two foreign suppliers were the only viable sources. The assembly of these products was also complex, requiring more than a hundred skilled workers more than three months to assemble one robot. Because of the high cost and the long purchasing lead time for securing the titanium alloy, and then the subsequent long production cycle, ATMAC negotiated progress payment contracts with both the navy and the air force. Both contracts were similar and worked as follows:

1. When ATMAC placed a purchase order for titanium or any other major quantities of supplies or materials required in the products, a clerk hand carried a copy of the purchase order to the local navy or air force procurement office. Within 30 days, a check for the full amount of the purchase order was in the mail to ATMAC.

2. Since delivery of most materials and supplies took between two and four months and the vendors invoices weren't payable until 30 days after receipt of the merchandise, ATMAC had the use of these progress payments for 90 to 150 days before the suppliers had to be paid. This slack period allowed the company to finance all of its purchases for other nongovernment product lines with these funds.

3. Direct production workers on the robot assembly and testing line accounted meticulously for their chargeable hours each week.

When the weekly payroll was drawn, a copy was delivered to the two military procurement offices, and within 30 days, a check was in the mail. There was no need to use collections from other receivables to meet this payroll, which accounted for 65 percent of the total ATMAC labor, and the company conserved additional cash for other product lines.

4. This labor also absorbed a portion of ATMAC's overhead, which was billed along with the payroll costs. In this way, progress payments provided working capital to finance indirect salaries and other overhead expenses.

5. As each robot came off the assembly line and completed testing, a government inspector signed off and a new billing was sent to the military. This time it was for the full contract price of the robot, less progress payments received to date against the product's cost. Because the government had already paid for the material, labor, and a good portion of the overhead content of its products, only the remaining overhead and profits had to be carried as a receivable—and this receivable was paid 30 days after invoicing.

6. Against each of the progress billings, a retention of 10 percent of the invoice was held back by the government. When the completed robot was accepted by the navy or air force, this 10 percent was paid within 10 days.

For ATMAC, progress payments on materials and supplies were received so early in the production cycle that by investing these funds in short-term securities, the company earned enough interest income to pay for a good portion of the labor content on other product lines. ATMAC never used outside financing for working capital to support commercial product lines, yet it maintained very conservative cash balances. Additionally, progress payments are interest free. This way is certainly cheaper and far less risky than borrowing working capital funds.

A second feature of selling to the government but not used by ATMAC is that, in some cases, if special equipment or facilities are needed to produce a government product, their cost can be built into the contract when it is negotiated. This way, the government pays for these assets and the producer does not need to obtain long-term financing elsewhere. Additionally, payments for such facilities and equipment can sometimes be included as progress payments. If not, negotiations can lead to receipt of funding in advance of the expansion.

Although ATMAC sold military hardware, the same type of progress payment procedures can be used for virtually everything the government purchases. To find out if any government agency purchases products or services that you produce, contact your nearest government procurement office and request a copy of the latest procurement bidding list or read the *Commerce Business Daily*. It lists all the requests for proposals (called RFPs) for everything the government buys. If your product or service is listed, check with your public accountant for assistance in putting together a bid. With few exceptions, all government procurements are made through the competitive bidding process. Once you land the first contract, however, follow-on orders can often be negotiated without going through the cumbersome bidding process a second time.

There are also "set aside" contracts specifically designated as small business allocations. Normally, a small business is defined as one with 500 or fewer employees. Because qualifications to compete in this program keep changing, however, check with your local procurement office for current regulations.

If you do end up selling to the government, be prepared to host an array of government auditors, inspectors, engineers, and, in the case of military materiel, army, navy, or air force personnel. They will camp in your facility either on a regular monthly, or quarterly, or full-time schedule. This might require setting up and furnishing an office for them; but then this can be included in the contract price so it's not an additional cost.

Government contract pricing

Once you decide to enter government markets, it's a good idea to understand how federal agencies view bid proposals and how contracts are actually priced and structured. Although variations occur between product classifications, certain similarities exist. The starting point is to understand that pricing for all government purchases must be based on the seller's cost. This doesn't mean that "cost plus" contracts are prevalent. What it does mean, however, is that the government is willing to allow the supplier a normal profit on his products, but not an excess profit. In many contracts, the current allowed standard is a pretax profit of 10 percent to 15 percent over the seller's cost.

When bidding on a government contract, special forms must be used to compile the bid package (which we'll get to a little later). Some of these forms deal with price and require a detailed analysis of the per unit cost build-up for the product or service. How much labor is used? How much and what types of materials? What are the elements of indirect costs chargeable direct to the contract? What elements are included in allocated costs, and how is such allocation arrived at? Are selling expenses or general and administrative expenses allocated? If so, how much, and on what basis? What other costs are either charged direct to the contract or allocated, and why? What profit percent is added to the total cost to arrive at a bid price per unit?

In addition to accumulating product costs according to the standards set forth by the federal government's Cost Accounting Standards Board (CASB), a business owner contemplating government contract work must:

1. have a cost accounting system that will yield sufficient detail to meet these requirements in place and working before submitting a bid; and

2. be prepared to verify the actual costs incurred in producing the product against his bid schedules when government auditors audit his books.

Though most manufacturers use some type of cost accounting system in their normal business activities, many other businesses do not. Retailers, service companies, resale businesses, and research facilities are often notoriously lacking in cost systems. Unfortunately, it's impossible to do business with the government without a cost system. If your business doesn't use a cost system that complies with CASB standards, then either hire a competent consultant to design such a cost system for you—and then get it up and running—or forget about doing business with the government, at least with progress payment contracts.

The second key pricing feature of government contracts involves verifying the actual cost incurred against negotiated prices. This is significantly different from doing business with the private sector. Seldom, if ever, does a commercial customer demand verification of actual cost build-ups to support the prices it pays. Even if it did, few business owners would be willing to open their proprietary accounting records to an outsider. But the government is different. Just as IRS auditors have the legal right to examine proprietary documents to verify income and expense items reported on tax returns, so do government auditors when you want to be in the government contracting business.

Following the basic principle that all prices to the government are based on cost—and not on what the market will bear—the actual costs incurred during a production cycle must be equal to, or more than, the estimates submitted in the bid package. If they are more than estimated, certain renegotiation procedures might apply to recover excess costs subsequent to audit verification. Usually, however, the seller bears the brunt of any cost overruns. On the other hand, if actual costs end up being less than those submitted on the bid, the contractor almost always pays back to the government proportionate shares of the contract price allocated to these cost savings.

The timing and frequency of government audits depends on several factors: size of the contract, type of materiel purchased, number of sources of the same product, and the government agency doing the buying. In some cases—notably for major military contracts—government auditors might maintain full-time residency at the seller's facility. For less critical products, or those with low quality standards, audits can be quarterly, annually, or at the end of the contract period.

By the way, just because you sell to the government doesn't mean the profits on these sales are tax exempt. Normal IRS regulations apply to profits on government sales the same as commercial sales.

One of the side effects of getting involved in government contract work is that to comply with all the paperwork, audit requirements, cost standards, and contract negotiation procedures additional personnel qualified to handle the administration of the contract might need to be hired. This added cost becomes overhead, which is not directly assignable to contract pricing, except as part of allocated costs. Many potential government suppliers are frightened off because of this additional overhead and miss a good opportunity, not only for added profits, but also for free financing.

The bid package

A third element of additional cost and effort in government contracting is the preparation and submission of a bid package. Because nearly all contracts are let on competitive bids, the company submitting the lowest bid and meeting the other requirements of the contract gets the order. This means that the preparation of the bid package is crucial to being in this market at all. A business owner unwilling or unable to make the effort and incur the costs of preparing such a package should not try government contracting. But what is this bid package, and how is it put together?

Although the size of a bid package varies with the product and the amount of the contract, it can range from several volumes of paper each several inches thick to 10 or 12 pages of forms and brief descriptions. The following six elements, however, are common in nearly all bid packages:

1. Cost build-up to contract price (which has already been discussed)
2. Description of company
3. Qualifications of management and technical expertise
4. Quality control program
5. Description of accounting/cost system
6. Description of facilities

Description of company

The history, business, and ownership structure of the company should be described in sufficient detail to give the procurement officer a clear indication that the company is qualified to do the job. It should emphasize the stability, reputation, and general market acceptance of the company's products or services. As with other customers, the government doesn't want to do business with any company sporting a shaky financial history or a poor industry reputation.

If the bid falls under the small business allocation regulations, care must be taken to clearly identify why the company qualifies as a small business. Too often, this element is neglected and a bid lost simply because the procurement office doesn't recognize the bidder as a small business.

The description of company ownership need not be elaborate. A simple explanation of percentage shareholdings is normally sufficient. On the other hand, if large corporations, pension funds, trusts, or investment bankers hold major interests in the company, qualification for the small business allocation might be lost.

Management qualifications

A description of management qualification and technical expertise must always be included in the bid package. The agency issuing RFPs wants to be certain that respondents have the ability to do the job. This makes the management and technical expertise section a crucial determinant in winning the bid. A company submitting a low bid without demonstrable qualified expertise will lose to a higher bidder with sound management and technical qualifications.

Brief profiles of experience and background of key management personnel should be included: jobs they have held, what companies they have worked for, and their education and technical training. It's also necessary to state which key personnel, if any, are not U.S. citizens. For critical, highly classified projects, a company with foreign citizens in management positions is frowned upon, and the bid can be rejected out-of-hand for this reason alone. Other bids for noncritical materiel or services, such as shoes or clothing, are unaffected by citizenship.

Bids involving engineered products require evidence of sufficient technical knowledge to design or produce the product. The package must include informative descriptions of technically qualified individuals proving this background. For instance, the project manager supervising the assembly of electronic instrumentation must have sufficient engineering background in this type of work to qualify him as an expert. On the other hand, if identical products are also being produced for commercial customers, such as generic office supplies, the only expertise required by management is knowing how to produce the products to schedule and to meet quality specifications.

Quality control

Products designed to meet specific government quality standards must be tested throughout the production cycle to be certain such standards are being met. This requires a comprehensive quality assurance program with specified testing procedures at each stage. Rework procedures for rejects must also be covered. Many government contracts require a formal quality control manual to be in place, and continually updated to meet quality standards. The bid package must identify that such a manual is in existence and describe briefly the methodology for updating it to current conditions.

When quality control is a critical issue, the company must present evidence in the bid package that a thoroughly qualified quality control manager supervises these activities. His technical background, quality control experience, and managerial abilities must be documented. For all except the most standard, generic products, government quality standards are substantially higher than most private sector requirements. Quality standards built into military specifications are especially hard to meet in commercial production. They are just too expensive to implement and maintain. The government is willing to pay the bill, however, for high quality, and as long as progress payments are available, and quality costs can be built into the contract price, you can't lose.

The government approaches quality with such a vengeance that for most military contracts, a government quality inspector will either be resident in the facility or make frequent and surprise appearances to audit quality control standards.

Cost system

When describing the cost and accounting systems, enough information must be included in the bid package to assure the procurement officer that cost and accounting systems are in place, working, and can substantiate the cost build-ups in the package. They need not be complex. You don't need a computer. The only requirement is the ability to track direct costs of the product to prove that the contract price isn't overstated.

Recent scandals surfacing from suppliers charging outrageous prices for products, such as the $250 hammer, cast fair warning to all government contractors to maintain an accurate cost system. As long as the actual costs can be documented to support the profit percentage in the contract price, the government has no complaint. It's only when the cost system fails that prices get out of hand and government auditors have a fit.

To prepare an acceptable bid package, reams of graphs and charts describing how a cost system works are not necessary. Most purchasers won't understand the details anyway. Simple statements will suffice as long as there is enough substance to assure the purchaser that costs for the project or products will be properly accumulated.

Facilities

A description of the facilities—both real estate and production capacity—must be included to assure the agency that enough capacity exists to handle the project. No agency procurement officer dares contract for products only to learn after awarding the contract that the winner's plant, warehouse, or office can't handle the volume. This would be an embarrassment that no one wants to experience. If additional machine or storage capacity might be required to handle the contract along with other business, the bidder should say so in the bid package. He should also include a request for additional funding to handle the order. Although he runs the risk of losing the bid to someone with excess capacity, that's a risk he must take.

In some cases, if additional equipment is needed and the contract covers a large quantity of production, the government will fund the extra capacity outside the base contract, requiring that the equipment be returned after the contract is completed. In other cases, the cost of capital additions is built into the contract price and the business owner can keep the equipment.

Should you try government contracting?

For a variety of reasons, many business owners shy away from anything having to do with government agencies. Impossibly inefficient bureaucracy is difficult to deal with. Quality standards and control procedures are expensive to install and maintain, and some products cannot be priced to cover the costs of such a program. Some political, moral, or religious belief might also keep a person from supporting government procurement. Maybe you just feel that dealing with the IRS is enough and you don't want other bureaucratic types prowling around your facility. For these reasons, and many more, otherwise qualified suppliers are kept from entering government contracts. Finally, there are those companies that would like to do business with the federal government, but the government simply has no interest in buying their product.

If your company does produce products or services the government can use, however, and you can put up with all the headaches of dealing with a bureaucracy, you'll find that financing through progress payments can be a lucrative way to build a business. Many small businesses in a variety of industries have experienced substantial growth in sales and profitability by financing their expansion through the government. Progress payments for government contract work continues to be an inexpensive method of financing. Additional information about qualifying for progress payment contracts, compiling bid documents, and participating in small business allocation contracts can be obtained directly from the U.S. Department of Commerce or Department of Defense, or through a local, federal procurement office.

The following is a brief questionnaire to help you determine whether government contracting is for you. Though not extensive, it's a handy method to review the risks and exigencies of financing expansion through this source.

Government Contracts
Questionnaire

1. Does my product line fall within the bid requirements for small business allocations?
2. How many competitors will be bidding?
3. If bidding on a military procurement, will quality control procedures and standards require additional costs to implement?
4. If yes, what is the cost?
5. Can I use the same quality system for other commercial products?
6. Can I pass the costs of this improved quality on to commercial customers?
7. Do I have technically qualified supervisors in place to meet government requirements?
8. Is my cost accounting system sufficient to meet government standards?
9. Is there enough excess capacity to take on the additional volume?
10. If not, what equipment or space must be added? At what cost?
11. Am I prepared to deal with government auditors and inspectors? Office space? Personnel? Time?
12. Does the financial performance of the company over the past three years meet government standards for financially viable suppliers?

SBA financing

The Small Business Administration (SBA), an agency of the federal government, assists small businesses in getting started, expanding, and entering new markets by providing consulting advisory services, educational classes, and financing. Advisory services are provided by retired executives from a variety of industries and skills, who volunteer their services through an SBA organization called SCORE, Service Corps of Retired Executives. Active business people also volunteer, although they are not as numerous as retirees.

Typically, when applying for financing from the SBA, the first step is an interview with a SCORE representative, who will make suggestions, help the applicant complete the loan application, and offer any assistance desired. There is no mandatory requirement to use SCORE volunteers. They are available solely for the benefit of the small business person, and if their services are not wanted or needed, they won't push. There is no cost if you do choose to use them.

The SBA also offers a host of educational courses for entrepreneurs ranging from elementary bookkeeping and inventory control to computer instruction and modern marketing techniques. Classes describing how to prepare business plans are extremely popular, as are courses involving current tax and legal subjects. Most of these classes are free, although a few charge a nominal amount to cover out-of-pocket costs.

The Omnibus Trade Bill of 1988 increased the maximum loan available with SBA assistance from $500,000 to $750,000 for working capital and to $1 million for other purposes. Obtaining this assistance can be accomplished in either of two ways: (1) by borrowing from a commercial bank with an SBA guarantee, or (2) by borrowing direct from the SBA. Either way, the starting point is to complete an application at your local SBA office and go through the interview process.

Just as with tax laws, the SBA's qualification criteria, loan requirements, and availability of direct funding continues to change. What is true today will undoubtedly change tomorrow, and availability of specific types of funding in one part of the country might be restricted in another. Therefore, it's virtually impossible to lay down hard and fast rules. There are some general principles, however, that have remained in effect for a number of years.

SBA criteria

Generally, to qualify for SBA financial assistance, a company must meet the current SBA definition of a small business and qualify under certain credit requirements. Any SBA office can fill you in on the current policies for each of these criteria. As of 1988, to meet the definition of a small business:

1. A manufacturing company must have under 1,500 employees.
2. A service business must have less than $14.5 million in sales.
3. A retailer must have sales under $13.5 million.
4. Transportation and warehousing companies must have less than 1,000 employees.

5. Wholesalers must have less than 500 employees.

6. A construction company must have under $9.5 million in sales.

These standards are not sacrosanct, however. The size range varies in certain states and, from time to time, the SBA changes its guidelines. The best way to know if your business qualifies is to check with your local SBA office.

In addition to meeting size criteria, a company must be creditworthy and meet five general credit standards:

1. The business owner must be able to prove that he has high integrity and character. The best way to do this is by references from previous lenders and business associates.

2. The applicant must be able to show evidence that he has the ability to operate the business successfully. Profitable historical financial statements are an excellent measure.

3. The business owner must have enough personal capital to demonstrate that, with the SBA loan, the business will be operated on a sound financial basis. (This criterion seems contrary to the purpose of SBA financing of small businesses who can't get their financial needs met elsewhere. The implication that a financially sound debt/equity ratio is required to get SBA help seems ludicrous. Nevertheless, that's what the SBA wants.)

4. To quote the Small Business Act, which originally formed the SBA, the loan applicant must be "of such sound value or so secured as reasonable to assure repayment." (This also seems inconsistent with the avowed purpose of the SBA to help small businesses find money. If there is sufficient collateral, the entrepreneur wouldn't have to go to the SBA in the first place.)

5. The company's historical financial performance and projected performance after receiving the loan must give reassurance that the loan can be repaid out of future earnings.

There are two types of financial assistance available from the SBA: direct loans and bank loans with SBA guarantees.

Bank loans with an SBA guarantee

Almost without exception, when a business owner applies for SBA assistance, he will be asked if he has tried other sources first, such as commercial banks. If the answer is no, then the SBA office will usually not talk to him until he makes this effort. SBA financing is supposed to be a "court of last resort," where small business owners or entrepreneurs can raise capital unavailable elsewhere. Therefore, if you're interested in SBA financing, the first step is to get turned down by the commercial banking fraternity. Current SBA requirements insist that an applicant be turned down by at least two commercial banks before applying to the SBA. That shouldn't be too hard. Chapter 1 has already listed the unreasonable demands banks make. Be careful though. The SBA will only guarantee 90 percent of a loan up to $155,000 and 85 percent of the balance up to $1 million. This means that the commercial bank will have to be satisfied that you're good for at least 10 to 15 percent of the loan balance. Even if the bank is satisfied with holding 10 to 15 percent, they still might refuse to participate because of onerous SBA restrictions.

Interest rates and payback periods for SBA guaranteed loans are fixed by law. The rate is usually higher than most commercial bank rates but the payback periods are substantially longer, from seven to twenty-five years. With this long amortization period, most commercial banks are not willing to even consider such loans. Without bank participation, this route won't work, but it must at least be tried.

Assuming you can find a commercial bank willing to loan under SBA regulations, the SBA guarantee takes the place of personal guarantees of the business owner. It also takes the place of unreasonable amounts of collateral usually required for security by commercial banks. That's why SBA-guaranteed loans are so popular with entrepreneurs just starting out with virtually no collateral as well as with business owners whose companies do not have many hard assets or substantial receivables.

Mitzy Scott started her photography studio in 1983 after serving an apprenticeship for 12 years with a large New York studio. In the beginning, between her own savings and a loan from her in-laws, she managed to stay out of the banks. Three years later, however, her business was doing so well that it seemed logical to hire an assistant, move to a larger studio, and diversify to a modest-sized, modeling agency specializing in children and teens. She judged she needed about $300,000 for working capital and photography equipment to make the expansion. Trying the local branch of Fidelity Bank, she quickly learned that regardless of the advertisements and proclaimed adherence to federal anti-discrimination laws, the bank refused her loan application—citing lack of credit experience. She knew better, and decided to try the SBA which she had heard would favor female business owners rather than discriminate against them.

The Philadelphia SBA office suggested she try one of the other banks in the area which they knew handled SBA loans. Mitzy complied. A branch of Meridian Bank welcomed her loan application. Within four months, she had a $300,000 loan at two points more than prime for 10 years. With SBA participation, her photography equipment sufficed as collateral and no one pressed for a personal guarantee.

After it was over, Mitzy took me to lunch to celebrate her new expansion and thank me for helping her with the SBA arrangements. Her comments were similar to many others I have assisted through the SBA, "I'll tell you Larry, I was pretty angry when Fidelity pulled their cheap trick, but the help and consideration I got from the SBA office more than renewed my faith. The next time I meet somebody looking for money, the first step I'll recommend they take is to see the SBA."

Mitzy's case was typical of the reception most of my clients have received from the SBA. Though all haven't been satisfied with the end result—some had their loan applications turned down—nearly everyone has complimented the SBA personnel and SCORE representatives on their courtesy and apparent desire to help. And that's encouraging in this day and age of bureaucratic indifference.

Direct loans from the SBA

If a bank will not participate with an SBA guarantee, the other option is to apply for a direct loan with the SBA. The availability of these loans is determined by how much the SBA has left in its coffers out of its annual allocation from Congress. During some periods, it's impossible to get a direct loan because there just aren't any funds. Other times, assuming you have been turned down by two banks, the agency can help.

Direct SBA loans are a marvelous way to raise capital. Even though interest rates are normally a bit higher than bank loans, the payback period of up to 25 years is substantially longer than anything you could get from a commercial lender. The funds can be used for virtually any business purpose. With such a long amortization schedule, monthly debt service payments become significantly lower than for nearly any other source. Collateral must secure the loan, but at least the amount won't be as unreasonable as that demanded by commercial banks.

Both SBA guarantees and direct loans favor minorities. If you are black, hispanic, American Indian, or belong to some other defined minority, the SBA will favor your loan application over others. This can be a terrific advantage because, as stated earlier, annual funding for the agency is limited by Congress, and if the funds run short, minorities get preference.

Every large metropolitan area and many midsized cities have SBA offices. An appointment with a loan officer will get you started. Some commercial banks will also help you get the process rolling, but because most won't touch an SBA deal, you're probably better off going directly to the SBA office. With a few exceptions, such as publishing, gambling, and investment or speculation in real estate, most types of smaller businesses are eligible for SBA assistance.

The SBA can also assist in financing small business export programs through direct loans of up to $750,000. These funds can be used to purchase equipment or materials to make products for export or for working capital to develop or maintain an export program. Chapter 11 explores SBA funding for export programs along with other sources.

Unfortunately, the SBA has recently fallen on hard times. Budget cuts have made the agency practically impotent. The SBA's report, *The State of Small Business*, states that small companies received nearly $300 billion in commercial and industrial loans in 1987 and about $540 billion in commercial mortgages. In 1988, the SBA guaranteed about 15,000 business loans totalling $2.4 billion. Obviously, with the SBA currently contributing less than 3/10 of one percent of the overall financing requirements of small businesses, its impact in the financing markets is negligible. Furthermore, direct loans from the SBA were, for all practical purposes, nonexistent during 1988 and 1989. What the future holds is anyone's guess. With the combination of continued budget deficits, however, there is nothing on the horizon to suggest an improvement.

As an experiment in helping small businesses finance their needs from budget drained federal coffers, the SBA has recently begun working with a few states to structure loans from commercial banks with SBA guarantees, which are subsequently sold on the open market to replenish the SBA treasury. A private organization called the Business and Industrial Development Company (BIDCO) originated in California where there are several such organizations. A few other states have followed suit and expanded the concept to include equity funding as well as debt. With the federal budget crunch continuing, other states will inevitably try this or similar means of providing SBA-assisted financing for small businesses. The best source of information in your state is, once again, the local SBA office.

If, for some reason, the SBA officer doesn't feel you qualify for either a bank loan with an SBA guarantee or a direct loan, he will probably suggest you try a Small Business Investment Company (SBIC). Chapter 10 examines how SBICs can assist in financing R&D projects. SBICs are privately owned financing companies, licensed and regulated by the SBA. SBICs provide capital for expansion of existing businesses, new company start-ups, or for developmental projects. They are the forerunners of venture capital firms and will finance a deal with either debt or equity capital. Normally, they take at least 15 percent or the company's ownership in exchange for providing capital. They're easy to work with, however, and because of the tie-in with the SBA, through licensing and regulations, are less prone than private venture capital firms to become offensive when operating problems arise.

Special SBA financial assistance

In addition to standard business loans through either the direct method or the guarantee procedure, the SBA offers special types of loans to meet specific needs. These loans can also be either direct or through banks with an SBA guarantee:

1. *Economic Opportunity Loans* for economic or socially disadvantaged entrepreneurs. Blacks, hispanics, American Indians, and native Alaskans are examples of those defined as disadvantaged.

2. *Disaster Loans* for businesses in federally declared disaster areas resulting from floods, earthquakes, tornadoes, and so on.

3. *Handicapped Assistance Loans* for either physically handicapped business owners or those companies where more than 75 percent of the employees are handicapped in some fashion.

4. *Economic Injury Loans* for businesses injured by some government action, such as the closing of military installations, federal acts involving pollution or safety requirements, and so on.

5. *Displaced Business Loans* for companies displaced by some government act such as building a road through the middle of your facility.

6. *Contract Loan Program* for businesses that have been in operation more than 12 months on specific government contracts to enable them to complete the contract. This only covers labor and materials, however. Not overhead and profit.

7. *Seasonal Line of Credit* for seasonal types of businesses.

8. *Contractor and Real Estate Loans* provide financing of up to three years for the construction of commercial or residential properties.

The SBA Surety Bond Guaranty Program

The Surety Bond Guaranty Program is specifically designed to assist small and emerging contractors to obtain bonding. The SBA will guarantee up to 90 percent of the losses incurred by the surety to a qualified surety bonding company. Losses might be related to bids, payment, or performance by the contractor. The maximum amount of the construction contract cannot exceed $100,000. The SBA will also issue a surety guarantee of up to 80 percent and, in unusual cases, 90 percent on contracts of more than $100,000, but less than $1,250,000. The percentage guaranteed will depend on the circumstances of the project and the creditworthiness of the contractor.

Economic Development Agency funding

The Economic Development Agency was conceived to provide business development loans to businesses, public agencies, or community groups to assist in the development or upgrading of a specific community, neighborhood, or area. These loans must be used primarily to develop business that will create new jobs and improve the income and conditions for local residents. They can be used either to establish new companies or to expand existing businesses. The only catch is that the business must be located in a redevelopment area, which is designated by the EDA. You can get a listing of redevelopment areas from any EDA office. The biggest advantage of an EDA loan is that there is no legislated upper limit to the amount, although EDA officials prefer to take on those projects that are already financed through the SBA and merely increase the amount of funding available.

Direct EDA loans are made for the purchase of hard assets by the business enterprise, such as machinery and equipment, buildings, and land. These assets must be used as collateral to the loan, and the EDA insists on a first position; that is, there can be no prior liens against the property. The EDA will loan up to 80 percent of the cost of these assets and the entrepreneur must come up with the other 20 percent independently. Interest rates range from prime plus 1.5 percent to 2.5 percent. The term of the loan is normally limited to the life of the asset being acquired, but no longer than 25 years. In addition to the interest rate, the EDA will want an annual placement or guarantee fee of one-half percent of the outstanding balance of the loan.

The EDA can also provide working capital funds in the form of guarantees to bank lenders. In this case, the EDA guarantees up to 90 percent of the loan with the private lender, risking 10 percent. The loan cannot extend beyond five years. As with every government agency, however, the rules keep changing, so if you are interested in pursuing EDA assistance, get in touch with your local EDA office and find out what requirements have changed. EDA loans are hard to get, and you shouldn't waste your time with an application unless you're sure you meet all of the requirements.

The business must be located in an EDA defined redevelopment area, and EDA loans cannot be used to relocate a business to such an area. The business must already be there or it must be started from scratch in the area. In addition to these restrictions, there are seven other criteria that must be met to qualify for financial assistance:

1. The project must be consistent with, and conform to, the existing EDA-sanctioned economic development program for the area, commonly referred to as the OEDP, or Overall Economic Development Program.

2. Each applicant must first get the approval of the state or municipal agency promoting or otherwise directly supporting the development.

3. The project will be disqualified if it is in an industry experiencing significant overcapacity. (It is unclear just how the EDA measures overcapacity, but such a restriction does exist.)

4. The EDA must be satisfied that the loan can be repaid by the business.

5. The applicant must provide at least 15 percent of the total capital required for the project from equity sources or subordinated debt.

6. Any construction contractors on the project must pay prevailing government pay scales.

7. Only those projects which provide an EDA exposure of $20,000 or less per job created, or saved, will be considered.

EDA financing clearly isn't for everyone. Most business owners who use this method are involved in some type of construction or contracting effort in an urban redevelopment program or a rural development project. Nevertheless, the EDA does serve a purpose in the overall financing market, especially for high cost projects that other financing sources find too risky.

Financing through other government agencies

There are a host of other government agencies with limited funding to finance specific types of projects. There are too many to list even a representative number here, but if you're interested, the fastest way to find out what agencies might finance projects from your company, call or write your U.S. congressional representative. All congressional offices have staff people specifically designated to assist constituents in any way possible. Just tell them what you're looking for and nine times out of ten, they'll be able to put you in contact with the appropriate agency. There are four major groups of federal financing programs for private industry:

Department of Agriculture   for projects having to do with agricultural conservation programs, environmental protection, crop insurance, wool, feed grain, cotton and wheat stabilization, forestry and fish conservation, and low-income farm housing repairs. Financial assistance from the Department of Agriculture comes through two agencies: the Farm Credit Administration and the Farmers Home Administration. You don't have to be a farmer to get financing from these sources. You do have to be located in a rural environment, however—in a town or city with a population below 50,000 people. A business located in this type of area can apply for Department of Agriculture financial assistance regardless of what product or service the company sells.

The Farm Credit Administration is responsible for federal land banks located throughout the nation that make long-term mortgage loans to assist in developing agricultural communities and farms. These federal land banks are administered by cooperative credit associations composed of farmers and others from the local area. To be considered for a loan, you must be a member of the cooperative. If you get the loan, then you must use 5 percent of it to purchase stock in the cooperative. These loans are relatively cheap. Currently, they are one percent over the rate paid by the member bank for its funds—and the term varies.

The Farmers Home Administration (FMHA) makes direct loans and bank guarantees for a wide array of purposes. In the business area, the FMHA will either make direct loans to businesses or guarantee 90 percent of a loan from a bank. Interest rates vary, and the maximum terms are 7 years for working capital, 15 years for equipment and machinery, and 30 years for real estate. Priority is given to applicants located in open country or in towns with less than 25,000 population.

Department of Labor   for projects involving employment and labor training, assistance to workers adversely affected by imports, and occupational and health programs.

Department of Transportation   for acquisition and construction of facilities for mass transit, merchant marine, and urban transportation; and to subsidize air service to small communities.

Local Development Corporations   are state or local organizations formed by local residents, businesses, and financial institutions to further the economic development of the area through assistance to small businesses. The SBA loans funds up to $500,000 directly to the Local Development Corporation for each small business company to be aided. Funds can be used to expand the equipment or real estate of a business or to start up a new business. Loan maturities extend to 25 years.

In addition, low cost loans or grants are available directly through the Environmental Protection Agency for special EPA projects and through the Department of Housing and Urban Development for construction of low-income housing. Currently, HUD is still trying to recover from the bribery, fraud, and payoff scandals that rocked the agency during the eighties, and until the smoke clears, it is uncertain exactly what funds will be available for what uses.

Financing through private foundations

If government money doesn't hold any appeal, how about a grant from a private foundation? There are literally thousands of private foundations promoting projects, regions, minorities, and special interest groups. Some offer technical assistance or counseling to small businesses trying to expand into a specific area or product line. All offer either very low cost loans or outright grants. Most business owners aren't aware that this type of financing exists because these foundations do not advertise nor are they well known in financial circles. Many have been established by wealthy philanthropists as a way to improve social conditions. Others have been founded by a few major corporations (Xerox, Ford, Butler Manufacturing, Kennemetal, Phillips Petroleum, Marathon Oil, H&R Block, and Hitachi are some of the better known companies) as nonprofit organizations to develop new products or new technologies. Still others have direct lines to universities or research labs to promote scientific exploration.

Private foundations are an excellent source of capital for a whole spectrum of businesses and projects. Sufficient investigation should uncover private foundations that can provide at least some funding for virtually any need. The trick is to locate the source that best fits your business. A sampling of foundations offering some of the larger grants is included in Appendix C. A comprehensive source of names and addresses of large and small foundations that offer financing assistance can be found in a current book, *Free Money for Small Businesses and Entrepreneurs*, by Laurie Blum listed in the bibliography.

There are two ways to get money from private foundations: (1) by loans or grants direct from the foundation, and (2) by using an intermediary, nonprofit organization. The first method is self-explanatory and not that difficult once you locate the right foundation, as Bob and Janet Wrenwright learned.

Bob and Janet ran a youth counseling clinic outside Atlanta. Most of their clients were troubled young people either addicted or still experimenting with drugs and alcohol. The couple received some financial assistance from local charity drives and a few small stipends from local churches and religious groups. It was enough to get by, but just barely. The clinic grew rapidly, and as additional staff people were added, Bob and Janet could easily see that they would never have enough working capital for the branch center they had planned for several years to open near downtown Atlanta. Then they heard about the Coca-Cola Foundation in Atlanta.

The Coca-Cola Foundation offered both grants and loans for socially beneficial projects, and within six months, Bob and Janet had obtained a direct grant of $80,000 to get their new center started and a low interest loan of $50,000 to help defray the cost of acquiring furniture, office equipment, and supplies in the new location. Thanks to the Foundation, the inner city branch of their counseling clinic not only survived the initial opening expenses, but has gone on to become a major force in fighting addiction in young people in Atlanta.

The second route to getting money from a private foundation involves locating a nonprofit organization interested in promoting the type of project you're interested in. Once the organization is contacted and approves your project, it can apply to the appropriate foundation for the funding. If granted, the nonprofit organization receives the money and passes it on to the business enterprise. Most nonprofit organizations involved in this type of private company financial support expect to be paid between five and seven percent of the grant or loan as a placement fee. Many don't insist on it, but all expect it. Still, a one-shot charge of five to seven percent is a lot cheaper than 10 to 12 percent interest for the life of the loan charged by commercial lenders. Also, because much of this money is in the form of grants, not loans, it never needs to be repaid.

It's not hard to locate a nonprofit organization as a sponsor. Any library has listings of charitable organizations. Chambers of commerce normally know of local, nonprofit groups. And area offices of the United Way maintain records of local charitable organizations and their objectives. Whitehall Foundation, Inc. in Palm Beach, Florida, and The Arca Foundation of Washington, DC are two of the better known foundations that offer this indirect way of financing projects.

The starting point with most private foundations, just as with commercial banks, the SBA, other government agencies, or any other financing source, is to put together a financing plan. As described in chapter 4, it doesn't have to be a complex plan, but should be inclusive enough to give the grantor a comprehensive picture of why you need the funds and what benefits will be derived from the project. If you go through a nonprofit organization, information about their tax status, management, purpose, and annual budgets should also be included. Additionally, if you can find newspaper or magazine articles extolling the work of the organization, this would be very helpful in generating interest from the foundation.

If you don't have the time or the inclination to put together a plan, solicit third-party, nonprofit organizations or search out applicable foundations. Your public accountant or a qualified management consultant can help. Many might not be aware of the opportunities or techniques for financing through private foundations, however, because their clientele have probably never thought of this source. In this case, check with one of the foundations listed in Appendix C. They should be able to refer you to a qualified professional in your area whom they have worked with before.

Government funding through progress payments, the SBA, or other agencies, as well as private foundations, can be a viable financing alternative to a commercial bank. The cost, payback period, qualifications, collateral, and application and reporting requirements vary, but there are some constants. The financing is more economical; getting it is less troublesome; and the risk is far less than borrowing from a commercial bank. If such financing schemes don't appeal to you, however, there are a host of other ways. Chapter 7 examines public stock offerings and partnerships as two other methods to raise that much needed capital.

7

Raising capital through an IPO or partnership

TCO CORPORATION SOLD SURGICAL SUPPLIES TO HOSPITALS, PHYSICIANS offices, nursing homes, clinics, and pharmacies in suburban Los Angeles. The board of directors of this $13 million distributor voted to begin a nationwide acquisition program by purchasing other small distributors who commanded prominent shares in each of their regional markets. Jerry Fuller, the founder, majority shareholder, and CEO of TCO Corp. agreed that the time was right to expand the business, and this seemed like a good way to do it. His investment banking partner, who was also a board member, pushed hard for a public stock issue, arguing that, with the company's profitable history, they should be able to raise $10 million. This would be enough to retire most of the existing long-term debt and still leave plenty for two or three small acquisitions. Jerry wasn't too sure this was a good idea but, inexperienced in financing matters, he acquiesced to the investment banker's opinion.

The TCO initial public offering (IPO) consisted of five million shares at $2 per share. The investment bank insisted on handling the underwriting itself. With the issue only 50 percent subscribed, the banker gave up and withdrew the offering from the market. Jerry was furious, but had little recourse. When recounting this experience to me 18 months later, he admitted that the issue failed for two reasons: (1) the investment bank didn't know what it was doing in the underwriting market; and (2) they attempted the issue when the public market for hospital supply and pharmaceutical companies was declining. Jerry never tried an IPO again. Two years after our meeting, he sold the company and retired to New Zealand.

Under the right circumstances, issuing stock to the public can be one of the best and most lucrative ways to raise major amounts of capital, assuming the issuing company can boast annual sales of at least $5 million. Smaller companies can make an offering, but it usually becomes prohibitively expensive. For a company with sales of at least $5 million, however, a public stock issue is a handy way to raise long-term capital for major expansions, business or product line acquisitions, recapitalizations, or to increase the value of management-held shares. Although going public is an expensive process that requires significant up-front expenditures, as well as on-going expenses to comply with SEC reporting regulations, the amount raised can far exceed opportunities in the debt markets. For many companies, the high cost of an IPO prohibits serious consideration. For others, compliance restrictions from the Securities and Exchange Commission (SEC) and state regulatory agencies preclude an owner from venturing down this trail. Nevertheless, many companies use this route to make a quantum jump in their expansion or recapitalization plans.

It's important to remember the matching principle when considering an IPO. Money raised from selling equity shares is long-term capital and should only be used to acquire or develop long-term assets. New shareholders will be looking for dividends or stock appreciation, or both, as the payback on their investment, and this can only occur through earnings generated by incremental business resulting from the addition of productive assets. Funds raised through an IPO should be used to acquire these new assets. Some companies violate this principle and issue stock to raise short-term working capital or to pay current dividends. This type of misapplication of funds inevitably leads to additional financing shortfalls down the road and creates more cash problems than existed before the IPO.

There are fundamentally three major problems in making an initial stock offering. First, you can't go public until you find a competent underwriter to handle the issue and complete all the paperwork to secure approval from the Securities and Exchange Commission. Even an intrastate issue requires approval from your state securities commission. With careful economic analysis you might decide that June 1 of next year, for example, would be an ideal time to make the issue. You get an underwriter, complete the myriad of schedules and filing applications, prepare the offering prospectus, and file your registration statement with the SEC. But the SEC is backlogged and can't get to your application for six months. Your economic window has closed, and all of a sudden, after spending thousands of dollars and untold man-hours, market conditions have deteriorated and now investors will pay only $6.60 a share rather than the $12 you had originally calculated. This is an uncontrollable event, and if you want to go public, it is a risk you must agree to live with.

The second major problem could arise after the issue is sold. Normally, one of the major reasons for going public is to utilize the trading of the company's shares to enhance the value of management's ownership of the company or to use them in lieu of cash for buying a company or product line. In either case, it's imperative that the market supports active trading in the company's shares. There is no guarantee of this, however. You might find that once the issue is sold there is virtually no market interest in trading. This can cause the value of the shares to decline to practically nothing. It can be a great way to raise initial capital, but might fall far short of serving as a mechanism for further actions or for enhancing the value of the company. Again, this is a risk that can't be avoided when going public.

The third problem also arises after the issue is on the street. Managements of many companies, especially smaller ones with less glamorous product lines, find that to keep the market price of the stock up, or rising, they need to take management actions inconsistent with the mission of their company. They find that they must continually strive to improve the earnings of the company over prior periods. They soon learn that the greater the earnings per share, and the sharper the company's growth curve, the better their stock performs. They are forced to take actions to increase earnings when the most logical move might be to temporarily retrench, trim product lines, or take a gamble on a new product. In other words, managements of public companies tend to spend a lot of time making their company look good to the market when they should be spending time strengthening the long-term prospects of the business.

A few innovative companies have recently tried a different approach to resolve this last problem. When making the IPO, the underwriter has explicit instructions to find shareholders who want to see their investment appreciate over a long period of time and are not interested in buying the shares for short-term speculation. If investors buy a stock realizing that in the short-run earnings and growth might fluctuate but over the long-term their investment will probably appreciate significantly, then the management of the company can concentrate on long-term goals, not short-term window dressing to keep the stock price up. Only time will tell if this policy attracts sufficient investors for the normal IPO. It's a relatively new approach and there are not enough companies trying it to know if it really works. Nevertheless, it's certainly something to consider.

The high cost of IPOs

There are two types of added costs an entrepreneur must evaluate before proceeding with an IPO: initial issue costs and compliance costs. Issuing public stock is not cheap. A host of up-front expenses must be incurred regardless of whether or not the issue is successful. And there is always the chance that the buying public will not purchase the entire issue or even a major portion of it. When that happens, the proceeds anticipated to cover these up-front costs don't materialize and the business owner gets stuck with paying them out of company earnings. If the issuing company is large enough, this won't be especially serious, but with a small company, such costs could easily wipe out one or two years of earnings. These up-front costs include:

1. *Attorneys* for assisting in writing the offering prospectus and SEC registration statement and for issuing legal opinions. Legal fees can easily cost as much as $75,000 to $150,000 or more, depending on the size of the law firm engaged and the complexities of the issue. Filing fees with the SEC can add another $50,000 to $100,000 to the bill. Also, additional filing fees in the state in which the company does business can add another $50,000.

2. *Public accountants* for audited financial statements and for assisting in compiling pro forma financial statements and summary financial statistics. Annual audit fees from a Big 5 firm can range from $20,000 to $150,000 depending on the size of the company and complexities encountered in the audit. Additionally, fees of $100 per hour or more are not uncommon for special IPO work.

3. *Financial printing companies* for printing the offering prospectus, SEC registration statement, and official notices. Though printing costs vary significantly in different regions of the country, budgeted amounts of $40,000 to $100,000 for all typesetting, printing, collating, and other clerical preparation costs should be conservative.

4. *Underwriters* for assisting in the preparation of the prospectus, registration statement, coordination with attorneys, accountants, and the SEC, marketing the stock issue, and providing a market for the stock after issuance. An underwriter will probably charge an initial fee of one to two percent of the issue value, plus commissions of seven to ten percent of the value of the actual stock issued.

It is not uncommon for a small IPO, say between $6 and $8 million to cost up to $500,000 before any proceeds are realized. In addition, preparing for an IPO takes a great deal of time from company personnel, especially the controller and the owner or president. Records to be assimilated, forecasts to be prepared, legal descriptions, and files to be resurrected from company archives, clearances from lease holders, copies of contractual documents, and many more administrative chores take valuable management time away from running the business. Though not an out-of-pocket expense, management time has a real cost to the company and must be considered along with other incremental expenses.

Administrative overhead costs can also run into substantial amounts once a company has issued public stock. Quarterly and annual SEC reports must be prepared. Annual certified audits must be performed. Proxy statements, quarterly financial reports, and annual reports to shareholders must be prepared, printed, and distributed. Shareholder meetings must be announced and held. If a stock is listed on a stock exchange, special exchange reports must be filed periodically. When dividends are paid, dividend notices, checks, and tax reports must be handled. All of these activities are time consuming and take away from valuable effort otherwise directed to managing the company. Most companies that go public realize quickly that additional financial personnel must be hired to cope with these continuing compliance activities.

Going public might be a terrific way to raise substantial sums of capital, but it is also a costly gamble. If the wrong economic conditions occur prior to the issue, if the underwriter can't live up to his optimistic marketing projections, if something happens to the company before the issue is consummated, or any number of other exigencies arise, then the issue could easily fail. If the issue fails to net expected returns, the company could be worse off financially than before starting down the public trail. For these reasons, it behooves every business owner contemplating an IPO to be absolutely certain that he chooses the right underwriter and that both his company and the economic conditions are right for the issue.

The best way to locate a qualified underwriter is to get references from either a Big 5 public accounting firm or through your legal counsel. Usually, accountants and lawyers with experience in SEC registrations are the first advisors to engage for an IPO. They will have worked with underwriters before and can suggest two or three who are qualified to handle your issue. Then it becomes a matter of chemistry between you and the underwriter—which can be resolved through interviews—and the fees he charges, which can be competitively evaluated.

Should you go public?

Assuming the added costs and SEC compliance procedures can be managed, the following guidelines should be helpful in deciding if an IPO might be worthwhile.

IPO Guidelines

Company structure

1. The company must be already incorporated.
2. If an S corporation election has been made and the new shareholders will total more than 35, the company must convert back to a C corporation.
3. The company must be large enough to be professionally managed by a controller, sales manager, chief engineer, and so on.
4. At least some of the products or services offered by the company should have high growth potential over the next five years.
5. This potential growth must be demonstrable, not the owner's dream.
6. A commanding market share or unique market niche is highly desirable.
7. The company must have three years of progressively improving profitability (two years if it's a small IPO under $7.5 million).
8. Projections for the next five years should show continued improvement.
9. The prior three years financial statements (two years for a small issue) must be audited by a reputable CPA firm.
10. The CPA firm must have issued a clean certificate for each of the years.

The economic picture

1. Stock exchange averages should be rising.
2. Per share averages should be running above 10 times earnings.
3. General optimism should prevail in the national economy.
4. Regional economic indicators should be at least stable, preferably rising.
5. Interest rates, national unemployment statistics, and inflation projections should be at modest levels.
6. Industry trade statistics should indicate favorable growth projections for the next three years.
7. Federal international trade policies should not be detrimental to the company's product lines.

Going public is not a decision to be made on the spur of the moment. A successful IPO requires extensive planning that should be started long before anticipating the actual issue. Most entrepreneurs who have been successful with an IPO began the process up to three years in advance. Obviously, with a two or three year certified audit requirement, a company not regularly audited must begin at least that far in advance.

Preparing to go public

The following are some of the other hints that smaller companies have found helpful in making a successful IPO, all of which dictate beginning the process early in the game:

1. Regardless of the specific products or services sold by the company, if its market is commonplace rather than glamorous, the chances for a successful IPO are substantially narrowed. You might make a high tech chrome-plated screw, but if it's used as a key part in making drop forges (a declining industry), the public won't have much interest in your product. On the other hand, a company producing relatively low-tech fasteners used in biogenetic diagnostic equipment would probably be received warmly in the financial markets. The industry into which a company's products are sold can be a deciding factor in going public. If you determine that your product fits but your market doesn't, perhaps you can penetrate a new, more glamorous market before writing the prospectus. At least it might be worth a try, provided you start soon enough.

2. A full complement of the management organization should be in place and functioning. This means that if you're lacking a controller, sales manager, production superintendent, or other key management person, or if you are not satisfied with the performance of existing key supervisors, recruit and train new people so that they can function properly long before going public. Step #6 describes public imaging as crucial to a successful issue. One of the features in successful imaging is the ability to promote the quality of your management team. If one of more are well known in the industry, in their specialty, or have uniquely applicable backgrounds, this can be enormously attractive to investors.

3. Clean up contingencies such as lawsuits, insurance claims, bank disagreements, IRS discrepancies, and any other potential problem that could cause the reader of the offering prospectus to question the viability of the company or management acumen. No reasonably smart investor wants to buy stock in a company with financial problems on the horizon. Even if you can't resolve all these contingencies on the best terms, at least get them resolved one way or the other. If you don't, then the prospectus will have to reveal the

substance and potential effect of any contingent liability, and this is never an attractive condition to an investor.

4. If you don't already have a five-year strategic operating plan in place, implement one as soon as possible. As noted later on, the offering prospectus and registration statement must include a strategic plan complete with pro forma financial statements. Rather than trying to implement a whole planning procedure at the last minute to meet this requirement, putting a workable plan in place ahead of time will smooth the way.

5. One of the "look right" features of a company going public is to have one or two new products or services on the drawing boards ready to be introduced within the next year. Investors are attracted to companies about to take a giant step forward in the marketplace with a spiffy new product. Whether its introduction actually brings a lot of new business or not, a new product with a snappy application looks good to the investing community. Reaching the point of being able to confidently announce such new products, however, usually takes two or three years of development effort. So be sure to start the process early in anticipation of an IPO.

6. Public imaging is more crucial for an IPO than for any other capital-raising endeavor. Certainly, a glamorous, high tech company with several hot new products has investor appeal. But so do less glamorous companies, providing the public knows about them. As mentioned in chapter 2, there are a number of ways to create a high profile company image. Advertising campaigns, new product introductions, trade association participation, market promotion activities, community involvement, and a host of other methods can be employed to bring your company into the public limelight. Effective public imaging will do more than anything else to ensure the success of an IPO. Therefore, it is extremely important not to overlook this relatively inexpensive method for attracting investors. People who can't even read a financial statement will invest in a company that is well known and has a good reputation.

7. Another way to enhance the company's public image and become known to the investing public is to have outside directors, who themselves are well known, sit on the board. Investment bankers, prominent lawyers, CEOs, or other officers of well-known companies, community or government leaders, philanthropists, religious leaders, even noted authors, can be of enormous help in lending their names to your stock issue. As long as the person brings public notoriety to the table, it's well worth the effort, and

the cost to persuade him to join your group. Unless, of course, his notoriety casts a pall on the investment community; in which case he can only hurt your cause. For example, many smaller companies trying to go public have learned the hard way that public activists of any caliber are harmful as board members. It might take a while to round up a cadre of available, publicly known board candidates, so once again, it's imperative to start early.

8. The economic flavor both nationally and in the company's industry can have a major impact on the success or failure of an IPO. Because the issuer cannot control economic performance at either the national or industry levels, it is important to start early enough so that the issue coincides with the most favorable economic curves. Although some companies successfully issue stock during a bear market, most are better off waiting for the market to turn. The best time to do it is with the financial markets rising; the worst time is when they are falling. Some companies, especially those in industries favored by investors as long-term growth markets, can do well during an economic trough. Investors see a bright future and are willing to take a risk as a ''flyer.'' From the company's perspective, however, this type of issue is usually underpriced, and the returns will not be as lucrative as they would be in a bull market. Generally, the higher the market's price/earnings averages, the better a new issue will do.

Preparing the offering prospectus

Once the decision is made to proceed with an IPO, and professional advisors have been selected, it is time to prepare an offering prospectus and registration statement. An offering prospectus forms a part of the SEC registration statement and becomes the primary selling tool for the underwriter to market the issue. In its final form, the prospectus gives the potential investor a clear, concise picture of the issuing company, its management, financial history, and the intended application of the funds raised through the issue. It also gives management's estimate of the financial results of the company for five years into the future (pro forma financial statements).

The offering prospectus and the registration statement must represent a conservative picture of the company and clearly identify risks to the investor in buying the stock as mandated by the SEC. There must be full disclosure of the company's financial condition, its management and their capabilities, pending lawsuits, claims, or other contingent liabilities, and a detailed explanation of how the proceeds of the issue will be used.

SEC regulations specify explicitly what items must be included in the prospectus and even how financial statistics will be displayed. A novice making a first stock issue might be able to follow the detailed SEC instructions but it's doubtful. I have never seen it happen. Everyone going public engages qualified professional advisors to offer guidance through each section of the prospectus and registration statement. In most cases, an experienced attorney or public accountant actually does the writing for the issuer.

The elements to be included in the prospectus are not much different from any other financing plan used for raising capital. The differences are in the format and in the words used to describe the company and events. As described in chapter 4, typical financing plans can be somewhat optimistic and emphasize the strong points of the company, its plans, and its management. An offering prospectus and the subsequent registration statement, on the other hand, must, by law, emphasize the risks to the buyer in making the investment. Optimism is kept to a minimum and descriptions and forecasts continually highlight how the investor might lose his entire investment. The following major topics must be included in an offering prospectus:

- Description of the stock offering—price per share, value of total issue, use of the proceeds.
- Name, address, and telephone number of underwriter and underwriter's commission.
- Description of company, along with its history and current ownership.
- Profiles of key management and any special board members.
- Product and market narratives.
- Description of facilities.
- Disclosure of contingent liabilities.
- Pro forma financial forecasts for five years into the future and underlying assumptions.
- Audited financial statements for the prior three years with the auditor's opinion letters.

The fear of losing control

A common misconception is that an owner loses control when taking a company public. Nothing could be further from the truth. In almost all cases, if an IPO is completely sold out, it will still account for no more than 25 percent of the ownership of the company. Of course, higher percentages can be sold if desired. In fact, when it comes time to retire, an owner might consider going public with 100 percent of the ownership. That certainly isn't necessary, however, nor even desirable for a small business. Actually, for the smaller business, it's easier to market the issue if the total issued shares represent less than 25 percent. If investors acquired the entire company, or even a controlling interest, then they would be responsible for the proficiency of the company's management, and that negates one of the main advantages in being an investor—to be able to sit back and clip coupons without incurring liability or management risk.

Even though it's an expensive, arduous undertaking, if it is done at the right time and for the right reasons, a public stock issue can fit the bill for raising major amounts of outside capital. Obviously, the corner grocery or video store are not large enough to use this means but any business doing over $5 million in annual sales can seriously consider this as a viable alternative to debt financing for major projects.

One attractive by-product to going public is the creation of a ready market for the balance of an owner's share in the company. When it's time to retire or to get out and do something else, a business owner should be able to sell his other stock holdings on the open market, assuming the price is right. Strict SEC insider trading rules must be followed, of course, including provisions against dumping large numbers of shares on the market at one time. This could destroy the price stability of the stock, so it wouldn't be in the best interests of an owner to do so regardless of the SEC. But nothing prohibits the gradual liquidation of shares over time.

Speaking of price, in a bull market, probabilities are high that an owner can get more through the public markets than by selling the company in total before taking it public. Unfortunately, the reverse could also happen; so timing the liquidation of shares over the right period becomes crucial to maximizing the gain.

A second interesting feature of owning a public corporation is that as long as the owner retains controlling interest—51 percent—shares are readily marketable as a private sale, outside the confines of the market. The SEC's full disclosure rules make such an acquisition attractive to potential buyers not wanting to spend the time nor the money in complicated due diligence procedures.

The following summarizes the major advantages and disadvantages of financing an expansion move, acquisition program, or recapitalization by going public:

Advantages:

1. A greater amount of money can be raised than through debt financing, grants, or from private investors.

2. No interest payments are required and the company can unilaterally determine what, if any, dividends to pay, therefore making the financing potentially cheaper in the long run.

3. Control of the company remains with the owner.

4. A ready market exists for the owner to sell shares when it's time to get out.

5. Even without selling shares on the open market, the owner can sell to a private investor faster than if the company was not a public corporation. The valuation of the company also becomes much easier.

6. Stock options can provide a valuable incentive compensation program for key employees.

7. It might be the only way to raise sufficient growth capital for internal expansion or business acquisitions. Most companies reach a point where additional growth cannot be financed internally. Going public adds financial stability to the company and increases additional borrowing capability.

Disadvantages:

1. The cost of going public is very high, and additional administrative overhead must be added to maintain compliance reporting.

2. SEC regulations restrict an owner's freedom of action.

3. The economic or market timing could be wrong.

4. Tax advantages of using an S corporation are negated.

5. Full financial disclosures reduce the degree of privacy an owner can maintain, and personal and company skeletons are revealed.

6. It usually precludes the use of venture capitalists or investment bankers for future financing.

7. New management techniques will have to be learned to fulfill a fiduciary responsibility to public shareholders.

Unfortunately, a business owner might be ready for an IPO but the market might not be ready for him, regardless of climbing stock averages and Wall Street optimism. For example, according to *The IPO Reporter*, published by Dealer's Digest, Inc., during March 1989, nine nonfinancial companies managed to raise a mere $47.2 million through IPOs, and in April the totals were nine companies and $164.2 million. Although still a fair amount of equity capital, this volume was less than one-fourth for comparable periods in 1988. Since April 1989, conditions have deteriorated, the window for IPOs seems to be rapidly closing. Many business owners looking to this source are holding their breath hoping that the future will show more promise.

Going public is certainly not for everyone. Up-front costs, continuing compliance expenses, and restrictive SEC regulations could make this move unattractive to many entrepreneurs. On the other hand, a public issue might be the only feasible way to raise large amounts of equity capital and, therefore, should not be discarded out-of-hand as impractical. There is another way to do an IPO which, although currently in disrepute because of federal investigations into fraudulent stock manipulations, offers most of the advantages of a standard IPO but at much less cost. It is called a blind pool merger.

Using a blind pool merger

Many smaller companies that are unable to afford the cost of an IPO or that are unwilling to invest the lengthy time involved in its preparation, find the answer in what is commonly called a blind pool merger. A blind pool merger works as follows:

1. An individual or group of individuals form a corporation, say XYZ Corp., with a nominal amount of capitalization—$5,000 to $10,000.

2. XYZ Corp. then makes a public offering of stock to raise, as an example, $500,000. The price of the stock will be high enough to leave the original shareholders in control of the company after the public issue. This is considered a small issue by the SEC (currently the top limit of a small issue is $7.5 million) and, as such, is filed with a document called Form S-18. The S-18 requires substantially less disclosure than a standard offering, although the basics of the company, its purpose, officers and directors, and capitalization are still required.

3. The issue is considered a blind pool because the prospectus discloses that, although the company doesn't have any operations at the moment, the purpose of raising the capital is to acquire other companies. The company(s) to be acquired may or may not be listed in the filing. If not disclosed, the investor has no idea what the company will do with the money raised, and recognizes that a market will be made by the brokers involved rather than on a national exchange. These inter-dealer markets, often referred to as penny stock markets, enable the investor to speculate on the eventual outcome of his investment.

4. Once the issue culminates, the public company then merges with an operating company, exchanging stock for stock, in such a ratio

that the shareholders of the private operating company gain controlling interest in the merged entity, which is now a public company. This process is often referred to as a reverse merger because the shareholders of the private company end up controlling the public entity. The owner(s) of the private operating company in effect get the amount of cash generated from the IPO of the blind pool company in exchange for stock, resulting in a net increase of the company's coffers.

5. Immediately after the merger, the public stock acquired by the previously closely held company has very little value because, unless an S-4 is filed with the SEC, the stock cannot be traded on national markets. Consequently, the company loses is advantage of being able to use this stock for additional acquisitions, operating bonuses, or other perks associated with publicly traded stock. A proxy statement and prospectus can be filed on Form S-4, however, which then makes the stock resalable on the open market. The S-4 is merely an extension of the S-18 and includes additional information and analyses about the company and its business.

Penny stock markets have experienced very rapid growth since the late 1970s. Currently, several penny stock brokers are under investigation by the SEC for two types of fraudulent actions: (1) relationships or arrangements between the blind pool and the company to be acquired by it have not been disclosed in the filing prospectus; and (2) market manipulations. A business owner who founds a blind pool specifically to acquire his operating company must disclose this fact to investors. Some owners have been unscrupulous, however, and have either omitted such disclosure, as well as their own participation as founder of the blind pool, or have used nominees to cover up their involvement. Consulting agreements or other management-type compensation programs have also been omitted from the prospectus.

Market manipulations have been varied, ranging from creating an artificially high market by a series of wash trades between insiders using brokerage accounts, to making misleading or false public statements about the blind pool or the operating company; to charging excessive mark-ups when selling stock to the public or demanding unreasonable discounts when buying the stock back from public investors. Fortunately, these shady brokerage houses and camouflaged blind pools are in the minority. Most penny stock houses are very reputable, and most blind pools offer full disclosure. There are three major advantages to going the penny stock route rather than making a standard IPO:

1. The cost of issuing stock in a blind pool and the subsequent merger and filings cost much less than a standard IPO.

2. The arrangement takes substantially less management time.

3. Because there is always a market for blind pool stock (the brokers) the business owner can be assured of an existing market after the merger.

Essentially there are no more disadvantages in a reverse merger through a blind pool than with a normal public offering. There is still the risk that the public might not accept the operating company as a viable investment, thus driving down the open market trading value of the stock. Quarterly and annual filings must still be made with the state securities commission and the SEC. Annual meetings, dividend announcements, and disclosure rules must still be observed. Nevertheless, for many business owners, the expense saved by going public through a blind pool and the assurance of a ready market outweigh the disadvantages of being a public company.

If a public issue, either through a normal IPO or through a reverse merger with a blind pool is too costly, time consuming, cumbersome, or restrictive, another less expensive way to raise equity capital without losing control is to sell a portion of your company to a partner.

Bringing in a partner

For entrepreneurs who have successfully managed their own business over a period of time, the idea of allowing a partner to have a voice in the decision-making process can be traumatic. It is, however, an inexpensive way to raise capital. A partner can be either an active working partner or a passive investor. Smaller companies, and especially those without hard assets or products attractive to the investing public, find that bringing in a partner is the only reasonable way to raise equity funds. Selling part of the business to a partner actually achieves two objectives: (1) it is an inexpensive way to raise capital; and (2) it provides the owner with a way to structure a succession arrangement for selling the balance of the business gradually over a period of time.

A partner can be an investor group, an individual, or another operating company. Chapter 8 examines how an investor group, such as a limited partnership, can be used to bring in additional equity.

An individual might be looking for a way to increase returns over an existing investment portfolio by becoming a passive investor. It is not uncommon for corporate executives retired from active employment to want to remain involved in the business world without actually taking part in day-to-day decisions. "Golden handshake" termination agreements often leave the ex-executive with a lump sum cash settlement to invest somewhere. Tax laws or current economic conditions might preclude regular investment channels and, as pointed out in another book of mine, *The*

Battle-Weary Executive, an equity position in a closely held company could be a very attractive alternative.

Usually, an independent investor wants either a board seat or a board advisor agreement to provide some measure of control over investment. This can result in a second advantage to the business owner. Not only does the investor's money flow into the company, the owner also gets access to invaluable business or technical expertise. For certain types of businesses, this can end up being worth more to the owner than the money.

The best way to locate independent investors is through personal contacts and references from attorneys, public accountants, or even bankers. Some people find a partner through an advertisement in the *Wall Street Journal*, a trade periodical, or local business newsletters and newspapers.

If you can't locate, or don't want, this type of partner, perhaps a working partner meets your needs. Working partners come from any number of sources—employees, competitors, customers, advertisements, college alumni organizations, or perhaps from a contact through trade or civic organizations. A partnership agreement normally specifies the sale of a minority share of the business—20, 30, or some other percentage—at a price based on the negotiated current value of the business plus an amount for future growth (goodwill) resulting from the owner's efforts. In addition to bringing cash into the business, a working partner can be an enormous help to the owner, especially if the business is growing rapidly or if the owner plans to get out of the business in the foreseeable future.

In the first instance, additional supervisory or technical skills can spread the management load and free up time for the owner to concentrate on new business—customers, markets, or products. Perhaps a partner can investigate expansion into a new market or product line unfamiliar to the present owner. A working partner might also bring industry expertise and make a growth plan viable that wouldn't be otherwise.

A working partner could also serve as a perfect successor when the owner decides to retire. Professional practitioners or small service business owners often find this is the only feasible way to dispose of their business when it's time to get out. If this possibility exists in your case, be sure to get an attorney to structure the partnership agreement in the beginning to take care of successor arrangements. *Getting Out: A Step-By-Step Guide to Selling a Business or Professional Practice* describes in detail how to structure a successor program.

A third type of partnership arrangement involves another company. Not a merger per se, but the sale of part of your ownership to an operating company rather than an individual. This scheme works especially well with a large corporation as a partner. You could sell 10, 20, or 30 percent of your company to a large corporation and utilize the resources of this partner to broaden market coverage or develop new products—and still retain controlling interest. Often, a joint venture can be structured in this manner to expand into global markets. An added feature is the clout that such a partner brings in the financial community. Now, if you need additional capital, for any purpose, the presence of a large "name" partner influences any lender or investor to seriously consider your proposal.

A corporate partner could be a current customer, supplier, or, in some industries, even a competitor. This arrangement is quite common in industries characterized by large customer/small supplier relationships, such as the aerospace industry. Each of the large corporate prime contractors such as Boeing, Lockheed, General Dynamics, Grumman, and so on, maintain a cadre of subcontractors, many of whom are privately owned companies. It makes a lot of sense for a small subcontractor to team up with one of these large customers as a means of financing expansion, research and development, or recapitalization plans. Also, by selling a minority share of the company, the chances of receiving additional business from them can be significantly enhanced.

If the purpose of a partnership sale is to raise capital as opposed to arranging for a successor or for technical assistance, keep in mind that this is equity capital, and by definition, equity capital is long-term money. This capital should be used only for long-term purposes, such as to acquire another company or product line, to purchase major production equipment, to expand to new facilities, or other long-term applications. Chapter 2 explains the matching principle of long-term versus short-term capital in more detail. Selling a partnership interest to raise short-term capital for operating funds or to raise personal cash, dilutes an owner's interest without doing the company much good in the long run.

The mechanics of a partnership sale

In a partnership sale, a partner buys an equity interest from you, not the company. Therefore, the cash realized from the sale ends up in your pocket rather than in the company's till. There are two ramifications of this: (1) the tax liability for any gain on the sale rests with you the seller, not the company; and (2) for the company to utilize the money, you'll have to transfer it to a company bank account.

For tax purposes, the sale of a partnership interest is treated as the sale of a capital asset. The difference between the owner's cost basis and the sell price is a capital gain. Should congress reinstate capital gains tax rates, you, not the company, will be taxed at that rate.

The next step is to transfer the cash to the company. One way is to contribute the cash as additional owner's equity. This might not be realistic, however, if the new partner has purchased a specific percentage of the company. By contributing additional capital, your share increases and his decreases. A better way might be to loan the company the cash on a long-term promissory note. Properly constructed, this type of loan need not be repaid until you decide to sell the business completely. Of course, the repayment of the loan is a tax-free transaction. Be sure to include an interest rate in the loan document, however, and pay yourself this interest at least once a year. This makes the transaction "arms length" and satisfies IRS requirements. You will have to report this as interest income for tax purposes but the company can deduct it, so it's really a wash. There are some real advantages to raising long-term capital through a partnership sale:

- There are no interest or principal payments to make.
- A working partner can bring new expertise or energy to the business.
- A getting out position is easy to structure.
- Continuity of the business is ensured in case of the owner's death.
- The increased net worth on the company's balance sheet increases its ability to borrow additional funds in the future. (Practically any lender considers a loan from a shareholder as additional shareholders' equity.)

Unfortunately, there are also some potential negatives in any partnership:

- Locating the right partner can be difficult.
- People change, and what was once a good personality fit might turn sour over time.
- Goals and objectives of the two partners could be divergent.

Even with these negatives, however, a partnership can be a good alternative. There are a couple of tricky issues to deal with right in the beginning though. The first is to determine a proper price for the partner's share. The second is to structure a partnership agreement to give you a way to break the partnership if it doesn't work out.

Establishing a price

Unfortunately, there is no universally acceptable way to value a partial share of a closely held company. There are a multitude of mathematical, actuarial, or other textbook approaches to valuing a business that are convenient for selling the entire company, determining insurance coverage, or structuring a partnership buy-back agreement. The standard assumption in any of these methods is that the valuation and negotiation process determines how much the company is worth. When the primary purpose is to raise capital, however, a reverse procedure seems to be more appropriate.

Starting with the amount of capital required, the owner then negotiates how much of the company must be given up to meet this need. In other words, raising capital this way is purely a matter of supply and demand. If you need $2 million, it doesn't really make any difference how you value the company. The important step is negotiating how much you'll have to give up to get the $2 million. This will vary with the economic conditions prevalent in the industry, the profitability of the company, and the availability of an acceptable partner. Some owners are willing to use a third party to establish a price, such as an independent business appraiser, which usually works well if both parties can agree on a designated appraiser.

The partnership agreement

Structuring a workable partnership agreement is a bit easier. Once agreement is reached on how much of the company is to be sold, both parties should have approximately the same interests in arriving at a meaningful contractual document. The agreement should include language to cover the following eight matters:

1. Price, terms (if not a cash deal), and ownership percentage.
2. Percentage allocation of the company's profits, losses, and assets.
3. Percentage allocation of the gain or loss if the company is sold or liquidated.
4. Right of first refusal, and the price for each partner's share should either partner want to sell out.
5. Conditions, price, and terms for the new partner to acquire additional interest in the company.
6. Whether arbitration or other means will be used to settle major disputes between the partners.
7. Conditions, price, and terms for admitting additional partners.
8. State laws governing the agreement.

The buyout agreement

The partners should also execute a partnership buyout agreement, preferably separate from the partnership agreement. This becomes a crucial document in four types of possible buyout arrangements:

1. If one partner becomes disenchanted with the other and wants to get out.

2. If one partner dies.

3. If one partner becomes disabled and cannot continue to assume an active role in the company.

4. If both (or all) partners die or become disabled either simultaneously or in close proximity to each other (such as in a plane crash).

There is no need to look at an example of a partnership buyout agreement here. Every one is different anyway, so any example would be unusable in practice. The best way to get it done right is to have your lawyer draft it up. Just make sure each of the possible buyout arrangements is covered.

A major problem can arise when a partner dies and the buyout agreement stipulates a fixed price for his or her share, payable in full, within a specified period of time. Seldom does a company have sufficient funds readily available to make the purchase, and it makes no sense for the remaining partner to encumber the company with additional debt to raise the funds. The most common answer rests with "key man" life insurance. The policy should be for the amount of the fixed payment or for approximately what a variable price would be. To qualify the premiums as a tax deduction, the company must own the policy, pay the premiums, and be the beneficiary. This means that the buyout agreement must be written so that the company, not the other partners, actually buys the departing partner's share.

Raising cash for a buyout in the event of a partner's incapacitating disability is a more difficult problem. I am not aware of any insurance policy that pays a lump sum for disability, although one could certainly exist. Obviously, this would be the best way to handle the problem. Without such a policy there isn't any clear-cut way to be certain cash will be available at the right time. Therefore, most partnership buyout agreements stipulate two types of payments for incapacitating disability: (1) continued monthly payments to the disabled partner for life, based on the partner's salary at the time of disability (usually financed through a "key man" disability insurance policy); and (2) a deferred payment for the disabled partner's share of the company stretching out over several years. The latter provision must be funded either out of company earnings or through raising additional equity or debt capital. Ideally, another partner would be standing in the wings and more than willing to buy the disabled partner's share. In that case, there is no financing problem.

Throughout this discussion, the terms *partner* and *partnership* have been used. This does not imply, however, that the business structure must be a partnership to use this technique. On the contrary, selling partial ownership interests are much easier and cleaner with a corporate structure than with a partnership. With a corporation the owner can sell specific shares of stock to represent ownership interests. In a true partnership, new partnership agreements, or addenda, must be written each time ownership changes hands and each time the percentage of ownership varies, which is a cumbersome task.

A partnership, in any form, is much like a marriage; it's a lot easier to get into than to get out of. And getting out can be a very expensive proposition. If both partners do not have the same values, the same goals and objectives, and the same moral standards, there are bound to be problems getting along. With two or more individuals as partners, dissimilarities can be guarded against in the beginning through the partnership agreement; or they can be reasonably resolved by negotiating the differences as they arise. With another company as a partner, however, it's more difficult to ascertain how its goals, values, and standards will influence the partnership. And when the CEO or other top officers of the company change, its operating characteristics or corporate policies might change. So when striking up a partnership with another company, be extra careful that the buyout agreement gives you an escape clause if your partner becomes unmanageable in the future. George Cannovan forgot to do this and paid a heavy price.

ArmoMac Corp. was a profitable, $10 million a year subcontractor making small assemblies for the navy's Trident submarine program. George Cannovan approached one of the major prime contractors, General Dynamics (GD), with a proposition for GD to buy 20 percent of ArmoMac's stock for $1.5 million. This additional capital would be used to expand ArmoMac's production and testing capabilities. Wishing to safeguard this valuable source of supply, GD agreed. A straightforward agreement was executed and George purchased the new equipment. A few years later, the GD division responsible for that portion of the Trident program using ArmoMac assemblies, underwent a management reorganization and George found himself with a partner whose management goals were diametrically opposed to his personal values. The new division management team was capable but they were more into partying and entertaining than the old group and this soured George. Unfortunately, when writing the original agreement, though there were buyout provisions for ArmoMac, no price was established. Ultimately, to get GD out of his company, George was forced to negotiate a buyout price substantially in excess of the original sell price and 50 percent higher than the current book value of ArmoMac.

Though no partnership agreement or buyout agreement can cover all eventualities, minimum provisions that allow an owner to escape an unwelcome partner should be included. Not doing so can only lead to misery later on.

In this chapter, we've looked at raising equity capital in two ways: by selling shares to the public through an IPO and by selling part of the ownership in the company to a partner. But there are other ways to get equity capital as well as long-term debt. Three of the more popular ways—forming a limited partnership, using state or municipal revenue bonds, and using the cash resources of customers or suppliers—are covered in chapter 8.

8

Using a limited partnership, revenue bonds, and other outside sources

ALTHOUGH THE TAX REFORM ACT OF 1986 TOOK MUCH OF THE GLAMOUR out of limited partnerships, they are still a useful vehicle for raising new equity capital. Limited partnerships were an extremely popular investment vehicle for wealthy individuals prior to 1986. Under the old tax laws, a limited partner could personally deduct his proportionate share of any losses suffered by the limited partnership. This made investments with potentially high returns over the long term but inevitable start-up losses, such as oil and gas drillings and real estate ventures, very attractive. It was not uncommon for a small investor to put $100,000 into a real estate development limited partnership and report tax losses of $300,000 over a four-year period. In effect, the government paid back the investment through reductions in personal taxes while the investor's return was achieved through long-term appreciation.

The Tax Reform Act of 1986 changed all that, however. An investor can no longer indiscriminately deduct losses from a limited partnership without actively participating in management or in other partnership activities. Partnership income is still taxed, but partnership losses in excess of passive income from other sources are not deductible.

Over the years, limited partnerships have been a major catalyst for investments in commercial and industrial real estate, hotel development, shopping centers, and oil and gas field development. Although the tax shelter advantages of limited partnerships have been at least temporarily abated, they remain a favorite vehicle to raise capital in closely held companies; especially for those businesses connected with development projects with potential long-term capital gain possibilities.

A limited partnership is a combination of corporate and partnership structures. Although there are large, limited partnerships whose partnership units are publicly traded in the financial markets, we will cover only closely held limited partnerships with units sold exclusively through private placements.

A limited partnership always has at least one general partner, although there might be more, and several limited partners. The general partner controls the management of the partnership and is responsible for all operating activities, and assumes full liability for the actions of the organization. If a suit is brought against the organization, the general partner must bear full liability. Limited partners, without any voice in management are, in effect, merely investors, much like preferred shareholders in a corporation. The term limited designates limited legal liability in the same way that the corporate shield protects corporate shareholders.

Typically, when a partnership is first organized, the allocation of profits and losses to limited partners and general partners is carefully defined, usually based on a straight percentage of partnership units owned. Different methods can be used, however. For example:

"Limited partners will receive 75 percent of the profits of the partnership allocated on proportionate shares of units owned, and 25 percent will be charged to the general partner. All losses will be allocated entirely to the limited partners on proportionate units owned."

Or a different example:

"All profits will be allocated to limited partners on proportionate shares and all losses charged to the general partner."

Additionally, in most limited partnerships, the general partner receives salaries, fees, cost reimbursements, and other forms of compensation for administrative and management efforts before profits or losses are determined.

Just as with an S corporation or a standard partnership, cash distributions to partners—limited or general—are independent of allocated profits and losses. The allocation procedure is for tax purposes only and reflects the amount of partnership profit or loss to be reported on the partners' individual tax returns. Cash distributions, however, are not taxable (except under unusual circumstances), and can be made at any time in any proportion called for in the partnership agreement. It's entirely possible for a limited partner to receive a share of partnership losses for tax purposes and still receive a substantial cash distribution in the same year. When the partnership is liquidated, however, limited and general partners pay taxes on the amount of liquidation proceeds they receive in excess of the adjusted cost basis of their capital accounts.

If a company forms a limited partnership with itself as the general partner, it can then sell limited partnership units to individuals, other corporations, investor groups, an investment bank, or a venture capital firm. Privately placed limited partnership units are a favorite method for raising significant sums of equity capital without the cost of going through a registered public stock offering. It is not uncommon for an investment bank to be willing to participate in a private sale of limited partnership units but be unwilling to become involved in a public stock issue. Investment banks prefer the benefits of equity participation without the risk of liability; but with provisions for reaping returns prior to, or in excess of, the owner and other common shareholders. Very often, they want a preferential position in the event of liquidation. Buying limited partnership units can resolve these issues.

Structuring the deal

There are three possible structures for raising capital through limited partnerships:

1. Liquidate the corporation and donate its assets to the limited partnership.
2. Contribute personal stock holdings to a limited partnership and then loan the funds back to the corporation.
3. Form a new limited partnership and loan partnership funds to the corporation.

The first method involves a two-step transaction. The first step is to transfer all the assets of the corporation to the corporation's shareholder(s) in exchange for the corporation's common shares, which are then retired upon liquidating the corporation. Second, the shareholder(s) donate these assets to the limited partnership, which increases the basis of their capital accounts in the partnership. This is a tax-free transaction as long as the corporation does not have a negative net worth, in which case taxes are payable on the amount of the shareholders' deficit.

The second method is even easier. Here, the owner contributes his shares of the corporation to the limited partnership, which increases his capital account in the same way as the first method. Again, no taxes are payable. Under this method, the corporation stays intact and everything else remains constant; except that the limited partnership now owns the corporation. When funds are raised by selling limited partnership shares, this new shareholder (the limited partnership) merely loans the money to the corporation, being careful to evidence the loan by a promissory note bearing an appropriate interest rate. There are no tax implications when using this method other than the interest income the limited partnership must report on its loans to the corporation.

The third method keeps the ownership of the corporation and the limited partnership separate. Funds raised by selling limited partnership units are loaned to the corporation just like the second method. The only tax implications involve the taxable gains of the owner when selling his shares to the limited partnership and the interest income he earns on loans to the corporation. Probably the easiest way to see how this might work is to look at a specific example.

Barry started with one corporation, RCRX, Inc., assembling short-wave radios. As the business grew, he started up an export company, Mid-Cor International, Inc., to handle shipments to the Middle East. Eventually, vertical integration was achieved by acquiring Flatrex Corp., which produced several components used in the radio assemblies. On the advice of his tax accountant, Barry formed an English company (BARTO Trading Company) to handle the shipping, credit, and collections from foreign customers. Finding this miniconglomerate too much to handle on his own, Barry sold 25 percent of RCRX to a group of investors and found a British partner to buy out 50 percent of the English company. Recognizing the benefits of an S corporation, he converted RCRX and MidCor. At this point, the multiple corporation holdings looked like this:

Company	Ownership	Percent
RCRX, Inc.	Barry	75%
(S corporation)	Five outside investors	25%
MidCor International, Inc.	Barry	51%
(S corporation)	Barry's wife	30%
	Barry's son	19%
Flatrex Corp.	Barry	100%
BARTO Trading Company	Barry	50%
(British corporation)	English partner	50%

Two years later, Barry decided to refinance his holdings. He wanted to salt part of the money away in an offshore trust for his retirement years. He also wanted to reduce existing short-term debt and to pay a modest dividend to his partners in RCRX and BARTO. To accomplish the refinancing, Barry formed a limited partnership with himself as general partner. He engaged an investment bank to handle the private placement. Once the limited partnership was organized, Barry sold all of his shareholdings to the partnership. The tax ramifications of this transaction were as follows:

A. Sale of 75% of RCRX, Inc.

1. Because only individuals and certain qualified trusts can be shareholders of an S corporation, the S status of RCRX was terminated on the date of sale. There was no tax effect except for the built-in gains provisions when, and if, assets of RCRX might be sold in the future.

2. An S corporation tax return (1120 S) was filed for the short period ending on the date of conversion back to a C corporation and another standard corporation return (1120) was filed from this date to the end of the corporation's fiscal year.

3. Barry sold his shares in RCRX to the limited partnership for $300,000, which was $260,000 more than his cost basis. This $260,000 profit was a capital gain to Barry, available to offset against his other capital losses. The net gain was taxed at ordinary income rates.

B. Sale of 51% of MidCor International, Inc.

1. The S status of the corporation was lost and short-period corporation tax returns were filed as with RCRX.

2. The sale of Barry's shares to the limited partnership resulted in a capital gain of $60,000, which was taxed in the same manner as the RCRX gain.

3. Barry's wife and son, while continuing to hold shares in MidCor, could no longer report the company's earning on their personal returns, so they became employees of MidCor, each drawing a salary. This salary was taxable compensation and payroll taxes were paid by MidCor.

C. Sale of 100% of Flatrex Corp.

1. The sale resulted in a capital gain of $320,000.

D. Sale of 50% of BARTO Trading Company

1. The capital gain of $35,000 was taxed the same way.

As a result of these transactions with the limited partnership, Barry showed a net gain, after taxes, of $450,000, which he used as follows:

1. To set up a trust in Grand Cayman with his wife and son as beneficiaries—$225,000.

2. To pay off existing short-term debt of RCRX—$75,000.

3. To pay dividends to the other shareholders of RCRX and BARTO—$150,000.

To get the money back into RCRX and the other corporations for debt repayment and dividends, Barry loaned $125,000 to RCRX and $100,000 to BARTO secured by demand notes with interest at 12 percent, payable annually. The tax ramifications of these transactions were as follows:

1. The dividends were taxable to each shareholder as ordinary income and not deductible by the corporations.

2. The interest paid to Barry was included as interest income on his personal return and deductible by the corporations.

3. The dividends received by the limited partnership were taxed to each partner at ordinary income rates according to the partnership agreement.

When all the transactions were completed, Barry still controlled all the domestic corporations and retained 50 percent ownership in the English company through his general partnership interest. All companies were now free of short-term debt, the outside stockholders were all satisfied with their dividends, and Barry netted an off-shore trust for estate purposes. His total tax bill, excluding the annual interest income, was $225,000. A totally satisfactory arrangement for everyone. As a footnote, the limited partnership is still holding the shares in the operating companies, and the limited partners have often expressed their satisfaction with the deal.

Limited partnerships are not only a vehicle to raise equity funds. Under certain circumstances, limited partners' cash contributions can be treated as loans to the partnership rather than equity capital. This can be accomplished by forming the limited partnership outside of the operating company, perhaps with the business owner as a general partner.

How a limited partnership works

Using a limited partnership to raise capital sounds complex but it really isn't. There are some expenses in the beginning, such as attorney's fees to draft the partnership documents, appropriate filing fees, mailing costs, and printing expenses, but none of these are significant in relation to the amount of capital that can be raised—and these expenses are much less than with a public stock issue. The limited partnership units must be registered with the state of residence and, if the units are sold interstate, with the SEC. A private placement memorandum, similar to an offering prospectus for an IPO, must be prepared, although it is not as inclusive. If you plan to sell units to other than close friends and associates, an underwriter should be hired to do the marketing. This involves the same type of commission fees paid for an IPO underwriting. As long as the limited partnership is a private placement, however, the total costs of selling the issue and collecting the funds aren't even close to those of an IPO. Each state has somewhat different regulations controlling registration requirements, and the best way to clear this hurdle is to get a competent local attorney experienced in this type of transaction.

The clearest way to illustrate how a limited partnership is put together is to use an actual case history. Though not a large issue, the limited partnership formed by Max Holland for $6,500,000 serves as a ready example.

Max Holland owned 80 percent of the stock of Ready Rubber Manufacturing Co., Inc. (RRM), and his wife owned the other 20 percent. As part of his five-year strategic plan for RRM, Max needed to raise new capital totalling about $2 million for two automated assembly lines, $2.7 million for a new warehouse in Florida, and $1.8 million to set up a small weaving plant in Taiwan. He estimated it would take about three and a half years to implement the three expansion moves. Rather than going at it piecemeal, Max decided to try the limited partnership route. He hired a controller for RRM who had experience in limited partnerships and, together, they came up with the following program for SQL Limited Partnership. The $6.5 million worth of limited partnership interests were issued in units of $100,000 each, to be paid as follows:

Capital Subscriptions	Per Unit	Total Offering
Payable upon subscription	$34,000	$2,210,000
Payable one year from date of offering	33,000	2,145,000
Payable two years from date of offering	33,000	2,145,000
	$100,000	$6,500,000

Max thought that locating 65 investors shouldn't be too difficult. Between his own business associates, his wife's friends, and the new controller's contacts in the investing community, there was no need to engage an underwriter. Max enlisted his company's legal counsel and Price Waterhouse, who did the company's annual audits, to assist in putting together the placement memorandum. Four months and a number of phone calls later, 42 interested investors had subscribed to the entire offering, several for more than one unit. Max also arranged with his commercial bank, First Interstate, to act as escrow agent for collecting the subscriptions. By the end of the year, all investors had made their payments and $2,210,000 was in the bank.

During this time, Max transferred all the company's assets to himself and his wife. They then immediately transferred the assets to SQL Limited Partnership. The value of these assets represented the couple's capital contribution as general partners. The new controller also got a piece of the general partnership as compensation for soliciting limited partnership subscriptions. SQL then set up a wholly owned subsidiary called Ready Rubber, Inc.

With the $2.2 million in hand, Max purchased the new automated production lines for Ready Rubber with SQL funds, setting up an intercompany loan for $2.2 million at 10 percent interest, payable on demand. The following two years brought in the balance of the offering, and by the end of the fourth year, Max's strategic plan had been fulfilled.

In 1988, I met Max at a Wharton alumni function and asked how he had made out with his financing scheme. "Terrific," was his response. "I raised $6,318,000, net of all expenses, which was more than enough to complete my three projects. Furthermore, my controller has been able to administer the partnership without any difficulty. This was the best advice I have ever received from any consultant or accountant. If you ever need a reference, be sure to let me know."

Using revenue bonds

Many state and municipal agencies issue revenue bonds from time to time to stimulate investment in a specific industry or area. The purpose of revenue bonds is to provide financing not otherwise available to private individuals and companies for the creation of new jobs, improving the environment, or for other projects to assist in the development and well being of a neighborhood, town, county, or other local demographic area. Projects to develop industry and jobs in a depressed section of a city, to clean up environmentally dangerous sites, or to bring industry into rural areas are favored candidates.

Companies engaged in the construction or development of commercial or industrial real estate, such as hotels, shopping centers, warehouses, or manufacturing plants are prime beneficiaries of such financing schemes. Firms involved in environmental projects such as river and stream cleaning and control, water purification, waste management, noise abatement, and clean air programs are also major recipients; as are businesses providing improvements in rapid transit, airport renovation, and major roadway work.

Unless a person has participated in a revenue bond issue at one time or another or happens to be bidding on a job for which revenue bonds have been allocated, it is unlikely such financing will even be considered. Yet, companies aware of this source of funding continue to take advantage of revenue bonds to provide all, or nearly all, of the money they need for working capital and expansion moves; and in some cases, recapitalization. Often, this is the only source of funding available to smaller entrepreneurs involved in a major project. Also, revenue bonds are normally long-term funds with an interest rate normally much lower than traditional debt. Buyers of these bonds find them attractive because they are at least partially, and many times fully, tax exempt; that is, the holder pays no taxes on interest earned from the bonds.

Once again, however, congress has seen fit to muddy the waters. The Tax Reform Act of 1986 and the Revenue Act of 1987 added a number of restrictions and limitations to the use of tax-exempt bonds to finance nongovernmental projects. The most restrictive feature classifies this type of bond issue as *private activity bonds* (formerly called industrial development bonds or IDBs). If the bond issue meets the following two provisions, it is a private activity bond issue:

1. Ten percent or more of the bond proceeds are used by a nongovernmental person in that person's trade or business. Use of bond proceeds, or bond-financed property, includes direct ownership of the property or beneficial use of the property through a lease or incentive payment contract.

2. Ten percent or more of the payments on the bond issue are made directly or indirectly by nongovernmental persons.

If a bond issue falls into this category it must meet additional tests to maintain its tax-exempt status:

1. Ninety-five percent or more of the proceeds must be used for the exempt purpose of the borrower. Less than five percent can be used in a trade or business not related to the government function being financed. For example, if $35 million was raised to construct a sewage disposal plant, and an adjacent parking lot for employees cost $3 million of this amount, the issue would still be tax exempt. But if a physical fitness gym was constructed alongside the disposal plant (for employee use) it would disqualify the issue.

2. No more than 2 percent of the proceeds of the bond issue can be used to finance certain costs of the issuance.

3. The bond issue must be issued for one of the following uses, or must qualify as a small-issue bond:
   ~ The proceeds can be used to finance a qualified exempt facility such as certain low-income, multifamily residential rental projects, airports, docks and wharves, mass commuting facilities, sewage disposal plants, solid waste disposal facilities, facilities for the furnishing of electricity, gas, or water, district heating or cooling facilities, and certain hazardous waste disposal facilities. In a number of these categories, the finished project must be owned by a governmental body.

~ The proceeds can be used to finance the development of a locally designated blighted area.

~ Small-issue bonds are part of an issue of bonds not exceeding $1 million. The proceeds can be used to acquire land or depreciable property. The maximum limit can be raised to $10 million under specific circumstances.

A private contractor might be able to use the proceeds of a revenue bond issue in an existing trade or business and still qualify the issue as tax exempt, provided the issue meets the requirements of qualified mortgage bonds. Qualified mortgage bonds are used to finance low-interest loans for certain (generally, first-time) buyers of single family homes. The buyer must meet certain government income criteria; however, if the development is in a blighted area these rules are relaxed. Ninety-five percent of the proceeds must be used for this purpose. Several tax Code revisions have created a few other changes in revenue bond financing but they are minor compared to the above.

There are two big non-tax drawbacks to using revenue bonds, aside from the fact that they apply only to specific projects: (1) getting the bond program set up in the first place can be extremely complex and expensive; and (2) the administration of the program can be a complicated, time-consuming process requiring the addition of financial and administrative personnel. There are a myriad of different formats for revenue bond issues. Actually, no two are alike. Some bonds are publicly issued and traded, some are privately placed. Municipal authorities might assist in arranging bank participation or they might not. An underwriter, trustees, and commercial banks could be involved in the issue or it can be handled directly from the issuing agency. Escrow reserves may or may not be required. There are so many variations that it is impractical to give even a representative sample of possibilities. To get at least some idea of how they work, however, let's take a look at a bond issue that provided financing for the development and construction of a large hotel in New York.

Rocco Hotel Associates project

Rocco Hotel Associates (the "Company"), a limited partnership, wanted to build a 350-room hotel in a borough of New York City that was financed by revenue bonds issued by the New York City Industrial Development Agency (IDA). The IDA was willing to handle the financing because the project would provide a sizable number of new jobs in the borough, as well as redevelop a blighted neighborhood. The bond issue totaled $37 million, the estimated construction cost of the project.

The bonds   The issuing price for the bonds was 100 percent of the face value of the bonds, which were due in 30 years from the date of issue.

Most of the bonds were issued in denominations of $100,000 (one for $150,000). A much smaller number were issued for $5,000 to attract smaller investors. Each bond bore interest at a daily, weekly, or long-term interest rate to be established by the remarketing agent as that rate sufficient to market the bonds at a price of 100 percent of face value.

Although the bonds were issued by an agency of the City of New York, a specific disclaimer stated that, "The bonds shall never constitute a debt of the State of New York nor of the City of New York, and neither the State of New York nor the City of New York shall be liable thereon, nor shall the bonds be payable out of any funds of the issuer other than those pledged therefore." In other words, once the bonds were issued, none of the participating government bodies or agencies took any responsibility for the payment of interest on the bonds, or for their ultimate redemption. Liability was further clarified with, "The Bonds are limited obligations of the Issuer, and, except to the extent payable from Bond proceeds and certain other moneys assigned therefor, will be payable solely from, and secured by, an assignment of payments to be made under a Lease Agreement with the Company and from funds drawn under an irrevocable Letter of Credit." The Lease Agreement referred to was a long-term lease of the land and ultimate hotel property to the Company from the City of New York. The City of New York would own the hotel, not the Company.

The Players   Chemical Bank of New York, designated as Trustee for the bond issue, was responsible for paying accrued interest to the bondholders and for redeeming the face value of any bond submitted by a bondholder. The money to make these payments came from lease payments to the Trustee, in escrow, by the Company against a long-term lease between the Company and the City of New York. If such payments were insufficient to meet either the interest or bond redemptions, the Trustee could draw the difference from an irrevocable letter of credit (L/C) issued by Banque Indosuez.

In exchange for placing an irrevocable letter of credit totaling $37 million in favor of the Trustee, the Company paid Banque Indosuez a placement fee of $100,000 and was further obligated to pay the bank annual L/C fees of 1.5 points per quarter on the outstanding L/C balance.

It's interesting to note that, at the time this agreement was drawn, Banque Indosuez, a French bank with major investments throughout the world, had total assets of approximately $40 billion. Its stockholders' equity (net worth) was less than $1 billion. That's a debt/equity ratio of 39:1, which is just another illustration of how banks themselves are poor credit risks.

In addition to drawing down on the letter of credit, the Trustee was commissioned to hold the proceeds of the initial issue of the bonds in escrow for release upon the presentation of formal construction draw requests by the Company. Unreleased funds were invested by the Trustee to earn interest income, which in turn helped pay the interest on the bonds. Therefore, until it began to draw down on the proceeds, the company's interest expense was covered completely by interest income on the investment of bond proceeds. Of course, the Trustee received substantial fees from the interest income proceeds in the beginning and from the L/C drawdowns (and hence, the Company) later on.

To sell the bonds, the Company hired Smith Barney, Harris Upham & Co. (the "Underwriter"). The Underwriter purchased the entire initial issue for $37 million and then created a market for these bonds to be sold to the public and traded. The Underwriter thus became the remarketer who established the interest rates to be paid to the bondholders previously referred to. Of course, the Underwriter received a substantial fee up front to handle the issue—about $5 million.

The attractiveness of this issue from the Company's perspective was that the interest rate on the bonds averaged about three to four points below prime—clearly the cheapest money available. The bondholders also benefited. Their interest income was tax free and, even though substantially below prime, the after-tax effect nearly doubled the effective rate. The issue was made before the Tax Reform Act of 1986, however, and therefore, as long as the interest rate was more than 50 percent of prime, the remarketer could attract buyers to the issue. Subsequent to 1986, with a maximum tax rate of 33 percent for individuals, the remarketer adjusted the rate upward to at least two-thirds of prime. Even at this higher rate, however, the cost of the financing to the Company remained significantly lower than other sources would charge.

A bondholder, at his option, can redeem a bond from the Trustee at any time for the face value of the bond. The Company can also redeem any or all of the bonds at prices established in the initial offering prospectus. These prices ranged as follows, based on the holding period of the bonds:

Less than one year	not redeemable
Between years one and two	100 percent of the face value
Between years two and four	100.5 percent of face value
Between years four and seven	101 percent of face value
Between years seven and ten	101.5 percent of face value
Between years ten and fifteen	102 percent of face value
After year fifteen	103 percent of face value

Although each municipal revenue bond issue has its own terms and conditions, interest rate, funding requirements, and redemption provisions, they are all similar. The issuing agency is never at risk in the deal, and has virtually no administrative burden. The municipality benefits from adding jobs and a tax base. For these reasons nearly every city, town, or county in the country uses this method from time to time to stimulate its industrial development.

Banks and underwriters like these deals because of the high fees they make—and at no risk. Of course, the bank issuing a letter of credit does have some risk. If the entrepreneur defaults in making his payments, the bank must make good on the L/C. In this case, the bank merely forecloses and takes over the property or project. The bondholders like municipal bonds because they are a risk-free investment with an interest rate as good, or better, than what they could get elsewhere. The entrepreneur makes out by getting the financing at a lower rate than normally available from other sources. Also, an owner doesn't need to bother about establishing a bond credit rating because the municipality is the issuer. All in all, municipal revenue bonds are as close as possible to a complete win-win financing deal for everyone.

The major drawbacks to using revenue bonds include:

1. The project must be large enough to attract the appropriate banks and an underwriter (generally over $5 million).

2. It must be beneficial to the municipality to initiate the project.

3. The project must qualify under a specific municipality's criteria.

4. It must meet IRS regulations. If these conditions are met, however, it's pretty hard to go wrong with this type of financing—assuming the IRS will continue to allow tax-free status.

There is one additional drawback aside from the substantial fees paid by the entrepreneur. Because the bonds are issued to the public, SEC regulations must be adhered to in preparing the offering prospectus. As in a public stock issue, this always involves the use of costly lawyers. Initial legal fees in the above example ran well over $200,000. Unless the size of the project justifies such expenditures, revenue bonds should not be used.

If municipal revenue bonds seem to be a viable financing scheme, the best way to find out about opportunities in any particular locale is to work through a local law firm experienced in bond issues. They'll be able to fill you in on the likelihood of interesting the local taxing authority in a specific project and put you in contact with the appropriate municipal officials. At times, some larger cities advertise the availability of revenue bonds and solicit bids for specific projects. It's usually easier and faster, however, to work through an attorney. A lawyer must be used anyway if you decide to go ahead with the financing, so a selection might as well be made right up front. Local CPA firms might also be able to help but most are unaware of the details or requirements of a potential bond offering.

Financing by customers

In some industries, notably those characterized by a few large customers and many smaller suppliers, customer financing can be a viable means of raising capital. In fact, customer financing might be the only reasonable source of working capital or expansion funds for small companies contracting for large jobs or projects. In the aerospace industry, for example, there are only a handful of large manufacturers or prime contractors: Boeing, Lockheed, McDonnell, Gates Learjet, Cessna, Rockwell, General Dynamics, Grumman, and Bell. There are hundreds of thousands of small firms, however, that design and manufacture components and assemblies for these giants. The same industry configuration can be found throughout the government contracting business. It is also common in the shipbuilding industry, major industrial and commercial construction projects, and portions of the petroleum industry. In each of these industries, a great many small suppliers provide products and services for a few major customers. Financing from these customers typically takes the form of one or a combination of advances, progress payments, or loans.

Advances are most frequently used when a company must incur substantial costs before the product is made or service rendered; such as large purchases of raw materials, the addition of a sizable labor force, or a significant labor training period. Advances are normally used only for working capital, however, not for the addition of machinery or production space.

Advances are favored by a supplier over either progress payments or direct loans for two reasons. Normally, no interest is charged, and because payment is received in advance of the sale, the company does not carry a receivable on its books. This has a double-barreled impact on working capital. By collecting in advance of shipping the product, it's easy for the company to keep current with its vendors. This keeps the balance sheet clean and attractive to commercial banks if additional short-term loans are necessary. Second, without receivables on the books, a company reduces its working capital needs. Assuming the customer/supplier relationship remains continuous and not a one-shot sale, regular advances can, in effect, eliminate the need for additional short-term working capital borrowings.

Progress payments are also very popular in those industries requiring a long production cycle to produce the entire customer order or a construction contract extending over several months or years. In the construction industry, progress payments have been used for years to provide working capital for the contractor. The mechanics are similar to progress payments used on government contracts examined in chapter 6. In the construction industry, however, payroll is the largest single element of cost, whereas in government contracts, materials are usually the major element.

Tom Rador ran a contracting company specializing in providing contract supervision for complex, long-term installation projects in the waste management industry; large waste incinerator plants, trash to electricity conversion facilities, and sewage treatment plants. As a prime contractor, Tom subcontracted all of the actual labor and materials required for the project to smaller firms but retained supervisory responsibility. His cadre of supervisors normally totalled about 25 to 30 electrical, mechanical, and civil engineers—each earning approximating $90,000 a year, plus fringes.

Most of Tom's jobs extended over one to three years, and specific milestones were mutually agreed upon during contract negotiations. Tom was careful to structure these milestones to occur approximately one each month for the duration of the contract. As each milestone was reached and approved by the customer, Tom received a payment equal to the total percentage of completion of the project. The percentage of completion was calculated as the actual costs incurred as a percentage of total estimated project costs at completion, less payments previously received. On some contracts, a 10 percent holdback was deducted from the milestone progress payments. The payments included amounts for supervision, labor, and materials purchased.

As the prime contractor, Tom then negotiated similar deals with subcontractors who would be responsible for providing labor and materials. Milestones were also negotiated with them. As long as the project remained on schedule, which was Tom's responsibility anyway, the progress payments received from the customer substantially exceeded amounts paid to subcontractors and provided him with working capital to begin other jobs. Of course, if the project overran the originally estimated costs, or if milestones were missed, then Tom would suffer the consequences and have to come up with operating cash somewhere else.

The major difference between progress payments for construction projects and progress payments for typical government contracts is that the former are measured on the percentage of completion at each milestone, calculated as the actual cost incurred compared to the estimated costs at completion. In the latter, progress payments are normally based on actual cost of material, purchase orders placed, and labor incurred.

Progress payments from commercial customers in other than the construction industry work much the same as government contracts. For example, when I ran the $50 million Aerospace Division for Aeronca, our biggest customer was Boeing. The contracts we worked against for both the 747 and 727 airplane programs usually extended for three years, with several overlapping follow-ons. The 747 program components, the entire wing-rib structure and two major sound attenuation structures for the engine assembly, were especially costly to us. We negotiated progress payments to purchase all the materials in advance of production and a major part of the labor during the production cycle. The payments for materials were based on actual cost. For labor, payments were based on a percentage of completion of the order calculated on specific finished units shipped each month. Without progress payments, it would have been impossible for us to carry the production costs of these large products.

Under certain circumstances, an entrepreneur might be able to convince a customer to loan the company working capital cash rather than obtaining short-term funds from a commercial bank or other sources. This scheme is not as uncommon as it would appear. Many large corporations have short-term excess cash to invest in marketable securities, treasury paper, or other short-term, secure holdings. A good working relationship with major suppliers makes loans to them as secure as other alternatives. The biggest drawback in this type of arrangement, however, is that often a customer will try to gouge you on the interest rate. This happened when we ran short of cash at Aeronca and asked Boeing for a six month loan for $2 million to tide us over until they were ready for the follow-on contract. They rapidly agreed, but demanded an interest rate of four and a half points above prime!

Even if the rate is higher than that charged by a commercial bank, it's usually better to use the customer's money than a bank's. It can be both easier and quicker. And tying the customer to your company for additional business is an indirect benefit. Not all customers are willing to loan money to suppliers, but it certainly can't hurt to ask.

Financing by suppliers

Financing through a supplier is just the reverse of customer financing. Every entrepreneur is familiar with using 30, 60, or 90-day trade credit. Suppliers expect you to use their money this way and normally don't object to a reasonable pay period for merchandise purchased from them. But many times you can go much further than straight trade credit. When my partner and I owned our screw machine company in the Midwest, steel bars were the major raw material. We purchased several million dollars worth every year. Most of it came from local steel distributors, but one product required a special alloy from a Swedish steel mill. We negotiated a deal with the Swedish firm to ship enough steel bar for six months, twice a year. The steel was stored in a bonded warehouse from which we could withdraw truck loads as needed throughout the year. Our supplier agreed to bill us only as we withdrew the bars from the warehouse and to carry the balance themselves. This meant we always had at least six month's supply of this specialty steel bar without paying for it until it was used.

Another variation of supplier financing was used by a wooden furniture manufacturer. The purchasing agent of this company contracted with a distributor on the West Coast for a three-year's supply of specialty hardwood imported from South America. He negotiated a fixed price for the entire period but, short of cash, he didn't want to take delivery until the plant needed the material. The distributor agreed to make his purchases through arbitrage to take advantage of wide pricing variations with his South American supplier, but to hold any excess material in his warehouse, at his expense, until the manufacturer needed it. Also, he guaranteed to always have at least three month's supply on hand. The controller of the furniture manufacturer calculated that on an annual basis, this arrangement saved his company over $50,000 in interest and inventory carrying charges.

Just in time (JIT) deliveries have become a way of life in many industries. No longer willing to carry large inventories, users are demanding that the supplier finance the inventory carrying charges and stocking costs. And most are getting by with the practice. Supplier financing has become more and more popular in recent years and any entrepreneur not taking advantage of JIT deliveries is missing the boat. This has truly become one of the premier ways of increasing working capital, at least for manufacturing companies.

Summary

So far, a number of sources of capital have been explored and it's probably a good idea to summarize and compare them in the context of the type and size of business most likely to use each source, the type of capital each source provides, and the relative cost of each alternative. Table 8-1 shows this information. For comparison purposes, costs are weighted as 0 for the least cost and 5 for the highest cost. Cost is defined as the combination of interest rate, dividend obligations, fees, and issue costs.

Although capital from these sources combines debt, equity, income, and trade credit, most entrepreneurs tend to use any one, or a combination of them, for working capital or general business expansion. But what if you need capital for a specific purpose not related to working capital or overall growth? What if you need funds to buy a specific piece of equipment or a warehouse, to develop a new product or process, to buy a company or product line, or to finance an export program? Perhaps the timing is right to open a branch office or plant overseas and take advantage of burgeoning foreign markets? Or maybe your company is in financial difficulty already and you need to figure out how to restructure the business knowing that a public stock offering won't work? These are all legitimate rea-

Table 8-1. Comparison of Sources

Source	Best Use	Cost
Government contracting progress payments	Working capital for material, labor, and overhead for specific orders. Most commonly used in businesses making products for one of the military arms. Also works for companies making non-military products. Any size company qualifies.	2 to 4
Small Business Administration direct loans and bank loan guarantees	Exclusively for small businesses, as defined by the SBA. Can be used for either working capital or buying equipment. SBA usually refers applicant to Small Business Investment Companies if equity funds are needed to start a business or for other uses.	3
Other government agencies within the departments of agriculture, labor, and transportation supply direct loans and some outright grants	To be used for working capital and development costs for projects directly affecting growing food products, training disadvantaged labor, and rapid transit, among others. Any size business qualifies.	0 to 2
Private foundation outright grants and a few small loans	Funds must be used for working capital, equipment acquisition, or other development costs to enhance business, products, or services that are socially beneficial. Any size business qualifies, although most grants go to smaller firms.	0 to 1
Initial public stock offering	These are equity funds and should be used only for long term applications such as acquiring a business or product line, major equipment and facilities expansion, or to recapitalize the company. The company should have annual sales of at least $5 million and preferably $10 million or more. Exceptions are made for early stage, high tech, rapid growth companies.	5

(cont.)

(Table 8-1. Cont.)

Sell part interest to a partner	Again, equity capital should be used for long term purposes. Any size or industry qualifies but it's especially applicable to professional practices or personal service type businesses.	3
Limited partnerships	Equity capital for long-term purposes or loans for short-term uses. Such loans normally are convertible to equity shares in the near future. The company should have good growth potential and be large enough to provide cash throw-off for limited partners. The company should have at least $5 to $10 million in annual sales.	2
Municipal revenue bonds	This is long-term debt used mainly for major construction projects. Can also be used for major expansions of equipment and real estate in underdeveloped areas. Bond issue should be at least $5 million and company's size must justify this amount of debt obligation.	4
Customer financing using progress payments or advances, both of which are earned income, or in some cases loans, which are usually short-term	Progress payments are common in construction industry and in manufacturing products requiring large advance purchases of materials or long production cycles. In all three categories, these funds are used for short-term working capital.	0 to 2
Supplier financing is straightforward trade credit extended for longer periods such as one or two years	Funds are always used for working capital. This is off-balance sheet financing and never shows up on the recipient's books.	0

sons for raising additional capital and all require a different approach than sourcing funds for working capital or general growth. The following chapters illustrate a variety of ways to raise capital for each of these purposes. After all, working capital is only one reason for outside financing. There are many other applications creating just as big or an even greater need.

9

Finding financing for internal expansion

"ONE-STOP SHOPPING FROM YOUR FULL SERVICE BANK" IS HOW COMMERCIAL banks like to advertise their wares. Chapter 1, however, revealed that with commercial banks, all is not what it seems. As an increasing number of commercial banks expand into financial services about which they have little or no experience, the business consumer must be constantly on guard against incompetent and ineffectual advice from these newcomers. A banker might have a pretty good idea of how to review an application for a $10,000 installment loan against an automobile. Chances are, however, that this same loan officer is a neophyte when it comes to assessing the validity of a request for a five to ten-year equipment loan, a mortgage against commercial property, or a lease to cover new machinery. Nearly all large commercial banks have branched out into these and other specialties. Millions of dollars have been spent on public relations advertising trying to convince us that because commercial bankers are somewhat competent in handling checking accounts, savings accounts, and perhaps short-term operating lines, they must also know what they are doing in these other areas. Some actually do, but more do not.

When the owner of a small machine shop, delivery service, computer distributor, or publishing house wants to expand the company's capabilities by adding additional equipment or space, a natural first stop is at a commercial bank that handles the company's checking accounts or operating line. This might be a good starting place, but that's all, just a place to begin the search for capital. If your bank has departments to handle real estate mortgages, equipment leasing, or long-term hard asset loans, then by all means check there first. A personal contact with a commercial banker might get you at least part of your needs. Even if your commercial bank can supply long-term loans or leasing programs, however, it might not offer the most competitive rates and terms. It always pays to shop around when you're in the market for a new car, and the same principle holds for borrowing money. This chapter addresses financing for three types of internal expansion needs: working capital loans, machinery and equipment purchases, and the acquisition of additional plant, warehouse or office space.

Working capital financing

There are two primary sources of short-term operating loans: commercial banks and commercial finance companies. Though many large commercial banks have finance company divisions or subsidiaries, loan policies and operating management are usually segregated. Therefore, borrowing from a finance company division or subsidiary of a bank is different than standard bank loans.

After World War II, a new breed of risk-taking banks came into prominence. These were called personal finance companies and became popular as a supplier of small, highly secured, high-cost loans to individuals with poor credit ratings, who could not get money anywhere else. As cousins to the personal finance company, industrial or commercial finance companies performed the same service to businesses rated as poor risks by the banking community. Factoring receivables was the most common form of financing. Walter Heller & Co. and the James Talcott company are examples of large finance companies that grew up through the factoring business. The principle of factoring involved a company actually selling its receivables to a factor (finance company) at a discount from the face value of the accounts, usually a discount of between 20 and 40 percent. Customers would make payments directly to the factor, who would then be responsible for the collection of the accounts. Because only companies in very bad financial shape would resort to such a means of raising capital, customers looked askance at any company factoring its receivables.

Though factoring still exists, there are two more common forms of financing receivables, both requiring the borrower to retain the ownership of its receivables and the responsibility for their collection. One form directs the customer to pay directly to a lockbox controlled by the finance company. This is the method normally used. The other allows payment directly to the debtor company. Both methods are risky, however, as the controller of CORNCO learned by using a commercial bank first and then a finance company.

Cornet Consolidated Corporation (CORNCO) needed to establish an operating line to finance increased receivables resulting from a substantial growth in sales. The controller negotiated an operating line with the company's commercial bank to loan CORNCO up to 85 percent of qualified receivables. Every month, CORNCO submitted an aged listing of all outstanding accounts. If any account had any portion of its balance extending beyond 60 days, it was excluded from the borrowing base. The rest of the accounts were totaled, and CORNCO was allowed to borrow up to 85 percent. As collections were received by the company, they were deposited immediately in a collateral bank account and used to pay down the outstanding loan balance. As new shipments were made, invoices were submitted to the bank and additional funds, totalling 85 percent of the invoices, were added to the company's operating account at the bank. The bank felt secure because they always had a 15 percent cushion. CORNCO was happy because with shipments increasing, new borrowings always exceeded collections, generating a net addition to the company's cash balance. The bank charged an interest rate of one and a half points above the current prime rate on the average daily balance of the loan. It looked like a win-win deal for both sides. But then conditions at CORNCO changed.

A recession hit CORNCO's markets and sales began to drop off. It wasn't long before monthly collections exceeded shipments. Now, although the loan balance continued to decline, CORNCO needed the extra 15 percent for its own uses and the bank no longer had this cushion. As monthly sales continued to drop, the loan payback exceeded new borrowings and this caused a severe cash shortage for CORNCO. More accounts began slipping into the 90 day category, forcing additional paybacks of loans on those accounts, which were excluded from the borrowing base. Four months after sales began dropping, the commercial bank told CORNCO that it no longer wanted to do business with the company and that the controller should look elsewhere for a new bank. In fact, the bank called the balance of the loan. CORNCO lasted two more months and then filed for protection under Chapter 11 of the Bankruptcy Code.

This is a perfect example of how borrowing working capital funds against receivables can easily lead to disaster and why borrowing even short-term money from a commercial bank is a bad idea. To finish the story of CORNCO, once in bankruptcy, they negotiated a new loan agreement with a finance company at five points above prime with collections going direct to the finance company's lockbox. Until the company filed a reorganization plan and emerged from bankruptcy three years later, a representative of the finance company took up permanent residence in the company's offices to perform daily audits of CORNCO's business. In effect, the finance company took over the financial management of CORNCO, even though they never admitted to such an unethical, and illegal, maneuver.

A second method to raise working capital from a finance company is by borrowing against inventory. In this arena, finance companies have nearly all the business to themselves. Few commercial banks venture into the high-risk realm of inventory financing. Occasionally, one will try it if the customer is large enough. Financing against inventory works much the same way as with receivables. A physical inventory count of raw materials, work in process, and finished goods substantiates what's on hand each month. A finance company usually loans up to 50 percent of the cost value of finished goods and 20 to 30 percent on raw materials that can be readily sold at liquidation. Work in process seldom qualifies in the borrowing base. As new materials are purchased and new finished goods are produced, the amounts are reported to the finance company and new loans are added to the operating account. As raw materials are put into production and as finished goods are sold, quantities of both are reported to the finance company and withdrawals from the operating account are made to pay down the loan balance.

There are two big problems with inventory financing. First, the low amounts loaned against the borrowing base don't cover the cost of buying or producing the goods. Second, a company must have an effective production reporting and inventory control system in place to account for the movement of materials and production within the plant, and most small companies cannot afford such an elaborate system. Only in rare situations will a finance company loan against the inventory of a manufacturing company, although they will always want inventory as additional collateral to a receivables loan. A retail or distribution company, however, whose inventory is all finished product, readily marketable at established prices, should have little difficulty raising operating funds to increase inventory levels. The process is the same as in a manufacturing company. But what about a service company? How does the owner of an auto repair shop, a trade school, or a bookkeeping practice raise capital?

Raising capital in a service business

Owners of service businesses or professional practices have a more difficult time interesting either a commercial bank or a finance company in granting operating loans. Most service businesses need outside operating capital for either: (1) the hiring of additional personnel to handle increased business; or (2) the purchase of an additional piece of equipment, vehicle, or other hard asset to keep up with expanded customer demand. In the first instance, existing receivables should be available as collateral to a short-term loan to get over the hump. A growing service business, however, should not have to consign either its receivables (through factoring) or collections (through a bank controlled lockbox) to a bank or finance company.

The term of the loan should be short enough to merely use receivables as collateral rather than assigning them. In most instances, the amount of the loan required will be relatively small and, with a growing business, the payback period short. Therefore, with virtually no risk involved, a commercial bank should be willing to handle your needs. The bank will probably insist on additional collateral from outside the business, however. Demanding the pledge of your certificates of deposit or money market funds is not unusual. It might even want a second mortgage on your house or car. Most certainly, a personal guarantee.

Financing a piece of equipment, a vehicle, or other hard asset for the expansion of a service business can usually be handled most efficiently through a lease with the seller of the asset. Later in the chapter, we'll take a look at different types of equipment and vehicle leases that might be considered. Of course, a commercial bank—or even a finance company—would love to structure an installment loan for such a purchase. As pointed out earlier, however, this is a costly way to go and should not be used except as a last resort. Although a service business would probably never need more than one or two pieces of equipment, of which probably are not very expensive, expanding a manufacturing business is a different story. In that case, either a finance company or long-term leases are usually appropriate.

Financing through an asset based lender

When the time comes to expand your manufacturing business with a new production line of milling machines, lathes, or CNC equipment, remember that these are long-term assets. They will be used to produce products over a long period of time—probably at least five years, maybe longer. As with other long-term assets, such purchases should be made with long-term capital—either equity or long-term debt. Previous chapters examined some of the sources for equity capital and chapter 11 examines additional sources. Most entrepreneurs aren't willing to incur the cost or loss of ownership accompanying equity capital for expanding the company's production capabilities, however. Instead, they use long-term debt.

One of the best sources of long-term debt capital to purchase costly production equipment is a finance company, or as they currently like to be called, an asset based lender (ABL). The rapid economic growth in many manufacturing industries during the seventies and early eighties, together with the popularity of leveraged buyouts (LBOs), encouraged a small number of finance companies to reassess their business base. This specialized group turned away from lending on receivables and inventory and concentrated almost exclusively on providing long-term debt for the purchase of equipment and machinery or the acquisition of businesses with these assets as collateral. Chapter 11 examines how ABLs are used to source financing for leveraged buyouts. They can also be used to finance the purchase of additional machinery, equipment, and other hard assets. ABLs usually finance the purchase of hard assets either through a term loan with interest and principal payable monthly or quarterly or through an installment loan. In either case, the payback period is normally five years, although it could stretch to seven years in some cases. ABLs charge a high interest rate, ranging anywhere from three to five points above the prime rate. And there is usually an up-front fee ranging from $5,000 to $25,000 depending on the size of the loan. ABLs generally require very little, if any, down payment, however, and therefore, are popular with rapid growth companies that are strapped for cash.

The difference between term loans and installment loans is the way in which interest and hence, monthly payments, are calculated. Chapter 1 discusses how monthly payments on installment loans are calculated. Now, let's take a look at a term loan. The $600,000 loan for the purchase of four computer numeric controlled (CNC) milling machines by Accutate Machining Corp. is a good example.

Accutate Machining Corp. of Jacksonville, Florida manufactured machined components for the navy and the air force as replacement parts on several models of fighter aircraft. Accutate's sales were about $15 million and the key production line consisted of a bank of 12 midsized and large CNC milling machines and seven CNC lathes. Upon booking a large order from the air force with deliveries extending over a four-year period, the owner of Accutate, Roy Attleby, realized he needed to add milling capability, and while he was at it, decided to purchase new, state-of-the-art machines. He ordered four, and then set out to finance the deal. With progress payments to handle his working capital needs, Roy figured he could buy the machines rather than lease them and, with financing plan in hand, approached the asset based lending division of Security Pacific Bank. After several negotiating sessions, the two parties finally agreed on the following terms and conditions for a six-year term loan:

1. The total cost of the four CNC machines was $635,000.

2. Accutate made a down payment of $35,000 and financed the balance for six years at an annual interest rate of three points above prime, as published by Chase Manhattan on the first Wednesday of

each month. This interest rate would not be less than 11 percent and not in excess of 16 percent over the life of the loan.

3. Fixed monthly payments included interest and principal with interest calculated on a declining loan balance.

4. Monthly principal payments were calculated on a nine year amortization schedule with a balloon payment due at the end of six years.

5. The four CNC machines secured the loan together with an additional lien against four of the CNC machines already owned by Accutate.

Although the deal Roy struck was not as good as it could have been, it was certainly better than an installment loan. Table 9-1 shows the differences between what Roy negotiated and two other possibilities—the installment method and the simple interest, single payment (allowing monthly payments) method.

———————————— Table 9-1. ————————————

Total principal and interest	Accurate Deal	Installment Method	Simple Interest Equal Monthly Prin.
Year 1	$113,400	$144,600	$140,694
Year 2	113,400	144,600	132,028
Year 3	113,400	144,600	123,361
Year 4	113,400	144,600	114,694
Year 5	113,400	144,600	106,028
Year 6	113,400	144,600	97,361
Total	$680,400	$867,600	$714,167
Total principal paid	$319,237	$399,600	$400,000
Principal Balance			
Due at end of Year 6	$280,763	$200,400	$200,000

Total interest expense to Accutate over the six-year period was $361,163, compared with $468,000 using the installment method and $314,167 using the simple interest, equal monthly principal method. Obviously, if Roy Attleby could have negotiated the third payment method, it would have cost his company $47,000 less in interest. However, he was unable to swing the asset based lender to this method. This is not surprising; very few ABLs will agree to the third method. A commercial bank might, but I've never seen an ABL go with anything but the equal monthly payment amortization method or the installment method. However, the larger the loan and the more clout a borrower has, the better chance of negotiating favorable payment terms. Unfortunately, ABLs are no different than any other bank in this regard. Clout means everything. A large borrower or a business owner who knows the ABL president, a high official in the parent bank, or someone on the lender's board of directors, nearly always negotiates a better deal than the little guy without connections.

If your company is not considered a large customer or if you don't know anyone with influence, there is one other way to coerce the ABL into negotiating a favorable deal, although it is risky. There is an axiom in lending circles: the more money a lender has outstanding to a borrower, the more difficult it is for the lender to pull out or force liquidation when something goes wrong. Even though they don't like to admit it, every smart lender knows that all collateral, except cash, can depreciate in value. Therefore, a liquidation of assets could easily result in taking a bath on a loan. If you borrow from either a commercial bank or an ABL, one way to gain some clout is to be into them for a large sum of money. In other words, the bigger the loan and the less equity you have behind it, the more unlikely it is that the lender can destroy your business. This can be a risky ploy, however, because, as everyone knows, the more a business is leveraged, the greater the risk of not meeting debt service payments. So if you're going to play the leverage game, be sure you can accept the consequences.

A second feature of dealing with asset based lenders has to do with the background of the ABL personnel and the level of interference an owner might expect should business conditions deteriorate. One of the real hazards in dealing with an ABL, whether it is an independent company such as Foothil Capital, or a subsidiary of a large commercial bank, such as Fidelity Capital, is that inevitably, when something goes wrong in the business, the ABL will begin to interfere. Whatever the reason—missed forecasts, late or missed debt service payments, poor publicity for the company, the loss of a key management employee, it is almost certain that a loan officer, auditor, or operating executive from the ABL will be on your doorstep asking questions. If not satisfied immediately that everything is under control, look for a representative of the lender to move in and assist with the management of the company. Although no lender will acknowledge this interference, asset based lenders do, in fact, make a concerted effort to stay on top of a borrower's business. When you take into consideration that many ABL loans are made with very little, if any, down payment, it's understandable that they would be nervous about getting repaid.

On the plus side, most officers of ABLs have some background experience in operating companies other than banks. They may have originally come from an industrial background, public accounting, financial services, or a commercial enterprise, but at least most of them have some knowledge of how an operating company functions. This is a far cry from commercial bankers who seldom know about anything other than banking. With a general business background, an ABL officer can actually be more of a help than a hindrance, if you're lucky enough to find one with background in your specific industry. He can be an excellent source of trade information, and his operating suggestions could be very helpful.

Advantages and risks of using asset based lenders

For many closely held companies, ABLs are the lender of last resort. That is, deficiencies in the company's credit rating, profit performance, or balance sheet preclude a more favorable source of funding. In other cases, however, even a profitable company with a good credit rating and clean balance sheet might find that there really isn't any feasible alternative if they want to make major additions to their production machinery and equipment. In either case, it behooves the business owner contemplating ABLs to be aware of the major advantages and risks of going this route. The following are six advantages:

1. Little or no cash down payment required.
2. Minor importance attached to credit or performance history.
3. Can be done in addition to existing balance sheet debt.
4. The right ABL can offer valuable assistance with specific operating problems.
5. Payback period longer than commercial bank.
6. Could be the only available source for larger purchases.

There are three risks:

1. Interest rate is always high—3 to 5 points above prime—and up-front placement fees are exorbitant.
2. Strong possibility of interference in operating decisions if financial problems arise.
3. Unfavorable stigma attached to finance companies could damage industry or customer reputation.

Some asset based lenders are willing to make long-term loans on real estate, but generally, unless they are part of a larger group with a mortgage banking subsidiary, the average ABL doesn't like payment periods much beyond five years. Most will look at a real estate proposal, however, and if they don't want to take the deal, might very well recommend a mortgage banker to handle it. When looking specifically for long-term mortgage money for additional plant, warehouse, or office space, your best source will probably be to work through a mortgage broker.

Buying real estate

There are several sources of long-term financing for purchasing commercial and industrial real estate. The advantages and disadvantages of each vary with the size of the deal, the type of property, the location of the property, the current state of the financial markets, the financial plan presented by the applicant, and last, but certainly not least, current tax laws. A further complication arises in the nomenclature of these banks. State regulations and historical precedent result in different names in different parts of the country. Bankers making mortgage loans in the Middle Atlantic states, for example, commonly use the name "mortgage company," "financial corporation," "bond and mortgage," or "mortgage investment company" in their names. In the Midwest, typically the words "capital corporation," "financial services," "thrift," or "savings and loan" designate mortgage lenders. The term "mortgage banker" generically describes these lenders throughout the country, however.

Some of the more common sources of mortgage funds are certain asset based lenders, mortgage divisions of commercial banks, and savings and loan associations. These banks are the best bet for small transactions when the property cost is under $500,000. They all generally require a minimum down payment of 20 percent of the purchase price or construction cost. The term of the loan is normally between 15 and 25 years, with interest rates comparable to the going mortgage rates for residential properties in the area. Most can be contacted directly for an application. In some parts of the country, however, it's a little faster to go through a mortgage broker (these can be found in any city telephone directory).

Financing larger real estate deals is far more complicated, and the tax reform laws add to the burden. There are four major ways to finance large real estate transactions:

1. Normal, long-term debt through a mortgage bank capable of handling industrial or commercial deals
2. Municipal revenue bonds (described in chapter 8)
3. Real estate syndications
4. Sale and leaseback arrangements

Prior to 1986, most real estate purchases were done through debt. It was not uncommon to buy a warehouse or production plant with 20 to 25 percent down and the balance on a 20-year mortgage. All types of organizations got into the mortgage lending act, including:

- Subsidiaries of corporate conglomerates
- Large commercial banks

- Commercial and industrial real estate brokerage houses
- Limited partnerships
- Large savings and loan banks
- Foreign investors

Some of these sources, notably the national real estate brokerages, are still heavily involved in new mortgage financing for large properties. Smaller properties can still be financed through divisions of commercial banks or pure mortgage banks. Interest rates and terms for the larger deals—in excess of $20 million—are negotiable. Interest rates for smaller deals tend to follow the mortgage market rates for residential properties. Terms on these smaller loans continue to range from 15 to 25 years.

Because real estate deals are so localized and depend, to a large extent, on immediate regional economic conditions, it's best to deal with a mortgage bank in, or near, the locale you wish to locate. If your CPA or lawyer doesn't have anyone to recommend, the Yellow Pages are full of them. Many have recognizable names and all are easy to check out with area real estate brokerage firms.

Real Estate Mortgage Investment Conduits

For larger deals, tax reform has encouraged another form of real estate financing from the investing community. It is called a Real Estate Mortgage Investment Conduit, or REMIC. REMICs can be formed or sponsored by a large commercial bank, a securities brokerage house, an investment banking firm, a group of local banks, or a private investor group. Profits or losses from the REMIC are passed directly through to its owners, just like a partnership, and therefore, the REMIC pays no taxes as an entity. The purpose in a REMIC is to act as a vehicle to create a pool of mortgage-based loans to a variety of borrowers on one hand, and to create a market for the trading of mortgage securities on the other. It does this by issuing its own marketable securities for trading purposes, using the mortgages it holds as collateral. It then makes a trading market for these securities.

The advantage to a business owner in using this source is that the mere size of a REMIC (accomplished by the pooling of many mortgage loans) and the income it can earn for its trading activities, provides it with a fairly sizable, constant source of money to invest in new mortgages. A good starting point to locate one of these new financing sources is through one of the larger securities houses—Merrill Lynch, Shearson Lehman, or PaineWebber, for example. You might also try a few of the more diversified investment banks such as Morgan Stanley or Bear Sterns, or a large insurance company such as Prudential or Aetna. If all else fails, a commercial real estate broker in your area should either have a REMIC already set up or know where you can find one.

Real estate syndications

Real estate syndications are another popular way to finance real estate deals. Prior to the tax reforms, syndications were almost synonymous with tax shelters. Small and large limited partnerships were set up to syndicate several real estate properties, passing the start-up losses on to the investors. Emphasis was placed on sheltering the investors' income rather than on making financially sound real estate investments. With the advent of PAL rules forbidding the use of passive losses to offset a partner's other income, the focus of syndications has passed to more economically sound investing.

Limited partnerships are a natural for raising financing for real estate acquisitions. Most real estate is reasonably secure over the long term, the market for resale tends to change only over very long economic cycles, and the management of a real estate limited partnership requires a relatively minor amount of administrative effort and time. Because of these advantages, limited partnership units in a real estate syndicate are much easier to sell than if the investment involved an operating company.

Although limited partnerships can also be effectively used to raise capital for the acquisition of product lines or entire businesses, as pointed out in chapter 11, using this technique to raise capital for expanding into additional plant or warehouse space can be done more quickly. Once the limited partnership is formed, there is nothing to prevent business owners, as general partners, to encourage investments by the syndication in other real estate properties as well as serving their own expansion needs. In fact, several entrepreneurs have used this method to actually start up another business separate from their operating company. As long as income-producing properties can be found to provide a positive cash flow to the limited partners it makes sense to expand in this direction.

Real Estate Investment Trusts

A different vehicle serving the same purpose as a real estate limited partnership, the Real Estate Investment Trust (REIT), has been a popular form of syndication in the past. It can be structured in either a corporate form or as a trust. A REIT works like a mutual fund. Several small investors contribute, or pool, their money to allow the REIT to acquire real estate. Income to the REIT is then passed through to its owners as income or losses. Tax reforms have simplified the mechanics of forming and operating a REIT, but it still remains a cumbersome vehicle compared to limited partnerships, and the benefits to shareholders are comparable. The REIT has yet to regain its popularity.

Sale and leaseback

The sale and leaseback of an existing plant, warehouse, or office building provides yet another source of capital to supplement operating funds or to acquire additional facilities. There are a number of existing real estate limited partnerships, large and small, publicly traded and private, that are always interested in picking up a viable industrial or commercial property on a sale/leaseback arrangement. The best way to find a large, publicly traded real estate limited partnership is through your broker. Any reputable brokerage house knows which syndications are in a buying mode in any particular area and which are the easiest to work with from the tenant's perspective. Small, private partnerships are more difficult to contact, although many people have fairly good luck working through commercial real estate agencies.

There are no common elements in sale/leaseback arrangements. Each is different and requires negotiation between the parties. Property values vary significantly depending on the age and condition of the property and its location. Market values generally establish both the sell price and the square footage rental value. If your property houses a manufacturing operation, you will probably want a long-term lease, say 15 years, with one or two five-year options tacked on. Most industrial leases are "triple net," with the lessee paying for everything except very major structural repairs. As far as taxes are concerned, when you sell the property to the lessor, your company will have a capital gain, which is calculated as the difference between the net sell price of the property and the depreciated book value. There are also recapture rules to contend with for that part of the gain representing prior year's depreciation. You might also have built-in gains to worry about if you are operating out of an S corporation.

A sale/leaseback of real estate can be a very viable way to raise capital for further expansion and for current operating needs. It's important, however, to remember that real estate is a long-term asset, and financing raised by a sale/leaseback should be used for long-term purposes—not working capital. This might not be possible if your company is already in financial difficulty but the principle should be followed whenever possible.

Leasing equipment and machinery

The leasing industry reached its pinnacle in the early eighties with favorable tax laws and outrageous market interest rates. Leasing companies benefitted by transference of the investment tax credit and favorable depreciation allowances. Entrepreneurs benefitted by using this source to finance expansion when interest rates prohibited bank financing. Now, with the prime rate hovering around 10 percent, abundant capital flowing from foreign sources, and the elimination of the investment tax credit and liberal depreciation deductions, leasing has lost much of its glamour. There are still several reasons why leasing remains popular as a means of financing hard assets, however:

1. Large cash outlays are not required either to purchase the asset entirely or for a down payment.

2. It eliminates the need to go through the lengthy and questionable loan application process with a lender.

3. The accounting treatment of leases on a company's balance sheet does not dilute the debt/equity ratio as severely as notes or mortgages.

4. Interest rates charged by some leasing companies are substantially below those charged by lenders.

5. Leases can be constructed so that, as the asset wears out and must be replaced, the new asset merely replaces the old one on the same lease without the need to search out new financing.

6. Some leases can be constructed so that at the end of the lease period, the lessee can purchase the asset for a dollar, or for a price significantly below market value.

7. Once established with a major leasing company, an operating business can raise emergency working capital through the sale and leaseback of hard assets already owned by the business.

8. Very often, a company in financial difficulty cannot borrow money from a bank, asset based lender, or other source to acquire new assets, but a leasing company will do the deal.

9. Most officers of major leasing companies have experience in business outside the financial services markets and, therefore, are easier to work with than many lenders.

There are also, however, some glaring disadvantages in leasing hard assets:

1. The total cost of the asset at the end of the lease will always be more than if it was purchased outright.

2. The sale or disposition of assets under lease requires the lessee either to pay off the balance of the lease prior to transferring title or to obtain approval from the leasing company to transfer the lease to a new owner.

3. Selling off assets to raise capital is not possible if they are leased.

4. Leased assets cannot be used as collateral for other financing.
5. Selling a business is more difficult with leased assets, and the gain on the sale will probably be less.

Nearly everyone is familiar with automobile leasing. This continues to be a popular way to acquire a new car every three or four years with little or no money down. Propaganda from leasing companies stating that it is easier to get tax deductions for leased cars is a fallacy, yet many people continue to believe the advertisements. Normally, automobiles are leased for either three or four years with an option to purchase the car at the end of the lease period for blue book value. Most auto leases are also structured to allow a fixed number of miles during the lease period, such as 15,000, with the lessee obligated to pay a fixed amount for every mile driven above this number when the lease expires. All major car manufacturers have their own leasing programs and thousands of independent automobile leasing companies exist throughout the country.

Business-asset leasing is an entirely different situation, however. The number of major leasing companies in this field are limited and the types of leases available are varied. Many companies negotiate a lease structure unique to that particular deal. Let's take a look at three types of business-asset leases, excluding automobiles.

Leasing through a manufacturer or dealer

If you need to acquire a single machine, a computer, or a piece of testing equipment, the normal leasing source remains either the manufacturer of the equipment or the dealer/distributor. If these companies won't do the leasing themselves, they certainly know of an independent lessor whom they do regular business with. Often, it is a firm that the manufacturer or dealer has ties with, such as a local finance company or the leasing division of a local bank. Although seldom admitted, several of these local leasing affiliates offer discounts, kickbacks, or other favors to companies sending leasing business their way. It's illegal, but it's done, as Matt Goldberg learned when he needed a new automated capping machine for his soft drink bottling company.

Matt contacted the sole source of the capping machines to get the specifications on the newest, state-of-the-art, computer-controlled capper. The sell price, after negotiating appropriate modifications to fit his production line, was $95,000. Already fully indebted on his operating line and unwilling to risk potential interference from an asset based lender in his business, Matt decided to lease the machine. He asked the manufacturer for recommendations of competent leasing companies. Matt was given the name of a small leasing company in Seattle, with whom he arranged a seven-year lease with an option to buy the equipment at the end of the period for $10,000. Matt had a feeling the monthly lease payments were rather steep, but not knowing where else to turn, he acquiesced. Six months later, Matt learned through a competitor of the customary arrangement between his leasing company and the manufacturer of his capping machine. In exchange for forwarding business to the leasing company, this lessor took out monthly, full-page advertisements in the local business newspaper and the trade association monthly magazine using the manufacturer's products as examples of products they would provide leasing for. The sales manager of the manufacturer also received season passes to the Seattle Seahawks football games.

In spite of the somewhat higher monthly payments charged by local firms leasing single pieces of equipment, it's generally easier and faster to go this route than to search out a national leasing firm. The amount of money just isn't enough to interest a larger lessor.

Leasing through a national lessor

There are several national leasing companies that lease large quantities of machinery, equipment, or furniture from a variety of manufacturers. They will handle either new assets or construct a sale and leaseback contract for existing assets. This type of leasing arrangement is used extensively in the hotel industry to raise capital for an existing hotel through a sale and leaseback or to furnish a new hotel. It is also used frequently to equip a new manufacturing plant, warehouse, or office complex. The economic justification usually hinges on the short, useful lives of the assets. For example, equipment with relatively short technological useful lives, such as computers, can be replaced with state-of-the-art equipment without renegotiating a completely new lease. If the equipment was owned, it would have to be sold, perhaps in a depressed market, before new computers were added. Companywide telephone systems are another example of technologically short-lived assets. In hotels, the wear and tear on rooms, lobbies, restaurants, or bar furnishings make these assets ideal candidates for a leasing arrangement that allows for replacement under a master lease.

There are many leasing firms that are more than eager to handle this type of large master lease. Some of the more reputable national companies are Leaseamerica, GE Capital, Equitable Life Leasing Corp., and Textron Financial Corporation. The secret in dealing with lessors is to negotiate a master lease rather than individual leases for each piece or type of equipment. A master lease is similar to a blanket purchase order. New assets can be added to the lease and old assets deducted from it without going through the expense of negotiating new leases each time. Of course, the lessor will adjust the monthly payment up or down depending on the collateral, but that's to be expected. Normally, master leases can be negotiated for 5 to 10 years depending on the type of collateral. The lessor gets the tax benefits of owning the equipment, so the rent he charges is seldom as high as straight debt financing. Of course, the lessee will never own the assets.

Leases with national lessors can also be structured for sale/leaseback financing. For example, let's take a look at how Quantum Hotel Associates, the owner of two, 300-room hotels on the east cost of Florida, raised capital when room rentals took a plunge.

The two hotels had a combined book value for furniture, fixtures, and equipment (FF&E) after depreciation of $8 million. Replacement of certain pieces of FF&E would have to begin in about two years with the total turning over during the ensuing five years. The season just ended had been disastrous, with room occupancy falling to less than 35 percent. Cash flow was extremely tight and the management of Quantum wasn't sure how they would keep going. Working with GE Capital, they structured a sale/leaseback deal to sell the lessor all of the FF&E from both hotels, including air conditioning and kitchen equipment for a total price of $7.7 million (which resulted in a small tax loss). A lease was structured to lease back everything on a five-year master lease with monthly payments of $130,000. The extra $6 million enable Quantum to survive the recession. By the second quarter of the next year, occupancy picked up. The hotels are still in business and, though expensive, the sale/leaseback arrangement gave the company an immediate injection of operating cash. Over the next five years, the company continued to add replacement FF&E to the lease as needed.

Leasing facilities

Not only can leasing be used to acquire assets or to supplement working capital, it can also be used to expand a business by acquiring a new plant, warehouse, or offices. In fact, most closely held businesses seem to favor leasing additional space rather than using borrowed or internal funds to purchase it. Leasing real estate has the same advantages as leasing equipment—little or no cash down, off balance sheet liability, flexibility to relocate at the end of the lease, and so on. It also creates similar drawbacks, however—the lack of a valuable hard asset to sell to raise emergency money, being subjected to the whims of a landlord, and reduced collateral for additional borrowing power.

Business real estate leases vary with the location, the age of the property, the use to which the property is put, and a variety of other considerations. Generally, however, the term of most real estate leases is at least five years with options for additional one or two five-year increments. Also, depending on the circumstances, the lessee might or might not pay the real estate taxes, utilities, and major or minor repairs. The lease might also have escalation clauses for increasing the rent based on an indexing scheme tied to published government statistics, such as the consumer price index, the cost of living index, or local ordinance indices. Typically, for a production facility, the lease will be net, net, net, which means the lessee pays everything except major structural repairs. An office lease in a shared building normally includes escalation clauses for increased costs of shared services, such as unmetered utilities, real estate taxes, and building maintenance.

It is also quite common in retail leases for landlords to charge a base rent plus an additional rent based on a percentage of the tenant's gross sales. Shopping malls frequently use this technique, as do large commercial properties renting retail space. There is no universal way to construct a real estate lease. Each situation is different and you should research what similar establishments in your area are paying, and at what terms, before you negotiate anything with a landlord.

The new tax laws have impacted landlords in a number of different ways—mostly unfavorable. As for the tenant, there is one major change that could preclude leasing real estate as an economically desirable option; the write-off of leasehold improvements. Prior to 1986, a tenant could write off leasehold improvements over the shorter of the term of the lease or the depreciable life of the property (calculated on the accelerated cost recovery system). If a business invested $100,000 in modifications to the electrical or heating system of its building, or installed a new roof, and it was leasing the property for five years, this amount could provide a tax deduction of $20,000 a year. Under the new tax laws, this is no longer possible. Now, leasehold improvements must be written off over the same depreciable life allowed for the building. For improvements to nonresidential property, this is currently a 31.5-year period. Using the $100,000 example, you could get an annual deduction of only $3,175. What impact this change will have on the future demand for leased property remains to be seen, but it is certainly possible that it could cause demand to slacken, forcing base rents for industrial property down.

Except in very remote, rural areas, if you want to lease additional space you should have little difficulty locating a real estate agent who handles this type of property. You might also inquire at the local office of one of several federal agencies managing government-owned properties acquired through foreclosure. Often, the government will lease foreclosed property for substantially less than that charged by a private facility. There are some very good bargains to be found in government foreclosures, and even though the agency will often try to sell the property, in the interim, it could be available for lease. Hotels that have defaulted on federally insured mortgages are an excellent example.

Although leasing isn't for everyone, it is often a far superior way to finance expansion than to incur additional debt. Forming real estate limited partnerships to acquire industrial or commercial property has slackened as a result of the PALs in the new tax laws. If the property is economically viable, however, this option is still the best way to get the best of both worlds: an owner can acquire a new facility with capital raised through his limited partnership and also conserve cash in the operating company by leasing the facility back from the partnership. For smaller properties, where the amount of cash needed to make the purchase fit the resources of a private limited partnership, this scheme can work wonders.

10

Locating money for R&D projects

MARY CRANSHAW HAD MANAGED THE BANQUETS DEPARTMENT FOR A MAJOR hotel in Center City, Philadelphia for nearly six years and, although she was very accomplished at her job, she longed to try her hand at entrepreneurship. In her spare time, Mary enjoyed experimenting with her PC computer, designing and programming her own computer games. She had also designed an analysis program to predict, with a fair degree of accuracy, the correlation of dollar exchange rates with trends in the Tokyo and London stock markets. Mary had no real use for the software but the challenge intrigued her.

After an especially frustrating week at the hotel, Mary decided she had had enough and quit her job. Free at last to choose her own destiny, Mary decided to open her own business designing and selling PC computer software. It didn't take her long, however, to learn that bankers weren't the least bit interested in providing money for her to refine and market her currency exchange program.

Mary was ready to give up her brief venture into entrepreneurship when a friend suggested she apply for a grant through the Small Business Innovation Research program. She completed the reams of application paperwork, and within six months, received a grant of $40,000 to do a market feasibility study for her computer program. Two years later, Mary's new company, Zactograph, Inc., was prospering. As she stated at a conference sponsored by the Ben Franklin Technology Center, "Without SBIR, I could never have gotten Zactograph off the ground."

One of the biggest problems creative entrepreneurs face is raising capital for developing and marketing new products. Most do not have sufficient collateral to borrow money from a commercial bank or an asset based lender, and without a profitable track record, they cannot interest an investment bank in taking the risk. Few of these budding entrepreneurs have enough personal cash to fund the market research and testing necessary to determine if there is any market demand for their idea. This chapter points to seven sources of R&D capital for the development of that new product or service:

1. Grants and loans from the Small Business Innovation Research (SBIR) program.
2. Awards from state sponsored R&D programs.
3. Debt and equity capital from Small Business Investment Companies (SBICs).
4. Equity capital from venture capital firms.
5. Joint ventures with customers and competitors.
6. Grants from the federal government.
7. Grants from private foundations.

Small Business Innovation Research program

The Small Business Innovation Research program (SBIR) is a federally funded program specifically designed to make grants and initiate contracts with small business entrepreneurs with 500 employees or less to develop new products and services, and then to bring these innovations to market. Every year, 11 federal agencies set aside a portion of their budgets for awards through the SBIR program. In fiscal 1989, over $400 million was allocated for this purpose. The names of the 11 federal agencies participating in the SBIR program are a good indication of the breadth of the projects that might qualify. These agencies include: the Departments of Agriculture, Commerce, Defense, Education, Energy, Health and Human Services (including the National Institutes of Health), and Transportation; together with the Environmental Protection Agency, National Science Foundation, National Aeronautics and Space Administration, and the Nuclear Regulatory Commission.

Funds are competitively awarded to sole proprietorships, partnerships, and corporations in the form of outright grants or contracts for the development of a specific product. Applicants must be more than 50 percent U.S. owned and operated, and the project must be the primary employment for the individual making the application. Primary employment is defined as more than 50 percent of the person's time and income.

Each agency publishes an annual list of topics for which they solicit proposals. The topics signify the agency's requirement for projects, products, or services that will not be met internally, or through contractual arrangements with outside individuals or companies. Each agency determines its own R&D projects or topics, sets its own date of publication of project lists, and establishes its own proposal deadlines and award dates. In other words, even though all these federal agencies support and participate in the SBIR program, each one handles its own segment independent of the others. This is both a bane and a blessing for the entrepreneur. Some agencies are much easier to work with than others, and if your specific project falls under the jurisdiction of an agency with difficult work standards, you might not want to proceed. On the other hand, with each agency setting its own project topics, it's entirely possible that what you are doing could fall under the jurisdiction of more than one agency. In that case, feel free to submit proposals to each agency calling for your project.

Once the project is completed, the developer retains ownership of the technology, not the federal agency providing the funding. The importance of this feature is obvious, especially if your product or service has commercial value and can be marketed outside of government circles.

SBIR funding for R&D projects is provided in two phases. In Phase I, applicants can receive awards up to a maximum of $50,000 for six months of preliminary investigation to determine the feasibility of the project. Those who successfully complete Phase I can compete for further funding through Phase II. This second phase consists of awards of up to $500,000 for developmental research. The research period can extend over a two-year period. Following Phase II, companies are usually invited to move into an extended R&D contract relationship with the federal agency. If they choose, however, they are free to secure funding from other sources to complete the development and sale of their product in the commercial market.

Awards for both Phase I and Phase II projects are made on a competitive basis. Each applicant must submit a complete proposal for the project directly to the federal agency making the solicitation. Each agency has its own review process. Some are significantly more competitive than others, but the designation of the most competitive ones varies from year to year. One way to get a jump on what topics are coming up in the next release of listings is to contact the SBA for a "pre-solicitation" list. Such a listing can be obtained from:

OFFICE OF INNOVATION, RESEARCH AND TECHNOLOGY
U.S. Small Business Administration
1441 L Street NW, Room 500
Washington, DC 20416
(202) 653-6458

Once you receive the list, you can then choose which topic or topics appeal to you and contact the appropriate federal agency directly to arrange to receive solicitations as soon as they are published. Appendix F includes solicitation dates and closing dates for each agency for fiscal year 1990. These dates don't change much from year to year and can be used as a guideline for 1991, and probably 1992 as well.

The contents of the proposal are nearly identical to those described in chapter 4 for financing plans. The only variations are: (1) in the SBIR proposal, special care must be given to describing your vision of the project and its benefit to the agency if it is successful; and (2) for a start-up company, there will not be any historical financial statements. Other than these two exceptions, everything covered in a financing plan should be included in your proposal. The more comprehensive it is, and the more professional the presentation, the better the chance of winning the competition. It should also be recognized that, similar to any other relationship with the government, political clout and influence help here also. If your project is supported by a congressman or someone from the applicable agency, and if your proposal submission is made under the guidance of a recognized advisor, your chances of winning improve markedly.

One of the best sources for assistance in preparing a proposal is your local state organization that works with SBIR projects. Most states have at least one such organization. Your state Department of Commerce can help locate one in your area. In addition to assisting in the preparation of the proposal, these organizations usually have contacts in Washington that can help you evaluate and select the most favorable solicitations for response. They can also arrange for confidential evaluations and locate expert reviewers in local universities to strengthen your proposal.

State-sponsored R&D awards

Many states and regions have recognized the need to assist small businesses and entrepreneurs finance creative R&D projects. Those states and regions with a preponderance of research and technology-based companies seem to be leading the way in this effort, but many states without a high technology base are also getting into the act. These state-supported agencies and organizations do not compete with the SBIR, SBA, or any other federally controlled research development program. They act as an adjunct to these other funding sources and provide funds to companies that otherwise do not qualify for federal assistance. The efforts made by Pennsylvania in this endeavor are certainly not unique, but they do serve as examples of what can be done independent of the federal government.

The Commonwealth of Pennsylvania, along with the support of private industry, has formed an organization named the Ben Franklin Partnership, to promote economic growth in Pennsylvania through science and technology. The Partnership's activities are administered locally throughout the state by regional technology centers. In the Philadelphia area, this technology center is called the Ben Franklin Technology Center of Southeastern Pennsylvania. In addition to assisting in the selection and evaluation of R&D projects for entrepreneurs and smaller companies, and in the preparation of proposals for SBIR funding, the Technology Center offers two forms of direct financial assistance for R&D projects: the Innovation Grant Program and the Challenge Program.

The Innovative Grant Program recognizes that many creative entrepreneurs, small companies, and university faculty often generate new ideas and concepts that have commercial potential. Typically, the cost of developing an idea to prove its value or to convert an idea into a product in its early development stage, must be borne by the person or company doing the research. It is not unusual for these private funds to run out before the product or service can be developed to a stage where it will attract investors, strategic partners, or government support. Awards from the Innovative Grant Program bridge this gap.

Applicants can include entrepreneurs, small companies with less than 10 employees, or faculty from academic institutions. The applicant must be structured as a small, independently owned business, and operated in Pennsylvania. In addition, it must provide the primary source of employment for the individual during the length of the project. Awards range from $10,000 to $25,000 for a three to six-month period, and the applicant must have identified where follow-on financing will be obtained (from the SBIR, for example). Awards can be used to pay salaries, consultants' fees, and other expenses directly associated with the project but cannot be used for indirect expenses or to purchase equipment. Not more than 50 percent can be used for the personal expenses of the applicant.

The Innovative Grant Program is a cost sharing program, and applicants must commit other non-state funds to the project. These matching funds can be expenses paid by the company to support the project, such as salaries, equipment time, direct materials, space rentals, and so on, or they might come from federal grants, foundations, or outside investors. The developer will own the rights to the product or service when the project is completed.

The Challenge Program of the Ben Franklin Partnership takes a different approach. It offers two separate options: funding for universities engaged in a R&D project (which is not examined here) and private company funding. The program awards grants of up to 1/3 of the project cost during a 12-month period, but not to exceed $150,000. Additional funding can be obtained, however, for projects of longer duration. It applies to companies operating anywhere within the commonwealth with 50 or fewer employees and capable of conducting their own research and technology development. These companies typically have a management team, R&D facilities, and operate on a sound business plan. The Partnership makes awards of between $25,000 and $150,000 direct to the company for a 12-month period. These funds can be used for direct research expenses including personnel, equipment lease (but not purchase), materials, and supplies. The company retains all rights to its developed product or technology. The catch to this program is that, in return for the cash award, the Partnership wants a royalty on sales of the product, technology, or service developed. It limits this royalty to three times its original investment, however.

These two state assistance programs for R&D projects are illustrations of what one state has done to help entrepreneurs and developing companies. Each state involved in technology development has a slightly different program. There are two similarities however, other than the fact that the recipient must reside and operate his business within the state: the financial assistance always takes the form of outright grants, which do not have to be repaid should the project fail, and the amounts are relatively small, generally limited to $150,000 to $250,000. Any entrepreneur or business owner seriously contemplating starting an R&D project should check with his state offices first to learn of similar free financing. It's usually far less painful working with state bureaucrats than federal officials.

If state awards of SBIR funding don't fill your needs, the next stop could be the venture capital fraternity. Venture capitalists fall into two categories: those who handle bigger R&D deals for larger companies, or for high-risk, but potentially high-growth, companies, and those who handle smaller deals for companies with less glamorous prospects. The latter are small business investment companies.

Small business investment companies

Small business investment companies (SBIC) have been around since 1958. Changes in tax laws and innovative financing schemes have caused the popularity of SBICs to fluctuate widely over the years. From a new financing source for small businesses to relegation as an also ran, SBICs have survived. Today, they remain an easily accessible source of funds, not only for small business start-ups, but for the financing of R&D projects for new as well as existing businesses. Originally, SBICs were conceived as off-shoots of the SBA, with charters to meld public and private money into a pool of equity and debt capital available to small, start-up businesses not able to raise financing through conventional commercial bank channels. Equity contributions normally ran to 15 percent ownership. Debt capital had to have a maturity of at least five years. Though licensed by the Small Business Administration, SBICs are privately organized, owned, and managed firms that set their own policies and make their own investment decisions. Therefore, each SBIC has different loan and equity criteria. Some might favor debt over equity; others, just the reverse. The amount of financing available varies as does the industry specialization.

A huge advantage in seeking financing from a SBIC rather than from a typical venture capital firm is that many SBICs are not after the fast buck, and shun investments promising 35 to 40 percent returns. Several of these SBICs are more than satisfied with 15 to 20 percent. The best way to determine if a SBIC might be right for you is to research the SBICs in your area listed in the membership directory of the National Association of Small Business Investment Companies, which can be found in the reference section of most public and university libraries; or you can write directly to NASBIC, 512 Washington Building, Washington, DC 20005. To qualify for SBIC participation, a business must meet the definition of "small business" as set forth by the SBA (see chapter 6 for a current definition).

All SBICs are not interested in funding R&D projects, but enough of them are to include them as a candidate. Financing through a SBIC has two additional advantages. First, if you can negotiate either a SBIC equity position or a subordinated loan, other financial institutions are usually more interested in considering additional financing at the appropriate time. Commercial banks, ABLs, even investment banks, love to see a SBIC financial commitment. It gives credence to the business owner's claims that he has a good, viable product and knows what he's doing. Second, to receive a SBIC license, the management of the SBIC must furnish evidence that they have a wide range of management talent outside of the banking fraternity. Having a SBIC officer sitting on your company's board can be a big help in bringing a new product to market.

SBICs were the forerunner of today's venture capital firms, and in many respects, they remain competitive with them. For years, it was relatively easy to enter the SBIC market. Federal regulations required a modest capital investment by the founder that was then matched with federal funds. Consequently, many entrepreneurs formed their own SBIC. Not to go into the banking business, but as their own private source of government money. Rules have changed, however, and today SBICs are owned by commercial banks and larger venture capital firms, as well as private investors. Consequently, it is increasingly difficult to segregate SBICs from other venture capital groups or even small investment banking firms. One of the premises of SBICs remains constant, however. They still provide high risk equity and debt financing to small businesses for development projects.

The preparation required before approaching a SBIC for R&D funding must be just as complete as if you were going to a commercial bank, investment bank, or an asset based lender. The starting point is preparing a financing plan (see chapter 4). If your company has been in business for a while and you are now looking for capital to support the design and introduction of a new product or product line, the financing plan should be compiled in the same format as if you were looking for expansion capital. The same section headings should also be used: capital structure, market position and characteristics, technical and management capability, production facilities description, historical financial statements for three years, and pro forma financial forecasts. The impact of the development effort, and the benefits derived once the products are marketable, should be highlighted in both the pro forma statements and within the body of the plan. Detailed descriptions of the new product should be highlighted. Why it is unique, the market demand for it, how it will be priced and distributed, and why the market needs and wants such a product. Competition for the new product, both direct and indirect, should be explained fully.

On the other hand, if you are just starting a business, then the financing plan takes on a slightly different character. Without an existing business to absorb some of the administrative, selling, and development costs, and without existing management personnel, this becomes a far riskier venture for the financier. Many SBICs won't touch a start-up situation, although some will. To convince a SBIC that you are not just blowing hot air and working out a dream, the financing plan must be fully documented, the markets and competition carefully researched, and the pro forma forecasts conservative. You'll never arouse interest in a start-up venture with a new product unless you can convince the SBIC management that:

1. you are an expert in the field and have outstanding technical and managerial abilities to develop and bring the product to market;
2. you are willing to risk nearly all of your personal assets on the venture; and

3. you are willing to give the SBIC an equity piece of the action in the event you are successful.

Reference letters are normally the best way to prove your expertise and management acumen. Ideally, these should come from persons or companies well known to the SBIC, such as bankers, key management personnel of large, well-known companies, and technical authorities in your field. Also, you must be willing to pledge your personal assets as collateral to either the loan or the equity contribution of the SBIC. Investment portfolios, real estate, pension proceeds, your stock in the business, and even your house, might have to be pledged as a personal guarantee. Finally, you should offer up front to give the SBIC at least 15 percent of the equity in the business with warrants to acquire additional interests if the product is successfully marketed.

Financing a R&D project through a SBIC can be an ideal situation for a small business trying to grow. Although restrictions can be severe, and the SBIC will want a share of the business, their willingness to offer management assistance and the clout such a partner could bring to the financial markets later on, might make this source a viable alternative to consider. If, however, you already have a substantial operating company whose size threatens the upper limits of the definitions of a small business or if you want to bring a glamorous, high tech product to the market, consider a private venture capital firm.

Venture capital firms

A SBIC is one form of a venture capital bank. Because they are supported by the government, however, they are limited to investing in small businesses that meet SBA definitions. They also have internal limitations imposed by federal regulations on what they can do in terms of structuring a deal. A privately owned venture capital firm has far more leeway in determining what projects and companies to finance and how to structure a deal because they are unregulated. There are a multitude of venture capital firms in nearly every state, ranging from one-person operations to divisions of large commercial banks. Non-SBIC venture capital firms are normally grouped into four categories:

1. *Investment banks.* Some active investment banks occasionally venture out into the never-never land of R&D ventures if the deal looks good enough and if the business owner comes highly recommended.

2. *Divisions of large corporations.* Nearly all Fortune 500 corporations either currently have venture capital divisions or subsidiaries or they have had one in the past. This is an excellent source of new

product innovation for a large company and these companies must have some place to invest their excess cash. Independent venture projects tend to cost less and provide greater coverage than strictly internal R&D departments.

3. *Family funds.* Many very wealthy families (Rockefeller, Mellon, Coors, Cudahy, and so on) have traditionally funnelled some of their wealth into small, high potential start-up companies with state-of-the-art product development ideas. They are primarily interested in products and companies that will have a positive social effect.

4. *Private investment firms.* These are limited partnerships and corporations that have the financial backing of insurance companies, pension trusts, and other large blocks of capital. Some are small funds ($2 million); some are larger (more than $100 million).

With the splurge in mergers and acquisitions during the past 15 years, venture capitalists have expanded into other fields including, investment banking, asset based lending, exploration, and even international projects (chapter 13). Today, it's hard to tell a venture capital firm from an investment bank. Often, the two are synonymous, as discussed in chapter 11 on buying a business. There is, however, one area of the financing spectrum in which venture capitalists predominate; supporting individuals and smaller companies undertaking a R&D project that will ultimately result in potential high growth. The financing of Silicon Valley computer-oriented firms was done almost entirely with venture capital funding.

Although the amount a venture capitalist is willing to invest and the terms of the financing vary, depending on the type of venture and the risks involved, most demand, and get, a healthy piece of the business in exchange for financial help. Whereas 15 percent is the norm with SBICs, private venture capital firms will often take up to 75 percent in the ownership of a business for a start-up, high tech venture. Another feature of venture capital financing is that the fundamental premise of investing in developing projects rests on the ability of the new company to go public within a reasonable time period—generally five years—at a price high enough to give the venture capitalist a significant gain on the investment and an assured getting out position. If you have no intention of going public in the future, stay away from venture capitalists.

Like SBICs, venture capitalists will also want to have a hand in the management of the company, usually through active participation in management operating decisions or through a board seat—either as a director or as an advisor. This type of assistance to a developing company can be extremely beneficial if the venture capitalist has a sound background in the company's industry or product line. Of course, such interference can have just the opposite effect if the venture capitalist isn't competent. Consequently, choosing the right one becomes a very crucial task for the business owner. J.P. Holleran found one with just the right combination of technical expertise and management savvy, and a willingness to gamble on a new electronic device to detect impurities in, and then automatically filter, ordinary faucet drinking water.

J.P. Holleran was a salesman for a large, bottled water company in the Los Angeles area when he invented his electronic water purifier. Excited and confident he could raise the financing to take the product to market, J.P. quit his job, rented a small shop, and assembled his prototype product, which he called a Lec-Fil. His next stop was at a local commercial bank where he hoped to secure a $1 million loan to acquire appropriate assembly and testing equipment and to hire three people. With only $20,000 of his own money and virtually no personal assets worth anything to the bank, quite naturally the bank turned J.P. down. Through a friend of a friend, J.P. finally contacted me to help with his financing problem. At the time, I knew of a small venture capital firm just getting started in Southern California. When approached with the proposition, the venture capitalist agreed to handle the deal with an equity contribution of $850,000 and a five-year loan for $150,000. In exchange, J.P. gave up 62 percent of the ownership of his company and agreed that, if the product line was successful, he would take the company public in three to five years. The venture capitalist also received warrants to acquire an additional 13 percent of the company within the succeeding six years.

A principal in the venture capital firm, Robert McCall, had a strong chemical engineering background and several years of managerial experience with a division of duPont. When it came time to line up orders for the first production run of the product, McCall, having taken a seat on the Lec-Fil Corp. board of directors, provided J.P. with personal introductions to some of the biggest names in the water filtration industry. With McCall's marketing and engineering assistance, the company took off, and in three years, was generating sales of over $4.5 million. Two years later, with sales continuing to climb, J.P. and McCall decided the timing was right to go public and put together their first public stock offering. The IPO was a success, raising over $5 million. The venture capital firm was paid off (they never did exercise their warrants). J.P. sold his stock in the company in 1988 and retired to Australia at age 52—with $8.5 million in his pocket.

Not everyone can be as fortunate as J.P. Holleran. Yet, the opportunity presented by the venture capital industry provides at least the possibility for making it big. Thousands of American entrepreneurs have been able to bring their dreams from the drawing board to the market with the help of venture capitalists, without whom the dreams would have died.

The availability of venture capital funds fluctuates with the current and projected condition of the national economy. Though known as risk takers, most venture capitalists will not take risks when the economy is down. In the past, whenever there has been even a mild recession, venture capital funds have tended to dry up. This lack of venture funds is probably why few new technologies ever get off the ground during recessionary periods, and few really new products are introduced to the market place. If it appears that venture capital financing can help get your new product or technology to market, watch the economic timing closely. If the stock market is bullish, economic indicators are in an upward trend and the federal government is in a pro-business mood—go for it. Chances are very high you'll find a venture capitalist to handle your financing. In good times, the money faucet opens and there is nearly always more money in the venture capital chain than can be effectively placed for R&D projects.

According to a survey in *Venture* magazine, a total of $970.2 million was invested in 1,336 deals by 25 of the leading venture capital firms in 1988. This total comprised the breakdown shown in Table 10-1.

Table 10-1. Breakdown of Funds Invested from Venture Capitalists

	No. of Deals	Millions	Percent of Total
Seed money and start-up money (the majority were for new product development in start-up companies)	162	$132.5	13.7
Later-stage	112	141.2	14.6
Follow-on financing	993	390.0	40.2
LBOs	69	306.8	31.6

Remember that these statistics represent deals done by only 25 of the largest venture capital firms, and that there are well over 1,000 firms in the industry. It is clear that R&D funding, at approximately 15 percent of the total, assumes a very important role in venture capitalist's portfolios.

It's easy enough to locate venture capital firms. They advertise in the local Yellow Pages and the *Wall Street Journal*. Any reputable merger and acquisition consultant can recommend at least two or three. Commercial bankers have pet venture capital firms they like to work with. There are many books listing sources of venture capital. *Venture* magazine can also provide assistance. If all else fails, you can always get a listing of venture capital firms from the National Venture Capital Association.

Joint ventures

Joint ventures with customers, and occasionally with competitors, can provide financing for a R&D program without ever going to the financial markets. Many Fortune 500 companies form joint ventures with small suppliers to develop new technologies and products that would be uneconomical to pursue themselves. General Electric has advocated this approach for years. Literally thousands of GE's technologies have been developed by small subcontractors and suppliers, all of which have been financed through advances and low-cost loans from GE. The aerospace industry is another excellent example of how large customers finance development projects of small subcontractors. Boeing, with an army of development engineers, freely uses their subcontractors to research and then develop technologies and products at a fraction of the cost of developing them internally. During the sixties, Boeing had difficulty resolving the aerodynamic design of the SST wing frame. Hundreds of thousands of dollars were poured into engineering efforts without yielding the right answers. Finally, agreeing to advance the funds necessary for a new approach to the technology, Boeing engineers turned the problem over to a small subcontractor. Within a year, the subcontractor's engineers had designed a state-of-the-art, aerodynamically acceptable leading-edge SST wing frame. Then in the early seventies, Boeing turned over the design of honeycomb sound attenuation structures to the subcontractor who once again, solved the problem for them.

Approaching R&D financing from a different perspective, several years ago, Mac Forsythe designed a new material for coating swimming pools but didn't have the capital to bring the material through the testing stage. He contacted a subsidiary of ITT, which was then producing and selling commercial pools, and negotiated a contract for an advance of $200,000 for testing equipment and working capital. In exchange, ITT became the owner of the technology to make the new material.

Competitors can also help finance development projects. Jim Archer owned a small company that manufactured automobile jacks, whose major customer was Sears. Designing a new type of jack specifically for smaller cars, Jim couldn't interest his banker, or Sears, in financing either the prototype or a trial production run of the product later on. His product drawings gathered dust for 18 months. While attending a trade show in Chicago, he mentioned his new product to a major competitor from Detroit. Before the show ended, Jim had negotiated a deal with the competitor to advance him $50,000 to build the prototype. If the competitor liked the result, it would take over the production and marketing of the product and pay Jim a 5 percent royalty on all sales. The product was successful, and eventually Jim made more money from his jack royalties than from the production of his other lines.

It's nearly impossible for an entrepreneur just starting out without an existing customer base to take advantage of this type of development financing. For those already running a company and want to bring a new product or technology to market, however, customer and competitor funding can be a boon. It works especially well for smaller companies with very large customers or for a company serving a very small market niche and several large companies as competitors on the perimeter. Customer or competitor R&D funding usually takes the form of advances or low-interest loans that are offset by the eventual sale of the product to the funding company. Often, a customer or competitor will insist on an exclusive right to the technology or on being the sole source for marketing the product in exchange for financing its development. Obviously, agreeing to such an arrangement precludes the developer's right to reap the profits in the open market. In some instances, this might exclude this financing source because it eliminates the opportunity for the company to grow using the new invention. For others, however, this is a good trade-off and results in added volume, even if it is only from one customer or from royalties.

For a new entrepreneur, however, customer or competitor funding isn't normally available and, for one reason or another, venture capital or SBIR funding might be inappropriate. In that case, perhaps a foundation grant could work.

Foundation grants

Chapter 6 examined private foundations as an alternative source of raising capital for a variety of purposes—starting a business, expansion, construction projects, and as an aid to companies suffering from foreign competition. Many of these foundations also extend grants or very low-interest loans to private businesses for developing new products, processes, or techniques. There is a catch, however; nearly all of the foundations specify that the development effort must be directed toward social benefits. A computer software package to more efficiently analyze stock market trends will never qualify. A nontoxic, biodegradable plastic container for infant's milk probably would. To be socially beneficial, the new product, process, or technology must relate to one of the following: ecological conservation, human health, renewal of blighted areas, improving the living standards of the poor, historic restoration, religious understanding, transportation improvement, agricultural development, or community service.

Private foundation grants or low-cost loans for R&D projects are usually for very small amounts. Foundations are seldom willing to fund a project costing more than $100,000. Several foundations will look at funding from $1,000 to $25,000. Few go beyond $50,000 except in unusual circumstances. Once the development project has been market tested, some foundations will increase their grants to $60,000 or $70,000. So, if you need big dollars, don't bother with private foundations.

Additionally, most private foundations want the business owner to complete at least the initial market feasibility study before applying for money. They will fund the building of a prototype model and assist in setting up a marketing effort but usually expect the entrepreneur to take care of the feasibility study himself. As seen in chapter 6, private foundations provide two types of financing: program-related investments to further the charitable objectives of the foundations and flow-through funding to existing, nonprofit organizations under Section 501(c)(3) of the Internal Revenue Code. Both channels are used for R&D funding as well as expansion or project financing. The best way to use private foundation grants for development projects is in conjunction with other financing from the SBIR, SBICs, or venture capitalists. Quite often, if a business owner can raise some money through grants or awards, one of these other organizations will be more interested in furnishing the balance required.

Choosing the right financing source

This chapter has examined seven sources for raising capital for research and development projects. All are not applicable to all businesses or all projects. Each has its place in the R&D financing spectrum. Some work well for the initial market research. Others are more advantageous in the later stages of product development. Some only finance very small amounts while others have no maximum limit. Some provide loans that have to be paid back. Other sources make equity contributions, direct grants, or advances against future sales. Some want part of the ownership of the new product or technology or a hand in the management of the business in exchange for financing the project. Others wouldn't get involved in your company if you wanted them to. Some specialize in products or technologies that will lead to a business start-up, while others only work if you already have a going business. With such a wide range of financing, restrictions, terms, and conditions it's difficult to know where to start looking. Table 10-2 should shed some light on the question. The idea in development financing is to choose the right source for the particular project you have in mind. Doing so increases the chances of getting the funding and, at a minimum, reduces the aggravation in the search process.

Each year, new efforts are made by major corporations, the federal government, state governments, and universities to come up with new ways to

Table 10-2. Financing Sources for Projects

	SBIR	State	SBIC	Venture Capital	Customers	Competitors	Private Foundations
Type of business							
Start-up	X	X	X	X			X
Existing	X	X	X	X	X	X	X
Type of project							
High tech	X	X		X	X	X	
Low tech	X	X	X				
Socially beneficial		X	X				X
Competitive		X	X	X	X	X	X
Size of project							
Under $50,000	X	X	X		X	X	X
$50,000 to $500,000	X	X	X	X	X	X	
Over $500,000				X	X		
Stage of project							
Feasibility study	X	X			X		
Prototype	X	X	X	X	X	X	X
First production run	X		X	X	X	X	X
Type of financing							
Short-term loans					X	X	X
Long-term loans	X		X	X	X		
Equity			X	X	X	X	
Grants/awards	X	X					X
Advances					X	X	
Terms and conditions							
Equity participation			X	X	X		
Management assistance			X	X			
Technical assistance	X			X	X	X	X

further the advance of technology and science in American business. Financial risks in research and development projects are formidable, and these major players recognize that ideas and creativity often flow from entrepreneurs and closely held businesses—usually without capital to bring their ideas to market. There is a high probability that new financing schemes are already on the drawing boards at one or more of these money centers. Lack of financing should never be an excuse to reject R&D efforts. The sources of cash are almost limitless. All one has to do is look.

11

Raising capital for a business acquisition

ENTREPRENEURS, BUSINESS OWNERS, PROFESSIONALS, MANAGEMENT EM-
ployees, and many others dream about buying a business at one time or
another. Some visualize retiring to Florida, Arizona, or the mountains and
buying a small business to keep them occupied. Others search for a way to
become independent or financially secure; to expand their business the
quick way by buying up their competition; or to enter the international
markets by acquiring a business overseas. Many just dream of being their
own boss. Whatever the reason for wanting to buy a business, the universal stumbling block is usually raising the capital to make the move. Few
people are willing to invest all of their own cash in a business—even if they
have enough stashed away to close a deal. In 99 out of 100 cases, a business acquisition is financed, at least partially, with someone else's money.

The business acquisition mania of the past decade has received wide
coverage in the media. Stories appear almost daily in the *Wall Street Journal* about one company or another floating junk bonds, borrowing millions in long-term debt, swapping stock, or planning a leveraged buyout.
Business acquisitions have enabled many Fortune 500 companies to
expand their businesses far beyond what was possible through internal
growth, and they've done it with other people's money. However, this
chapter is not about financing megabuck acquisition deals but where

private companies can raise capital for private acquisitions. Many of the techniques employed by the big boys are also available to smaller purchasers—but some, such as the infamous junk bonds, are generally not. This chapter includes raising capital for business acquisitions through:

1. Asset based lenders
2. Limited partnerships
3. Mergers
4. Investment banks
5. The business seller
6. IPOs
7. Other sources

Matching the use with the source

Eight primary criteria determine which one, or combination of, sources to choose:

1. *The size of the deal.* Certain lenders or investors might be very interested in a deal totalling $20 million but completely ignore anything under $10 million. Some participate if the acquisition price is $1 million but cannot handle anything above $5 million. Others only handle megabuck deals in excess of $100 million. An acquisition deal of less than $1 million is probably the hardest to put together because very few financing sources are interested in incurring the cost and the risk of administering a small deal when the overhead cost is the same, the risk less, and the returns significantly greater for a bigger deal.

2. *The size of the buyer.* The size of the deal and the size of the buyer really go hand in hand. A buyer whose annual sales are $5 million has a difficult time raising capital to buy a company with sales of $50 million. The financier logically assumes that the dearth of management personnel in the acquiring company precludes a smooth integration of the larger, acquired company. On the other hand, a buyer with $50 million in sales could easily finance the acquisition of a target of $5 million from several different sources.

3. *The type of business being acquired.* Some financing sources specialize in a specific industry or group of industries, such as computer hardware and software or electronic capital goods. Some handle retail acquisitions but not manufacturing, distribution, or service businesses. Others specializing in geographic areas jump at a farm equipment distributorship in the Midwest but scorn the

same deal in the Northeast. Generally, however, the major concern of a financier is that the buyer and the target be in the same type of business. They usually do not like to get involved, for example, in a deal where the buyer manufactures automobile parts and the target sells hospital supplies.

4. *The amount of equity contribution from the buyer.* This is a key issue. Most lenders or investors look more favorably on a buyer who can make a substantial equity contribution relative to the total price. A few, however, are willing to go into a deal with practically nothing down from the buyer.

5. *Current balance sheet of buyer.* If the buying company's balance sheet is debt free, it has significantly more flexibility in structuring the financing than if there are already substantial debt obligations.

6. *Profitability and cash flow of both the buyer and the target company.* All lenders or investors are interested in making money on their investment. This is determined by the profitability and the cash flow of both the buying company and the target. The better the historical cash flow from both companies, the more flexibility in financing the deal.

7. *Economic conditions in the financial markets.* A recession or a bear market preclude using certain financing sources. If the economy and financial markets are both upbeat, however, a greater number of options are available.

8. *Management capabilities of both the buyer and the seller.* With a sound management team from both the buyer and the target, a lender's or investor's confidence in the probability of actually realizing the projected cash flow escalates. This also opens doors to financing options that would otherwise be closed.

Asset based lenders

In addition to being a popular source for financing the purchase of equipment, as examined in chapter 9, asset based lenders (ABLs) have also been an attractive source for financing certain types of business acquisitions. From 1979 through the mid-eighties, and before the advent of smaller investment banks, ABLs were the prime funding source for small leveraged buyouts. As long as the target company had hard assets—machinery, equipment, vehicles, or real estate—ABLs were more than happy to loan money for LBOs. When the bottom fell out of the used machinery and equipment market in 1984-85, ABLs found themselves holding long-term notes with less than 100 percent collateral, and they began to withdraw as prime sources of acquisition funding.

As more small investment banks and venture capital firms started up in the early eighties, asset based lenders found themselves in partnership with these investors in acquisition funding. The investment bank provided the equity and mezzanine money and took the lead in putting together the total package. ABLs continued to lend money on hard assets but with an investment banker as an intermediary, they felt more secure than doing the whole deal themselves. This continues to be the posture of most ABLs today. They are still very active in high-risk, small LBOs, but in most deals, they require an additional outside source of funds; preferably an investment bank or a venture capitalist.

Since the early eighties, more and more ABLs have been swallowed up by commercial banks, large savings and loans, Fortune 500 conglomerates, and insurance companies. Few are independent anymore.

This bodes well for the private company because now when it uses ABLs for acquisition financing, it knows they have vast resources to draw upon and are less restricted to maximum loan limits. This consolidation has also permitted ABLs to become active in the short-term working capital markets. From a buying company's perspective, this means that it won't need to use a commercial bank to finance growth in receivables or inventory but can use the same lender it uses for long-term funding. Chapter 9 covered the dangers of such concentration, and it is still expedient when buying a business.

Asset based lenders never take an equity position. Their funding takes the form of five to seven-year term loans, secured by the hard assets of the acquired company. Interest rates are usually quite high, ranging from three to five points above prime. Additionally, ABLs require an up-front application or commitment fee ranging from $5,000 to $25,000. Monthly payments normally include interest and principal; and financial reports must be submitted at least monthly—sometimes weekly.

Asset based lenders normally pay less attention to a company's financial performance and more attention to the liquidation value of its underlying assets when deciding whether to participate in an acquisition deal. They are ready, willing, and able to step in and liquidate the company to get their money back if they deem such a move necessary. They all work closely with professional auctioneers and know exactly who to contact to get a liquidation rolling in a very short period of time.

Nearly all ABLs require a first position on all hard assets of the target business and normally a second position on working capital assets (if another bank has the operating line). The owner of the buying company is usually required to sign a personal guarantee for the entire loan balance, and the lender tries very hard to get a buyer's spouse or other outsider to co-sign as well.

The major advantage in using ABLs for acquisition funding is that they usually require less equity contribution from the buyer and, thus, are willing to do high-leverage deals. The biggest disadvantages are the high fees and interest rates and the extreme difficulty in working with these institutions. Some are worse than others and, of course, their policies vary over time.

High-leverage deals are always very risky. They are even worse when an asset based lender is the only available source of funds. The odds are high that within a short period of time, debt service payments will begin to strap the company and the ABL will quickly move in to dictate operating policy. Because they make loans nobody else wants, however, there are occasions when an ABL is the only viable source of financing and, although risky, highly leveraged deals do sometimes work out. There have been several highly leveraged deals financed by asset based lenders that have turned out very well. But be careful. As in any industry, there are reputable ABLs and there are those with questionable credentials. When choosing an asset based lender be sure to look at several before choosing which one to do business with. Check the company out with several customers before signing a loan agreement. A current debtor will be quick to reveal whether or not you can work with the lender.

Limited partnerships

Chapter 8 examined limited partnerships as a viable means to raise capital for a variety of uses. Even though new tax laws have eliminated the use of limited partnerships as a tax shelter, their popularity, especially in high growth situations, remains unabated. Instead of looking for investments to yield large tax write-offs, investors now look to limited partnerships as a viable way to invest in profitable, high-growth companies.

Buying stock in the public market can only benefit the investor through dividends or by realizing appreciation gains when the holdings are sold. Investing directly in growth companies as an equity player only generates returns when the company goes public or when the investment is sold. Buying units in a limited partnership that invests in growth companies, however, enables the investor to make annual cash returns on the investment and still retain ownership interests for further appreciation gains.

Funding acquisitions of operating businesses remains one of the major purposes for private placement, limited partnerships. Though owners of closely held businesses remain reluctant to enter what they consider to be the arena of high finance, setting up a private limited partnership is really very simple. And it is far more attractive than a private placement of common stock. Let's compare the benefits to private investors of buying $5 million of limited partnership units with the same investment in common stock of a closely held company.

Rachett Roller Rinks

Rachett Roller Rinks, Inc. designed, manufactured, and installed a patented floor covering for roller skating rinks. Sales in 1984 totalled just under $14 million. The company was owned by two brothers, Jan and Emil Dobrchek. Rachett earned about 15 percent profit and economic conditions indicated a substantial growth in demand for its floor covering both for new roller skating rinks and as replacement covering for existing rinks. Flo-Well Rinks Corporation also produced a rink floor covering and, although the brothers didn't acknowledge it as superior to theirs, it certainly was competitive, cutting into a segment of Rachett's market. The decision was made to offer to buy Flo-Well for $5 million, which Jan and Emil estimated was about 12 times earnings. The owner of Flo-Well was exuberant at the opportunity to retire, and he accepted Rachett's offer. The next problem for the brothers was to raise the $5 million.

The lead partner in Rachett's CPA firm was also the chief financial officer of a small, privately held investment banking firm. When approached with the financing problem, he immediately suggested forming a limited partnership to raise the capital. He was sure they could sell $5 million of partnership units to the principals as well as several investors in his investment bank. Roller Coverings LP was formed with Jan and Emil as the general partners. Within five weeks, the limited partnership units were sold to 14 investors for the full $5 million. The partnership agreement called for the limited partners to receive 85 percent of the profits and no losses. The general partners would receive 15 percent of the profits, all the losses, and a management fee of $500,000 per year. The proceeds of the offering were then used to acquire Flo-Well, and the brothers were off and running with a $20 million company.

For the first two years after the acquisition, Roller Coverings earned profits of 14 percent of sales, totalling $2.8 million each year, of which the general partners received their management fee and an additional $345,000 (15 percent of $2.3 million). The limited partners received the balance of $1,995,000. During each of the next three years, the company earned profits of $3 million, of which the brothers received a total of $875,000 and the limited partners $2,125,000. Over the five-year period, the limited partners received a total of $10,285,000 on an investment of $5 million for a compound annual return of just over 15 percent. The gains were taxed as ordinary income to the limited partners and, because none were active in the operations, all income was construed as passive.

Clowell Manufacturing

Martha Cunningham was the founder and sole shareholder in Clowell Manufacturing Company, Inc., a manufacturer of wicker porch furniture. In 1985, one of her suppliers of webbing fabric used in the production of the furniture came on the market and Mary decided the opportunity was too good to pass up. Clowell realized annual sales of $15 million in 1984, with profits of $2 million. Mary estimated that she could leverage up the earnings base of the combined companies to more than 25 percent on sales of $25 million if she could make the acquisition with equity capital rather than debt. The price of the webbing company was $5 million, and the seller wanted all cash at closing. After consulting with her attorney and her CPA, she polled her key employees, friends, business associates, and even a few major customers, and learned that there was substantial interest in investing in this acquisition. Afraid of the complexities of a limited partnership, she decided to issue a new class of stock in Clowell which would carry restricted voting rights, a noncumulative dividend yield of 5 percent, and warrants to convert to one share of Class A voting stock for every four shares of the new Class B stock (after the first four years of ownership). The new Class B stock would also be callable after the fifth year at a price equal to the then book value per share plus a premium of 15 percent.

Clowell's private placement brought in $4 million from 30 investors and Mary purchased the webbing company (Clowell contributed $1 million of its own equity to the deal). By the fifth year after the acquisition, the book value of Clowell's Class A stock had reached $3.35 per share. If Mary had decided to call in the Class B stock at this point, for each dollar of invested capital from the 30 Class B shareholders, Clowell would have paid a price of $2.01, amounting to a compound annual return of 15 percent to the investors—practically identical to the investors in the case of the limited partnership of Rachett Roller Rinks. This would have been a capital gain to the investors for tax purposes. Even with the urging of her attorney and CPA advisors, however, Mary refused to call the stock and instead opted to allow the Class B shareholders to exercise their warrants, which most of them did. This resulted in decreasing Mary's ownership of Clowell to 53 percent.

From the investors' perspective, the Rachett case was far more beneficial than the Clowell investment. In the former, the company was obligated by contractual agreement to distribute profits annually. In the Clowell case, no such agreement existed. In both cases, the investors earned their 15 percent per year, but in one case, they received the cash; in the other, they didn't. From the business owners' perspective, Jan and Emil continued to be the sole owners of their company; in Mary's case, she lost 47 percent of her equity. On the other hand, Mary did conserve her operating cash for use elsewhere in the business.

Each acquisition is different. There is no universally best way to raise acquisition capital. These cases represented two contrasting ways with different results to the business owner as well as the investors. Private placements of both stock and limited partnership units remain viable means to raise acquisition capital; although, the limited partnership route is often easier to sell to investors.

Mergers

A much less expensive way to make an acquisition of a going business is through a merger. No capital is required and there is no need to spend the time and money searching out investors. Chapter 7 examined a reverse merger through a blind pool IPO as a way to raise capital. But a straight merger is often the choice for acquiring a company. Although mergers are continually practiced by large public corporations, unfortunately, many owners of closely held businesses regard this maneuver as being reserved for the big boys and too complex for them. This is a shame because merging with another company can often be not only the fastest and least expensive way to make an acquisition, it can also be the smoothest. Management personnel can be integrated between the two companies in an orderly fashion; banking relationships remain stable; no additional debt is incurred; customers are left unaffected; and supply lines remain intact. Nothing really changes for either company, initially, except that they are now commonly owned.

Whether your company has already gone public and has stock traded in the open market or whether you remain a privately owned company, the techniques for merging remain similar. This is also true whether merging with a publicly traded company or with a privately owned business. The only difference is in the techniques used to value each of the companies.

In the case of a publicly traded company, either yours or the one you are merging with, the valuation process is relatively simple. The trading price of the stock is always the starting point. If the price has rapidly accelerated or decelerated over the past 12 to 18 months, a moving average might be used. If rapid change is projected for the next 12 months, perhaps a price established on a trend line would make the most sense. Beyond establishing the current (or projected) price of the stock, it's just a matter of negotiating how much of a premium (or discount) will be involved. The premium or discount takes into account the market position of the company, management capabilities, current balance sheet ratios, and good old Kentucky windage.

If either or both companies are privately owned, the valuation process is slightly more complex. Values are always based on a combination of profitability, cash flow, asset values, and economic conditions in the marketplace. To get some ideas on practical ways to value privately owned companies, pick up one of my other books: *Buying In: A Complete Guide to Acquiring a Business or Professional Practice* or *Getting Out: A Step by Step Guide to Selling a Business or Professional Practice*. Each book covers the valuation subject from a different perspective and both can be valuable aids in determining reasonable prices for a merger.

Once the valuation of both companies is established, the merger merely involves a trade of one company's stock for another. If done with competent advice, there will be no tax implications for either party. The biggest advantage to merging with another company rather than doing an outright purchase is that no cash is required, but a second benefit could come later. If you own a private company and see an advantage in being publicly traded, a merger into a public company, regardless of its size, can provide an immediate way to reap the benefits of public ownership without incurring all the costs and aggravation of making an IPO. Of course, there are also the risks of public ownership to consider.

Investment banks

Chapter 5 explored the benefits and risks of using investment banks as financial advisors to locate capital sources. A second role for this new face in the financial fraternity is as a financing packager. Investment banks, large and small, have emerged during the eighties as the primary source of funds for financing all types of business acquisitions. Giant firms such as Goldman Sachs, Merrill Lynch Capital Markets, and Bear Sterns, to mention but a few, have taken over as the principal creative force in sourcing funds for giant acquisitions such as the R.J. Reynolds and Eastern Airlines deals. Many smaller investment banks have done the same thing for thousands of smaller acquisitions.

As the stock market turned bullish in the early eighties and price/earnings ratios continued to climb, business buyers found that earnings and cash flows were insufficient to service the large amounts of long-term debt required to fund astronomical purchase prices through traditional debt markets. Financing from asset based lenders or commercial banks became unrealistic and equity funding emerged as the logical alternative. Investment banks, willing to provide such funding, have been able to buoy the acquisition market in the face of these high prices because investors continue to be optimistic about the American economy. The tried and true principles of valuing a business have been severely violated by these manipulations. Of course, the bubble must eventually burst, but in the meantime, prices remain inflated and many entrepreneurs wishing to expand their operation through a business acquisition must either go along with the investment banking community and pay the higher prices or retreat until the financial markets settle down. Through 1990, the acquisition market remains strong even though some serious holes in the dike are beginning to show.

The mechanics for using investment banks are relatively simple. Typically, an investment bank is the primary or lead source in putting together a financing package for an acquisition. It finds an appropriate commercial bank to take the working capital loan, an ABL to take a long-term secured position, and sources the mezzanine financing—if required—from its own funds. The balance of the purchase price is financed by the investment bank's equity contribution to the deal. In exchange for this contribution, the bank's share of the company ranges from 15 to 75 percent, although the higher percentages are reserved for very special deals. Most investment bankers do not want the responsibility that goes along with owning a controlling interest in a company; however, they do want a seat on the board or at least to be a board advisor.

Many small investment banking houses specialize in specific industries or types of product. These smaller houses are invaluable if you can find one with a specialty fitting your company or industry. Such a "boutique" investment bank understands the peculiarities of financing in your industry for companies of your size. If you're having trouble putting together a financing package for an acquisition, this is probably the fastest way to arrange it. Most of these smaller houses also employ people who have backgrounds in the business world outside of banking, and that in itself can help create a helpful atmosphere rather than an adversarial one. Given a choice, if a buyer has less than $100 million in sales or an acquisition deal of less than $50 million, one of these small houses contributes more to the efficacy of the deal than a larger investment bank. The larger the bank, the less personal attention you get. And in the acquisition financing game, personal attention to the deal at hand makes a big difference in the success or failure of it.

In addition to "boutique" houses, there are three distinctly different types of investment banks used by closely held companies for acquisition funding:

1. the large ones (James River, Narragansett, and Sprout, for example) who handle deals up to $100 million but prefer those in the $20 to $50 million range

2. the midsized investment banks (Golder Thoma, Howard Lawson, and, in certain cases, Bear Stearns) specializing in deals from $10 to $20 million; and

3. the smaller houses such as TDH and Wissahickon who package deals of up to $10 million but prefer to stay with those ranging from $500,000 to $8 million.

When selecting an investment bank for acquisition financing, it is imperative to choose one that fits the size of the specific deal. Otherwise, a lot of time, money, and effort can be wasted chasing ghosts. The best way to illustrate how investment banks function as a financing packager is to look at an actual case history, such as Barco Engineering Corporation.

Barco Engineering Corporation (BEC), with annual sales approaching $25 million, designed and manufactured electric and electronic control and measuring devices for monitoring traffic flow in several larger cities, including Chicago and Los Angeles. BEC was a closely held company owned by Roger Clavin, president (35%), Moury Greene, vice president of sales (30%), Shrak Amir, vice president of engineering (30%), and Clavin's son Robert, plant superintendent (5%). The company had always been profitable, and over the past five years, had doubled its sales volume. Competition was getting keener, however, and the partners saw that to continue on their self-proclaimed growth curve, new product lines and management talent must be added. They decided that the fastest way to obtain these resources was through an acquisition.

Through an intensive search effort, I was able to locate what seemed to be the ideal candidate for BEC—Radio Graphics, Inc. With sales of more than $18 million, Radio Graphics sold three proprietary lines for the computer graphic display of measurement data in the liquid and gaseous flow industries. It was a natural fit and we proceeded with preliminary due diligence investigations, culminating in a negotiated price of $12.3 million, cash at closing. The next step was to line up the financing. With business plan in hand, Roger and I approached three investment banks. We finally settled on a small, privately owned bank in Princeton, New Jersey—Wacklin Partners, Ltd.

For a placement fee of $250,000, Wacklin agreed to take the lead in putting together a financing package sourced from a commercial bank, an asset based lender, an insurance company, a secondary investment bank, and Wacklin. Their initial plan was to make a private placement of convertible debentures to take out their mezzanine loan about nine months after the acquisition. As we'll see, these plans changed. The financing package was structured as follows:

	(million)
Equity contribution from BEC	$1.2
Long-term loan from asset based lender, with interest at 2 points over prime. Interest and principal payable quarterly based on a seven-year amortization schedule with a balloon payment due at the end of the fifth year. Secured by a first position on the machinery and equipment and a second position on the real estate of Radio Graphics.	5.6
Long-term mortgage loan from an insurance company, with interest at 10.5 percent for 30 years. Interest and principal payable monthly. Secured by a first position on the real estate of Radio Graphics.	2.7
Preferred stock issue to a secondary investment bank (which remained unknown), and assigned for administrative purposes to Wacklin with a dividend rate of 5 percent. Cumulative and callable at face value plus accrued dividends, carrying warrants convertible to common shares after the fourth year at a ratio of ten shares of preferred to one common share.	1.0
Mezzanine loan from Wacklin with interest at 12 percent, payable on demand, and secured by a promissory note from BEC.	.8
Equity contribution from Wacklin, with warrants to purchase additional common shares within seven years at a price equal to the lesser of market value or BEC book value.	1.0
Total acquisition price	$12.3
Short-term operating line from a commercial bank, with interest at 1.5 points over prime, and secured by receivables and a demand note.	$3.0

The acquisition closed and BEC went on to become a significant force in the graphics display market for monitoring water contamination, chemical analysis, and hazardous gas detection. The company also remained a strong force in the electronic traffic control and measurement markets. Debentures were never floated as Wacklin had planned because the market for such issues dried up. The mezzanine loan was eventually converted to long-term debt with a second position on the machinery and equipment. Four years after the acquisition, BEC went public with a $15 million issue for 40 percent of BEC common shares. Eventually, both investment banks cashed in their warrants and everyone came out of the deal a winner.

The BEC case is just one example of how using an investment bank to package acquisition financing worked out well for everyone. Unfortunately, such is not always the case. The BEC market was growing rapidly and the public issue was a natural extension of their growth financing. Many companies, however, either cannot or will not go public and eventually get into trouble with their investment banker. The whole purpose behind an investment bank participating in a deal is twofold: (1) to earn a sizable return on its invested dollar—usually 30 to 40 percent per year over the term of its participation; and (2) to realize substantial appreciation on its equity investment over a five to ten year period. To reap a 30 to 40 percent return, the company must remain in a strong cash position. Many companies can never afford such an exorbitant payout.

The second objective is normally achieved by issuing public stock in an actively traded market, and whether the company reneges on going public or whether the market will not absorb such an offering, if a public issue is not forthcoming, the investment bank probably won't realize its investment appreciation. Additionally, the smaller the deal, the harder it is to interest an investment bank. The BEC deal for $12.3 million is an attractive size. At $1 million, it would have been much harder to place.

The following are guidelines to help determine if an investment bank should be used for financing an acquisition.

Guidelines for Using an Investment Bank for Acquisition Financing

The acquiring company should:

1. Have a profitable history and a recent upward trend in sales, profits, and cash flow.
2. Have a sound business reason for making the specific acquisition.
3. Have a strong management team.
4. Be willing to take the company public within five years.
5. Demonstrate the ability to integrate the acquired company with existing marketing, engineering, production, and management activities.
6. Be willing to give up an equity share.
7. Be willing to accept operating recommendations from the investment bank.
8. Be unable or unwilling to finance the deal with the company's own equity contribution.

The acquired company should:

1. Be able to demonstrate the ability to generate enough cash flow after the acquisition to make required debt service payments.
2. Be on the same growth curve, or better, as the acquiring company.
3. Be in an industry that is compatible with the acquiring company.
4. Have a strong management team.
5. Have a good reputation in the industry, the marketplace, and the community.

The combined companies should:

1. Be able to demonstrate the cash flow to return 30 to 40 percent per year to the investment banker.

2. Be able to demonstrate that combining the two companies will result in cost savings, additional growth potential, management efficiencies, and other benefits not attainable by the two companies separately.

These are the main criteria for using investment banks for acquisition financing. If there is any question about being able to comply with any of these guidelines, don't even consider using an investment bank. If the decision is made to go ahead with one, how do you choose the right one to match your objectives? Unfortunately, just because a specific investment bank might seem to meet your objectives, they might not be interested in financing your deal simply because their portfolio is already full. On the other hand, you never know this until you try, so if you have any inclination to go this route, the following criteria for choosing the right investment bank should be followed:

Criteria for Choosing an Investment Bank

1. *The size of the deal.* The size of the deal should match the range of activity of the investment bank—up to $1 million, up to $10 million, $10 to $20 million, $20 to $50 million, over $50 million.

2. *The size of the acquiring company.* Although it's possible to buy a business much larger than yours, an investment bank usually frowns on this. Look for a business smaller than your own.

3. *The financial history of both the acquiring and acquired companies.* If both companies are not on a growth curve for sales and profits, don't go to an investment bank. Some will consider a modest growth curve, but most will not. It's necessary to find one that likes the growth curve you are on.

4. *Type of industry.* Although recently more investment banks are looking at low tech or mundane industries, it's still much more difficult to interest one in this type of market than in a high tech, environmental, or other visibly rapid-growth industry; and they don't like companies in the government contracting business at all. Finding an investment bank that specializes in your industry is the best idea.

5. *The personality match of investment bank principals and yourself.* It goes without saying that to get into bed with an investment banker for a long period of time, you better be able to get along with each other.

6. *Geographic proximity.* Larger companies can afford to have management fly around the country for meetings. Smaller ones cannot. It's better to choose an investment bank near the home base of either the acquiring or acquired company.

There is no surefire way to get the right investment bank the first time around. You'll probably need to talk to at least three or four to find out whether there is a match or not. Take the time to contact and interview as many as necessary before signing up with one. Appendix B lists some of the large and small investment banks currently active in acquisition financing.

Seller financing

For some business acquisitions, especially smaller deals, none of the conventional sources of financing are available. Either the target company doesn't have hard assets; the profitability is low; the cash flow won't meet debt service; or the size of the deal is too small or not glamorous enough for investment banks. In those cases, the only way to arrange the financing is through the seller. This is a very common practice with purchase prices of less than $500,000. Seller financing can take one or more of three forms:

Promissory note

A promissory note is a promise from the buyer to pay the purchase price in monthly, quarterly, or annual installments. In the parlance of the merger and acquisition game, this is called buyer paper. Normally, the seller will want a complete payoff within three to four years. He or she might settle for lower monthly payments and a balloon payment at the end. Interest rates are normally negotiated at one to two points over prime. Some sellers want the buyer to secure the note with collateral outside the seller's business, such as the stock of the buyer's company, personal guarantees, or other collateral. The theory behind using buyer paper is that financing cannot be arranged anywhere else. From a practical perspective, it's a lot cheaper if you can get a seller to carry paper for the entire purchase price and pay for it out of the acquired company's earnings than using a lender or other third-party financing.

A contingency contract

A contingency contract stipulates that the purchase price, or part of the price, be paid only if certain conditions occur in the acquired company after closing. Typically, this type of an arrangement is used when the seller claims that a specific contract will be booked at some time in the future, a large customer account will be settled next year, or some other transaction to take place in the future makes the company worth more than its value today.

Contingency contracts are frequently used with companies that do a lot of government contract work, such as when the seller claims he will be getting the bid for a job but it isn't booked yet or a follow-on order is certain to be received next year. If these transactions occur, the volume, profitability, and cash flow of the business make it worth more than today's value. Obviously, however, a buyer won't agree to a higher price until, and if, these transactions really do occur. Therefore, the price is negotiated based on the resolution of a contingency, and a contingency contract finances the deal. A contingency contract normally doesn't carry any interest rate.

An earn out contract

An earn out contract is when the buyer agrees to pay the seller all or part of the purchase price when, and if, profits materialize in the future. This is really a form of profit sharing. If the buyer successfully generates a specific profit from the acquired company, the seller gets a share. Otherwise, the seller gets nothing. Normally, however, an earn out contract specifies a minimum annual payment if profits fall below a certain level. Because earn out contracts are merely a sharing of profits, they carry no interest rate.

The buyer's cost basis of the acquisition for tax purposes—whether buying assets or common stocks—is the amount paid with a promissory note or cash. Contingency or earn out payments are considered dividends to the seller, not part of the purchase price. The seller can report the sale on an installment basis for that part of the purchase price assignable to the buyer's paper and classify any gain as capital or ordinary depending on the circumstances. A seller must treat both contingency and earn out payments as dividends, which are ordinary income.

Most deals that use seller financing end up being a combination of the above methods, often combined with an allocation of part of the purchase price to a management consulting contract for the seller or to a not-to-compete covenant. Both conditions result in ordinary income to the seller. A management consulting contract is not part of the tax basis of the purchase price for the buyer but a not-to-compete covenant is. The buyer can write off the cost allocated to this noncompeting contract over its life as a tax deduction.

IPO financing

Chapter 7 outlined how to raise capital for a variety of purposes by issuing stock to the public. One of the most common applications of the proceeds of a public issue is to acquire another company, either with the cash raised through the offering, or by using the newly traded stock as payment (or part payment) of the purchase price. Some companies have been successful in combining both of these methods with outside participation by an asset-based lender or an investment bank. Generally, however, once a company has gone public, investment bankers are not eager to get involved unless there is a good probability of making a secondary issue in the future. As pointed out earlier, a public issue is about the only way an investment bank can be reasonably assured of significant appreciation on its investment, and unless this possibility exists, it won't be interested in participating.

Using the cash raised through an IPO to make an acquisition is a straightforward cash transaction. Using a company's stock to pay for the acquisition, however, can be a lot cheaper, and in many cases, more welcome to the seller. The biggest disadvantage in such a maneuver is that by issuing more shares to the seller, the per share equity of existing stockholders becomes diluted. Additional issues from a public company also require formal Security and Exchange Commission notification and preparing and filing another registration statement. This makes an IPO more costly up front than other financing sources. If you plan to go this route and you already have an investment bank as a partner, it can handle the deal for you. Normally, however, you'll be on your own, and all of the up-front costs and aggravations of dealing with the SEC discussed in chapter 7 will have to be repeated in an acquisition stock swap.

Other sources

In addition to asset based lenders, investment banks, seller financing, and public stock issues, there are a number of other possibilities for locating long-term acquisition financing. These sources almost always involve debt capital, however, and only rarely equity. Most of these funding institutions remain fairly specialized, and each has its own unique criteria for making secured loans. These sources are used infrequently because initial contact must be made through personal references. In addition, financing conditions and loan portfolios keep changing, so what might be out of the question today, can be the best source tomorrow. There are too many possibilities to be inclusive, but the following institutions are a few you might consider depending on the specific deal. If one of these looks promising, the best way to make contact is through an attorney, CPA, management consultant, or investment banking contact. They will probably know of at least one of these sources that is currently interested in your type of deal.

1. *Insurance companies.* Very large insurance companies such as Prudential or Aetna, or those specializing in life insurance such as Northwestern Mutual or New York Life, are a great source for large amounts of capital. They can be difficult to approach, but with the right references, you might be able to interest one. They have substantial funds to lend, are patient, and generally won't interfere in your business. Many insurance management people are fairly knowledgeable in the business world too.

2. *Pension funds.* Like insurance companies, pension funds are difficult to interest without a direct line through a third party. Preferred stock issues are a favorite of pension funds and most of them will seldom interfere with company management. A word of caution, however. Although most large pension funds are extremely reputable and easy to work with, others, especially some of the union funds, can become overbearing. With pension funds, the best bet is to let an asset based lender or investment bank be the lead lender with a pension fund participating with them.

3. *Foreign sources.* Since the development of oil resources in developing countries in the early seventies and the stabilization of the U.S. economy in the eighties, foreign investors have been eager to invest huge sums of ready cash in secure, high-return American companies. Several investor groups, principally in New York and Los Angeles, keep surfacing as eager sources of acquisition capital. A competent Mergers and Acquisitions consultant should know who to contact for information or be able to put you in touch with a third party money broker to source the funds.

4. *Trusts.* Several very wealthy families and individuals have allocated part of their fortunes to be invested in a variety of business activities, including acquisition funding. Many of these families have established independent trusts specifically for this purpose. They do not advertise, are very secretive, and demand confidentiality in their dealings. Don't try to contact one of them directly. The best way to tap these funds is through a well-connected, private, financial advisor. If you're really interested in doing this, inquire from some of the smaller investment banking houses.

Choosing the right source

This chapter has examined a number of potential sources for raising acquisition capital. Some are applicable only to larger companies, some only to smaller ones. Most require appropriate collateral as security to loans and

_____Table 11-1. Capital sources and uses_____

Characteristics of Deal	Source
Hard-asset value, close to price	Asset based lender
Low, hard-asset base, equity required	Investment bank
	Seller
	Insurance company
	Pension fund
	Private trusts
Glamour industry, high-growth curve	Investment bank
Mature industry, modest growth curve	Asset based lender
	Merger/IPO
	Seller
Target image or industry attractive to public financial markets	IPO
	Investment bank

Amount of Purchase Price	
Up to $1 million	Seller
	Asset-based lender
$1 to $10 million	Investment bank (small)
	Asset-based lender
$10 to $50 million	Investment bank
	Merger
Over $50 million	Investment bank (large)
	Insurance company
	Pension fund
	Private trust
Publicly traded target or acquirer	Merger
Synchronistic management and markets	Merger
	Investment bank

equity contributions. The amount of loans or investments they are willing to make varies widely.

Therefore, choosing the right source for a specific deal can be an awesome task. Going after the wrong one can be costly, time consuming, and if unsuccessful in raising the funds, the acquisition could fall through. So it is extremely important to look in the right place in the beginning without spinning your wheels trying to accomplish an unworkable deal. While not foolproof, Table 11-1 eliminates at least some of the variables. Also, as discussed in chapter 5, it's always a good idea to use professionals in sourcing funds, especially large amounts of acquisition capital.

12

Financing an export program

"ALL THIS TALK ABOUT EUROPE OPENING UP HUGE NEW MARKETS FOR American products sounds great for General Mills or Kraft, but I'm just a little guy selling mustard. I don't know how to market internationally," bemoaned Harry Torkul, president of Specialty Seasoning, Inc., a manufacturing company in Eau Claire, Wisconsin. "I can't afford to ship overseas anyhow. And I certainly can't afford risking not getting paid even if I could put the financing together. Still, a couple million dollars a year in extra sales would sure help use up my excess plant capacity."

Knowing Harry for several years and assisting him in his original acquisition of Specialty Seasoning, I offered to help him put together an export program with a U.S. trading company and then assist him in arranging financing through several government agencies. Two years later, Specialty Seasoning was exporting to countries in Europe and Latin America, and had just started shipping to Australia. Harry never used his commercial bank for export financing and never lost a nickel on collections.

Dispelling the export myth

Exporting remains a mystery to many American companies. Prevalent arguments against exporting personify the lack of understanding of global economics by many small and midsized company executives. They argue that domestic markets provide all the volume they can handle, and they can't see the need to get involved in complex international trade. Others are afraid of losing money through currency exchange fluctuations; are unwilling to tie up cash for long periods waiting for foreign collections; or continue to practice isolationist attitudes traditional in American business. These fears and old wives' tales result in many growth companies suffering financially and losing market share to competitors who do recognize the shrinking of domestic markets.

To stay competitive, many American businesses of all types and sizes have already entered the global marketplace. Large corporations have been active in international trade for decades. Through finely honed export programs, they are already firmly entrenched overseas in such diverse markets as aircraft engines, computer hardware and software, soups and cereals, paper products, pharmaceuticals, and candies. Now it's time for the rest of American businesses to step up to the global market-place and get their fair share of the burgeoning markets in Europe, the Pacific Rim, Central and South America, the Caribbean, Africa, and the Middle East.

Business owners tend to shy away from exporting for four major reasons:

1. They don't know how to locate foreign markets or how to sell their products to foreign buyers.
2. They don't know how to handle the myriad of shipping and customs paperwork, the intricacies of packaging for overseas shipments, or the legal and tax aberrations in exporting.
3. They don't know how to finance an export program other than through internally generated funds or through their commercial bank.
4. They fear foreign expropriation, currency fluctuations, and foreign credit risks.

Overcoming the first two obstacles is beyond the scope of this book, and for anyone seriously considering beginning or expanding an export program, my book, *Going Global: New Opportunities for Growing Companies to Compete in World Markets*, provides a ready answer to these questions. This chapter, however, examines a variety of ways to finance an export program and to take appropriate measures to eliminate most of the foreign risks. Chapter 13 examines ways to finance a physical presence overseas by opening a plant, warehouse, or sales office. There are principally four ways to finance an export program:

1. Using trade credit, with or without government support.
2. Through government agencies established specifically to help U.S. exporters.
3. A joint venture with another U.S. exporter.
4. Countertrade measures with the customer.

Some of these financing schemes and government programs tend to overlap. These same sources might also finance exports from the U.S., imports into the U.S., and the establishment of U.S. investments on foreign soil. This chapter deals with financing sources that primarily deal with finance exports. Chapter 13 deals with foreign investments and imports.

Unfortunately, establishing an export program of any size requires working with a commercial bank that maintains an international department. There just isn't any way to avoid it. You'll need their services for handling letters of credit, wire transfers of funds, currency conversions, and possibly even bank loans with SBA or other outside guarantees. On the plus side, you will be working with people well versed in global banking, not the typical loan officer. Don't fall into the trap, however, of choosing a bank for international trade simply because it handles your company's checking account or short-term operating line. It is essential to use a bank with an experienced, diversified international department. Without this expertise, the bank will be forced to act as an intermediary with another larger bank. This only confuses the issue, adds significant time to transferring money worldwide, and makes banking transactions more costly.

Financing with trade credit

To master the use of trade credit in the international sphere, it's necessary to understand the vocabulary used in global finance circles. There aren't too many terms, but without an understanding of at least a smattering of the international finance vernacular, a person can get very confused when talking to international bankers, government agencies, trading companies, and even customers.

Buyer credit refers to credit extended to the buyer by someone other than the supplier. This third party to the transaction could be an American or a foreign bank, a U.S. government agency, or a foreign agency. Buyer credit might come with or without third-party guarantees. The exporter does not record the receivable on his books because he receives cash, or cash equivalents, at the time of shipping.

Supplier credit refers to credit extended to the buyer from the seller (exporter). It doesn't make any difference if the exporter, in turn, obtains outside financing from government agencies, banks, or elsewhere. As long as the receivable resides on the exporter's books —even temporarily—it is referred to as "supplier credit."

In trade credit, the term *recourse* measures the degree of responsibility for paying off any indebtedness incurred by the buyer in an export transaction. *Full recourse* means the seller takes full responsibility for such obligations. A *nonrecourse* document means that he has no responsibility for payment and is completely off the hook if the buyer defaults. Residing in no-man's-land, a *limited recourse* obligation means that, if there was fraudulent representation in any of the export documentation, the seller has full responsibility to make good to the financing agency on any default deficiency from the buyer. If there is no fraud, then there is no recourse. Limited recourse documents that restrict the exporter's liability to a specified percentage of shipping values is used infrequently and, except in very rare instances, the exporter should avoid such conditions when negotiating the sales contract.

Financing with letters of credit

The most common financing instrument used by American exporters is the letter of credit. In international trade, a letter of credit (L/C) is universally accepted as a normal form of payment. A L/C comes in many forms and can have a variety of provisions attached to it. It can be revocable or irrevocable, confirmed or advised, a straight or negotiated letter, or payable at sight or over an extended period of time. A L/C might also be transferable.

Frequently, a L/C is payable upon presentation of bills of lading or other transport documents. These documents might read "clean on board," "about," or "approximately" (referring to quantities shipped), and cover partial or full shipments or transshipments. The L/C can be for one shipment or it can be revolving.

Properly preparing and executing L/Cs and their supporting documentation is such a crucial part of exporting that entire books are written with complete instructions for handling the various options. A full dissertation of the interaction of L/Cs and shipping documentation is far beyond the scope of this book. It is such an important subject, however, that if you are going to start exporting, check out the details in one of the many publications and books available. Two of the best are, *Going Global: New Opportunities For Growing Companies to Compete in World Markets*, and *Exporting from Start to Finance*.

There are four ways to use L/Cs to obtain working capital for manufacturing products or performing services to be exported:

1. Back-to-back L/Cs.
2. Off-balance sheet credit extension
3. Assigned proceeds
4. Transferred L/Cs

Back-to-back L/Cs

Assume you have a contract to ship rubber gaskets to a customer in Belgium. The customer places a L/C for the full amount of the order with a U.S. bank, allowing partial drawdowns against three separate shipments. Prior to the first shipment, the customer issues orders to hold the gaskets at the dock until it requests their release and extends the expiration date on the L/C accordingly. But your suppliers are unwilling to wait for your customer's orders and want their payments within 30 days. You then take the Belgian L/C to your bank and ask it to issue new L/Cs to your suppliers to be drawn down as they deliver their material to you using the Belgian L/C as collateral. These are called back-to-back L/Cs.

Banks normally don't like to handle back-to-back L/Cs because it puts them at risk for your performance on the first L/C. If a banker thoroughly understands the complete mechanics of L/Cs, however, he should go along with it. The reason is simple. L/Cs are not recorded on the bank's financial statement, and therefore, do not affect capital ratios or reserve requirements. Small banks are usually more willing to use back-to-back L/Cs than larger ones, not only because there is generally a close relationship with the customer, but also because issuing L/Cs requires less internal approval than making a loan.

Off-balance sheet credit extension

Off-balance sheet credit is a variation of back-to-back L/Cs except the bank does not use the customer L/C as collateral, and therefore, is not boxed in to your performance against it. Instead, the bank issues L/Cs to your suppliers backed by your general creditworthiness. In other words, it agrees to an extension of your open line of credit. The bank is willing to do this because it knows that when your customer's L/C is drawn down you will deposit these sums in the bank and use them to reduce your other outstanding bank debt.

At first glance, this doesn't seem like a very important financing scheme to the exporter. It really is helpful, however, because the issuance of supplier L/Cs will normally draw down on your working capital line of credit. By supporting specific export transactions and issuing supplier L/Cs without a corresponding reduction in your working capital line, the banker is, in essence, granting additional credit. Like back-to-back L/Cs, these L/Cs do not appear on either the bank's or your balance sheet, and thus, do not infringe on balance sheet ratios or debt limits for other purposes. As additional security, the bank can make a filing under the Uniform Commercial Code against the goods to be shipped to assure that you really will deposit the proceeds of your customer's L/C in his bank.

Whether you use back-to-back L/Cs, or get a bank to extend your line of credit by issuing supplier L/Cs, expect to pay the bank for its efforts. A commercial bank seldom, if ever, does anything free. They charge for issuing L/Cs just like any other service. Rates vary considerably but expect to pay between 1/2 to 2 percent of the value of the L/C. Some banks charge as much as 5 percent. There is also the possibility of a commitment fee for another 1/2 to 5 percent.

Assigned proceeds

Assigning the proceeds from a customer's L/C is probably the easiest way to finance supplier payments. The proceeds from any L/C can be assigned without permission from anyone. Just tell the bank holding the L/C that it should pay the entire proceeds, or a percentage of the proceeds, drawn on the L/C to a specified supplier rather than to you, the exporter. Neither notice of assignment to the buyer nor additional bank credit are required.

If a supplier insists on verification of the existence and the terms of the L/C, copies of the L/C documentation can be forwarded with the name of the buyer blacked out. The only potential disadvantage to a supplier is if the shipment is held up for some reason or if there is an imperfection in the customer's L/C preventing drawdowns. There is no additional cost involved in assigning a L/C. The completion of a simple assignment form is the only requirement.

Transferred L/Cs

Transferring a L/C is slightly more complicated than a straight assignment. In some instances, an exporter might require certain materials, assemblies, or components to be shipped direct to its customer as part of the complete order. If the exporter does not manufacture these items but merely buys them complete from a supplier, then the exporter's function becomes that of a middleman, or broker, in the transaction. If the components delivered direct from the supplier are high value items, the supplier might want the customer's L/C transferred directly to avoid relying on the exporter's performance as a condition of getting paid.

To transfer a L/C, either partially or in its entirety, the exporter must get permission from the buyer. This automatically informs the buyer that the exporter is not the original supplier of these goods or that he is not financially viable in the eyes of his supplier. The foreign buyer has the right to refuse such a transfer, but normally, unless the exporter-buyer relationship is antagonistic, the buyer shouldn't object.

All terms of the L/C (e.g., total value, shipping date, insurance requirements, special shipping instructions, and so on) transfer intact. One provision, however, saves the exporter from negotiating a new L/C with the foreign buyer for merchandise not supplied by the specific supplier receiving the transferred L/C. The exporter can instruct the paying bank to limit payment on the L/C to the amounts due a supplier and substitute the exporter's invoices for the balance of the L/C. This is common practice and, although it creates additional paperwork, most banks allow it for a small additional charge, or none at all.

The name of the foreign buyer can also be hidden from the supplier receiving the transfer. In this case, when invoices are presented for payment, the documentation must call for the notification of the original exporter, or his freight forwarder, rather than the buyer. Again, this is not an unusual request and most banks and buyers go along with it.

If a foreign buyer has cash problems of his own and can't raise the capital or credit to place a confirmed, irrevocable L/C as immediate payment against the exporter's shipping invoices, there are other ways to make the sale and still obtain working capital financing. One is through the use of a documentary banker's acceptance.

Using a banker's acceptance

A documentary banker's acceptance (BA) can be used to collect on a foreign sale to a buyer who has a poor credit rating or is short of cash. By using a BA, an exporter agrees to extend the exporter's credit to the foreign buyer. Once the sale is made, the exporter then sells the buyer's receivable at a discount. This is similar to factoring domestic receivables. The mechanics of this type of transaction work as follows:

1. The buyer draws a time (or usance) letter of credit for the full amount of the sale price with the specific provision that it is payable in a specific number of days after the exporter presents shipping documentation. Normally, an exporter insists on a fixed date, usually not in excess of 180 days from the date of sight. This is the maximum time frame that a BA remains in effect.

2. When the exporter presents shipping documentation, the bank issues a BA in place of cash. The BA is nothing more than the bank's marking "accepted" on the exporter's draft presented for payment against the L/C. This marking means that the bank promises to pay you, or any other holder of the BA, on the fixed date of the L/C.

3. The exporter then presents this BA to the same bank issuing it and requests the bank to discount the document, paying the face value minus the discount interest. Though the amount received is less than the invoice price, the exporter compensates for this up front when the deal is negotiated with the foreign buyer by increasing the price of the products by an amount approximating the discount rate. The buyer conserves cash for up to six months, and the exporter gets paid immediately—a win-win deal.

Even without an increase in the sell price to cover this discount, the interest rates (discount rates) charged on BAs are usually the least of any type of financing. The bank also charges an acceptance fee for handling the transaction (naturally!). This ranges between 1/2 to 2 percent per annum of the face amount of the L/C. Sometimes, a buyer might be willing to pay this acceptance fee but not a higher price for the goods.

Clean banker's acceptances

A clean banker's acceptance differs from a documentary banker's acceptance in that it is not supported by a buyer's L/C. Instead, it is arranged by the exporter with his own bank for his own use. A clean BA relates to a specific transaction or shipment, however, just like a documentary BA. The exporter discounts the BA with his bank, and then the bank takes this readily negotiable instrument and sells it in the secondary bond market. The BA never hits the bank's balance sheet and it is always readily negotiable. Because the borrower's performance on the specific transaction supporting the BA underlies the borrower's credit with the bank, however, very few banks grant clean BAs to smaller companies. On the other hand, large corporations use them all the time. If you can sell a bank on the concept of a clean BA, however, it is a cheap way to finance working capital needs for either imports or exports.

The normal size of a clean BA is $500,000, although some banks go as low as $100,000. Normally, only very large regional banks or money center banks work in this area. Interest rates on clean BAs are normally less than the *London Interbank Offer Rate* (LIBOR), which is almost always less than the U.S. prime rate. Acceptance fees range up to 2 percent per annum on the face amount of the BA.

Some companies negotiate export orders with shipments extending over several years. A typical example would be for equipment and components for the construction of an electric power plant or a large factory. The construction of the facility and the installation of equipment might take three to five years. The high cost of the equipment and its installation usually precludes such a long-term transaction from falling within the confines of typical L/C trade credit. More ingenious financing schemes must be found. One method used throughout the world to finance long-term exports is called "forfaiting."

Financing with forfaiting

Forfaiting, a French term, is a process whereby the exporter forfeits his rights to receive future payment in exchange for immediate cash. The process was developed years ago by large corporations exporting out of Europe and has become a popular means of providing supplier credit for large or long-term export projects. Although most Americans have never heard of either the term or the process, forfaiting is becoming acceptable to some of the more progressive international traders. The transaction should be at least $250,000 and normally doesn't exceed $10 million. The discount rate ranges up to 2 points above LIBOR, and commitment fees go up to 3/4 percent per annum. The financing period is one to ten years, although five or six years is the most common. Forfaiting works as follows:

1. The exporter and the buyer, who, for his own reasons, wants long-term credit for the deal, negotiates a series of notes, drafts, bills, or other instruments to pay off the balance due the exporter over the term of the transaction.

2. The exporter contacts a forfaiter and the forfaiter and the buyer negotiate with a foreign bank to provide a guarantee of the buyer's credit as an endorser of the note, draft, or bill. In the parlance of international finance, this endorsement, together with a promissory note or bill from the buyer, is called an "aval." The simplicity of this transaction has great appeal to bankers and buyers alike because no contracts are involved that could require litigation in the event of default.

3. When the exporter presents the forfaiter a complete set of shipping and customs clearance documentation, the forfaiter makes payment.

There are three broad advantages to the exporter is using forfaiting:

1. It is medium to long-term financing and for large transactions, short-term credit often won't work.

2. It covers the entire sale, not just 85 percent (the maximum for an Eximbank guarantee).

3. It costs less than borrowing from an American bank.

The primary disadvantages are that it cannot be used for short-term credit and many American banks just don't understand the mechanics yet. In addition, banks in some developing countries are still reluctant to handle the guarantee portion of the deal for the buyer. Any large money center bank should be able to help locate an appropriate forfaiter and assist in arranging the deal. Most have their own internal forfaiting departments, which eliminates the need to hire one from the outside. Chase, Citicorp, Bank of America, and Security Pacific are all experienced in this technique. Most major European banks with branches in New York or Los Angeles can also act as forfaiters.

Using leasing for exporting capital assets

The same type of leasing used domestically and examined in chapter 9 can be used to structure supplier credit for the sale of capital assets. In export trade, however, the exporter either does the leasing internally, or arranges for a leasing company to buy the goods and structure a lease with the foreign buyer. International Leasing Corp., one of the largest and well-known companies in the international leasing game, handles most of the foreign leasing for Boeing and other aircraft manufacturers as well as many other exporters. As popular as leasing is in this country, many smaller U.S. leasing firms have ignored the international market because they fear buyer credit risk or potential foreign government expropriation of the assets. The Federal Credit Insurance Association, which will be examined later in this chapter, provides insurance coverage for both of these risks, so there really isn't any reason for being afraid to enter into a long-term lease with a foreign buyer. It's not a bad idea for an exporter to hold the lease rather than selling it to a leasing company. With minimal risk and an opportunity to increase his profits on the transaction, it could be a very desirable way to go.

Leasing can be especially beneficial when exporting to developing countries that have soft currency (not readily convertible into one of the traded currencies, such as dollars, pounds sterling, yen, or deutsche marks). Payment terms can be structured over a period of time to meet the needs of both the buyer and seller. With a little ingenuity, an exporter should be able to arrange for a countertrade or barter payment to permit translation into hard currency or goods. Many large corporations finance their export programs to developing nations almost entirely with leases and countertrade arrangements.

During the past 20 years, entire infrastructures of developing nations have been built with products and services, many of which have been furnished by American companies. Most of these long-term projects have been financed through government agencies with little or no financing provided directly by the exporter. Even though an exporter often initiates the financing scheme, it's really up to a foreign buyer—many times a foreign government—to arrange its own financing, and this has frequently been done with U.S. government assistance.

Financing through Eximbank

American exporters of nearly any type or size learn quickly that financing export sales through trade credits is the least expensive and easiest way to do business with foreign customers. On the other hand, for a variety of reasons, many privately owned businesses are unable to compete in the world market using only trade credit. Something else must be arranged to match the subsidies offered by many foreign governments to their own companies. Eximbank is the first source of help.

In order to at least partially compensate for foreign government subsidized financing schemes, congress established the Export-Import Bank. Originally founded in 1934, the principal legislation governing its operation is the Export-Import Bank Act of 1945, as amended through October 15, 1986. Eximbank is an independent, corporate agency of the U.S. government. Eximbank coordinates its policies with other government agencies to ensure consistency with overall foreign policy and objectives. Normally, it will not support exports to communist countries or finance the sale of military products or services. To be eligible for assistance from Eximbank, a company must export goods or services with at least 50 percent U.S. content. The following five questions are asked about each transaction:

1. Is there a U.S. export involved?
2. What foreign competition exists, and is it officially subsidized?
3. Is the transaction economically feasible?
4. Is there reasonable assurance of repayment?
5. Would voiding the transaction create an adverse effect on the domestic U.S. economy?

A negative response to any of these questions usually exempts an export transaction from Eximbank assistance. The one exception relates only to small businesses. Evidence of foreign competition is not required for exports from small businesses when Eximbank supplies less than $2.5 million in guarantees or loans.

Eximbank supplements and fosters private capital for export business, setting fees and interest rates based on the risks involved in each foreign country. Although it does not receive congressional appropriations for its operations, the Bank's annual financing support authorization ceiling is established by congress. Through fees and interest charged on its guarantees and loans, and recoveries on previous claims, Eximbank has been largely self-sufficient and not financed by tax dollars since its inception. Because it is self-sustaining, Eximbank cannot always compete effectively with the rates and terms offered by foreign export credit agencies. By and large, however, it has remained in the running in most transactions.

Eximbank services are available to any American exporter of any size and in any industry. As with many government agencies, most of the support from Eximbank has gone to large corporations. Within the past 15 years, however, in an effort to brace against increasing foreign trade deficits, Eximbank has established several programs especially helpful to small and midsized exporters. Part of this effort has been the establishment of a "hotline" counseling service to answer questions smaller businesses might have about financing assistance for export products or services. The toll-free number is (800) 424-5201. Four of the most popular programs offered by Eximbank to help smaller exporters are: the commercial bank guarantee program, the foreign credit insurance program, a cooperative financing facility with overseas banks, and the discount loan program with U.S. banks.

Eximbank preliminary commitment

A preliminary commitment is an offer from Eximbank to finance a specific export transaction in advance of the transaction. It outlines the Bank's willingness to participate, and the terms and conditions for loan or guarantee support. It covers all products and services eligible for Eximbank participation. Any business can file an application for commitment. The only cost is a $100 fee accompanying the application. The commitment remains valid for 180 days but can be extended by Eximbank. With this commitment, an exporter, borrower, lender, or other responsible party to the transaction can then establish terms and conditions of financing for planning and marketing purposes. Obviously, a foreign buyer who is assured of Eximbank support should be more likely to negotiate a contract with a small exporter than if only trade credit were offered.

Eximbank Working Capital Guarantee program

The Eximbank Working Capital Guarantee program was designed specifically to help smaller U.S. exporters obtain bank-provided working capital financing for funding the production of export products and services. These loans are made to the exporter directly, not the foreign buyer. All eligible products and services are covered. An exporter should first obtain a preliminary commitment from Eximbank and then shop for the best credit line from commercial lenders. Any commercial lender willing to extend export-related working capital loans to small and midsized businesses is eligible for the guarantee. The guarantee covers up to 90 percent of the principal balance and interest up to one point over the U.S. Treasury rate. Repayment by the exporter must be made within 12 months, unless previous arrangements are made with both the lender and Eximbank. The cost to the exporter for this guarantee is a $100 processing fee, an up-front facility fee of 1/2 percent of the loan, and quarterly usage fees of 1/4 percent of the loan's average outstanding balance.

The guarantee is with recourse to the exporter, who must provide the lender with adequate collateral—usually inventory used to produce the products—so that the loan balance never exceeds 90 percent of the collateral value. An Eximbank working capital guarantee can be used either for a single export transaction loan or for an export revolving credit line. It can also be combined with the SBA's Export Line of Credit program. Approved lenders can receive Eximbank's guarantee on loans of up to $300,000 on a discretionary basis.

Eximbank guarantee for medium and long-term loans

Eximbank's Medium (1 to 7 years) and Long-term (7 to 10 years) Guarantee Program was created specifically for the export of capital equipment, including U.S. products made with foreign components. Eximbank covers up to 100 percent of the American content of the product only, but with two provisions: (1) the U.S. content does not exceed 85 percent of the contract price of each item; and (2) the total U.S. content is not less than 50 percent of the total contract value. This guarantee can be used only for loans made by either a U.S. lender or a foreign lender to a foreign borrower for the purchase of American goods. It cannot be used to guarantee loans to American exporters directly. The foreign buyer must pay 15 percent of the contract value as a down payment, either in the form of cash or an irrevocable, confirmed L/C.

A guarantee can be obtained for 100 percent of the financed portion. For medium-term loans, Eximbank guarantees up to $10 million. Either the exporter or the lender must counter-guarantee Eximbank for 2 percent of the commercial risk. The interest rate charged for fixed rate loans is the lesser of the U.S. Treasury bill rate plus 1/2 percent, or the U.S. Treasury note rate minus 1/2 percent. On floating rate loans, the interest rate is the lesser of the U.S. Treasury note rate minus 1/2 percent or a preselected rate from the following—prime minus 2 percent, LIBOR minus 1/4 percent, or U.S. Treasury bill plus 1/2 percent. The repayment period must comply with the following schedule:

Contract Value	Maximum Term (years)
$50,000 or less	2
$50,000 to $100,000	3
$100,000 to $200,000	4
$200,000 or more	5

Under exceptional cases, Eximbank will go seven years for larger loans. Prenegotiated long-term loans for over $10 million can be repaid over 10 years.

The cost to the exporter for medium and long-term guarantees for foreign buyers are: a $100 processing fee; an up-front exposure fee based on the term of the loan, country risk, and category of borrower, paid on each disbursement; a commitment fee of 1/8 percent per annum on the undisbursed balance of the guaranteed loan.

The Eximbank guarantee remains unconditional and freely transferable. Claims must be filed between 30 and 150 days after default by a buyer. This guarantee can also be combined with an intermediary loan. A preliminary commitment is available to any responsible applicant.

Eximbank direct loans

Eximbank provides two types of direct loans: loans direct to the foreign buyer of U.S. exported goods and loans to intermediaries who, in turn, fund the foreign buyer. These intermediaries are usually financial institutions—either American or foreign.

Intermediary loans are structured as "standby" loans, which means the lender can draw down on the loan at any time during its term. This provides flexibility to the lender because he is free to take advantage of lower rates than those established by the Organization for Economic Cooperation and Development (OECD), if he can. OECD is an organization of 22 developed nations that sets parameters for interest rates and terms applicable to its members' export credit activities. Maximum coverages and repayment terms for both categories of loans are the same as for the Eximbank guarantee program. Both require 15 percent down payments by the buyer.

Both intermediary loans and direct loans to foreign buyers are made at fixed rates established by OECD; but they do vary between the two programs. Under the direct loan program, the rates are established by the type of country the buyer is located in according to the following schedule:

Country Category	Up to 5 years	Over 5 years
I (Rich)	CIRR	CIRR
II (Intermediate)	9.15%	9.65%
III (Poor)	8.30%	8.30%

CIRR stands for the Commercial Interest Reference Rate and is revised monthly. Appendix I defines which countries fall into each category.

For intermediary loans, the following rate schedule is in effect, assuming the intermediary loans to the foreign borrower are at the minimum OECD fixed rate:

Loan Commitment	Eximbank Interest Rate
Less than $1 million	OECD rate less 1.5%
$1-$5 million	OECD rate less 1.0%
$5-$10 million	OECD rate less 0.5%

Additionally, if an intermediary loan is not combined with a guarantee, Eximbank waives the commitment fee. Otherwise the guarantee fee is the same as for a direct loan to the buyer—1/2 percent per annum.

Engineering multiplier program

Surprisingly, the engineering multiplier program has not received wide use by American exporters. It has been designed specifically for two purposes: (1) to provide funding for engineering firms and other preconstruction service companies; and (2) to fund feasibility studies by architectural and design firms. It also serves to promote the exporting of goods used in the construction of these projects. The program provides medium-term loans of up to $10 million direct to foreign buyers. If the engineering contract results in the export of American-made goods for the project, the engineering contract can be rolled into a long-term project loan. The criteria calls for the export contract to be the greater of $10 million, or twice the value of the engineering contract. Rates, repayment terms, and fees are similar to those of other programs previously described.

Other programs sponsored by Eximbank include financing for U.S. costs of operating and maintenance contracts for foreign projects and Foreign Credit Insurance Association (FCIA) guarantees covering leases, foreign expropriation, foreign currency translation, and coverage for export-related foreign currency swaps, as well as several specialized insurance coverages to reduce the risk to American export companies. The entire FCIA program will be examined later in this chapter. Before looking at foreign credit and risk insurance coverages, however, an additional, and relatively new export financing medium should be mentioned—PEFCO.

The Private Export Funding Corporation

The Private Export Funding Corporation (PEFCO) is a private organization closely associated with Eximbank. It has been formed and is owned by several U.S. banks and large corporations. Its purpose is to supplement long-term financing for foreign buyers of American exports. Typically, PEFCO becomes involved in financing programs for exports requiring longer terms than a commercial bank will handle but shorter than those funded by Eximbank. PEFCO also works with exporters and foreign buyers to structure financing packages with unique interest rates and repayment stipulations. PEFCO receives its investment funds from selling Eximbank guaranteed negotiable debt instruments on the open market.

Though PEFCO is not widely used by smaller exporters, the facility is available if needed. It handles projects exceeding $1 million and makes loans to foreign buyers for periods exceeding five years. It's just another way to promote American competitiveness in the global marketplace and gives the exporter one more option to plan financing.

The U.S. Department of Agriculture

Several specialized export assistance programs are administered by the Department of Agriculture. Exporters of agricultural products of all types should contact their local Department of Agriculture office to learn which programs apply to their product lines. One agency, however, supports universally applicable programs, regardless of product—the Commodity Credit Corporation (CCC). The CCC offers financial assistance in the form of buyer credits based on government-to-government agreements. Two of the most popular programs are the Export Credit Guarantee program and the Intermediate Credit Guarantee program. Both programs issue a CCC guarantee against a foreign letter of credit for up to 98 percent of the value of the product. The Export Credit Guarantee program issues these credit guarantees for up to three years. The Intermediate Credit Guarantee program extends credit to 10 years. Both programs specify unlimited amounts of credit and are intended to assist those countries with major economic problems.

A third CCC program, the Bonus Incentive Commodity Export Program, enters the picture when the CCC determines that, in order for the exporter to compete with foreign government subsidized companies, the U.S. company must be subsidized also. This subsidy takes the form of a certificate—an Export Enhancement Program (EEP) bonus certificate—with a value equal to what the exporter needs to effectively compete. Redeemable for any surplus commodity held by the CCC, and EEP certificate can be sold or traded in secondary markets. When an exporter enters into such a transaction, this certificate can be as good as cash. In many cases, the sale or trade value of the certificate exceeds the certificate value by a substantial premium, thereby permitting the exporter to make a profit on this transaction as well as on his original export sale.

Using the SBA for export financing

The SBA is also involved in export financing, but to a very limited extent. Chapter 6 explored the various facets of doing business with the SBA domestically, but the agency also offers assistance for financing smaller export transactions. The SBA's special Export Revolving Line of Credit program (ERLC) has been in effect for years but has received little emphasis from agency offices, hardly any publicity, and very little use from exporters. Provisions in the Omnibus Trade Bill of 1988 theoretically improved the program to be a viable source of export financing for small businesses. Congress has given the SBA a mandate to support small exporters, and hopefully, small and midsized companies will begin taking advantage of the program.

In August 1984, in an effort to reach more small businesses with its Working Capital Guarantee program, Eximbank reached an agreement with the SBA to extend co-guarantees under the SBA's ERLC program. Under this agreement, Eximbank participates equally with the SBA to guarantee working capital loans to small businesses for export programs. The effect of this participation was to increase the loan limit to $1 million. Thus, if an exporter qualifies as a small business under SBA criteria, and needs $1 million or less, the resources of both the SBA and Eximbank are available. The SBA continues to handle amounts below $200,000 solely through its ERLC program, and Eximbank supports the difference. Other qualification requirements and definitions fall within the same SBA parameters as those established for domestic assistance.

Through 1990, many local SBA offices have tried to recruit staff personnel who are familiar with international trade. So far, however, most have fallen short. This lack of exporting expertise coupled with the stringent budget cuts stressed earlier, cast a gloom over any significant active participation by the SBA in export financing in the near future. As increased allocations become available from congress and more qualified staff are hired, the SBA will probably be a good place to start looking for export financing. In the meantime, other facilities can be more helpful. It can't hurt to try your local SBA office, however. They might be able to get you started. If the SBA can't help, perhaps they can direct you to one of the several, recently established state export finance programs.

Eximbank's City-State Cooperation program

Early in 1989, in an effort to encourage the private sector of American business to begin helping the smaller exporter, Eximbank launched its City-State Cooperation program in California, Massachusetts, Maryland, Tucson, Arizona, and Columbus, Ohio. City and state agencies were asked to participate with Eximbank in its loan guarantees and its foreign credit insurance. The idea was to open up export financing direct to the small exporter rather than to the foreign buyer or to large corporations. Eximbank's traditional preference for the latter two heaped public and congressional criticism on the program and this was an attempt to rectify a badly skewed export financing system. The fact that Eximbank has operated at a loss since 1982 might have opened some eyes to the fact that, to be financially sound, Eximbank would have to get more involved with smaller exporters.

The new City-State Cooperation program started as a marketing tool for Eximbank. City and state agencies market Eximbank guarantees and Federal Credit Insurance Agency credit insurance through direct mailings, calls to local banks and merchants, seminars, and a modest advertising campaign. These agencies also provide the technical support to smaller companies. This makes exporting more assessable and creates less confusion and wasted time for local banks. A few wise Washington bureaucrats finally realized that commercial banks throughout the country had drawn away from smaller businesses, concentrating their efforts on larger corporations. The time finally arrived to try to change their minds about their smaller customers. And it seems to be working. Eximbank approved over $95 million for more than 100 working capital guarantees in 1988. Under this new pilot program alone, the Bank has approved 36 deals worth $25 million. This isn't all that encouraging, however, when one realizes that 80 percent of this volume was in credit insurance. Loan guarantees amounted to only $5 million for 18 deals with an average transaction size of about $275,000. It does seem to be a step in the right direction though.

The City of Los Angeles has taken Eximbank's program one step further. It formed an agency called L.A. XPORT to handle the marketing of Eximbank guarantees. L.A. XPORT has obtained a separate line of credit specifically set aside for small exporters from a local bank for $15 million. The Los Angeles LDC, Inc. functions as the administrative arm for the program, and through April 1989, had completed four transactions worth $1.2 million. Eximbank reports that through mid-1989, 15 states and cities have applied to the Bank to become part of the City-State program. Eximbank officers are confident that many of these applicants will pick up on the scheme worked out in Los Angeles. Before applying for any assistance from the Eximbank directly, it wouldn't hurt to check with your state department of commerce or city chamber of commerce to see what similar programs might be available locally.

Reducing foreign risk with FCIA

The Foreign Credit Insurance Association (FCIA) is an agent of Eximbank. Its purpose is to provide insurance coverage for foreign risks not normally available through private carriers. Policies available from FCIA cover a wide range of foreign risks, including expropriation, bad debts, and currency fluctuations. Eximbank lists the major objectives of FCIA as follows:

1. To protect the exporter against failure of foreign buyers to pay their credit obligations for commercial or political reasons.

2. To encourage exporters to offer foreign buyers competitive terms of payment.

3. To support an exporter's prudent penetration of higher risk foreign markets.

4. To give exporters and their banks greater financial flexibility in handling overseas accounts receivable.

To meet these objectives, the FCIA offers eight different insurance policies: new-to-export, umbrella, multi-buyer, short-term single-buyer, medium-term single-buyer, lease coverage, bank letter of credit, and financial institution buyer credit.

New-to-export insurance coverage

New-to-export insurance coverage is available to companies just beginning to export or that have an average annual export credit sales volume of less than $750,000 for the past two years. A company can qualify in this program for a maximum of five years. The coverage is a one-year blanket policy insuring the collectibility of short-term credit sales. It protects 100 percent of political risk and 95 percent of commercial risk (but drops to 90 percent after 2 years). Interest payments due on debt obligations of up to prime rate minus 1/2 point are also covered. Credit terms must be 180 days or less for most products; extended to 360 days for agricultural commodities and consumer durables.

Although the fees and insurance premiums vary with each transaction according to repayment terms and type of buyer, the FCIA has a rate schedule available for the asking. There is, however, a minimum annual premium of $500. Policy proceeds are assignable and no annual commercial risks, first-loss deductible applies for the first two years. If commercial risk coverage is not needed, political risk alone can be covered.

Umbrella coverage

Umbrella coverage is provided to an export agent who has the capability of administering the policy on behalf of multiple exporters, such as an export management firm. The policy provides one-year coverage for short-term export sales from exporters with average annual export credit sales of less than $2 million for the past two years and who have not used FCIA during this period. Covered risks include 100 percent of political risk and 90 percent of commercial risk. Interest coverage, maximum payment terms, and assignability are the same as the new-to-export policy. There is a minimum annual premium of $500 payable by the policy administrator.

The advantage in this type of policy is that it can be carried by the export management company or other export representative responsible for the entire administration of the policy, including reports to the FCIA, paying premiums, and filing loss claims. Obviously, this relieves the small exporter of a sizable administrative chore.

Both the umbrella coverage and the new-to-export coverage insure sales of consumables, raw materials, spare parts, agricultural commodities, capital goods, consumer durables, and services.

Multi-buyer coverage

The multi-buyer policy insures all exporters of goods and services who ship to more than one foreign buyer. The advantage of this policy is that it forms a blanket coverage so that each new buyer does not have to be qualified by the FCIA. It's a one-year blanket policy for short-term or medium-term credit sales, or a combination of both. There are two coverage options: (1) Spilt: after an annual commercial risks first-loss deductible: 100 percent political and 90 percent commercial; and (2) Equalized: for political and commercial after all risks first-loss deductible: 95 percent short-term and 90 percent long-term.

Criteria for interest coverage, repayment periods, minimum annual fee, and assignability follow other coverages. No cash down payment from the buyer is required under short-term coverage, but 15 percent must be made for medium-term.

Short-term single-buyer coverage

Short-term single-buyer coverage insures short-term credit sales from all U.S. exporters shipping to a single buyer. Political and commercial coverage are equalized based on the following schedule:

- Sovereign buyers—100 percent
- Private sector and non-sovereign public-sector buyers—90 percent
- Letter of credit transactions—95 percent
- Bulk agricultural sale—98 percent

Premiums are determined by type of buyer, repayment terms, and country of destination. Current minimum premium rates are:

- Sovereign buyers and political risks only—$2,500
- Letters of credit, transaction with bank guarantors, and non-sovereign public-sector buyers—$5,000
- Private sector buyers—$10,000

Medium-term single-buyer coverage

Medium-term single-buyer coverage includes 100 percent of the political risk and 90 percent for commercial risk. Repayment terms follow standard criteria. Premiums are based on the type of buyer and the country of destination. A foreign buyer must pay a 15 percent down payment before shipment.

Lease coverage

Insurance coverage provided by the FCIA for foreign leases often determines whether or not a lease transaction makes sense. Coverage is available for both operating leases and financial leases. Operating lease coverage insures both the stream of lease payments and the fair market value of leased products. Financial coverage covers only the total payment under the lease. Product coverage extends to new and used capital equipment and services, including automobiles, agricultural, processing, and communications equipment. Any leasing company, manufacturer, or financial institution qualifies as an eligible applicant. Coverage is equalized between political and commercial risk, with 100 percent protection for sovereign lessees, 90 percent for all other lessees, and 100 percent protection against government repossession. Buyer down payment requirements are 15 percent for finance leases and none for operating leases. Proceeds can be assigned, and no first-loss deductible is required.

Bank letter of credit coverage

A bank letter of credit coverage is available only to lending institutions. The exporter does not have to worry about this policy except to know of its availability to his lender. All banks dealing with L/Cs should know about this coverage and use it.

Financial institution buyer credit coverage

Buyer credit coverage is another policy available only to financial institutions extending direct credit loans or reimbursement loans to foreign buyers of American exports.

Using private insurance companies

Very few private insurance companies are willing to cover export risks. AIG Political Risks, Inc., 70 Pine Street, New York, NY 10027, is one of the few major private carriers willing to participate. AIG has been in the export insurance business for years and offers coverages priced competitively with FCIA. They offer policies covering political risk for export transaction, expropriation, money transfer, contract repudiation by foreign governments, and performance bonds required in bidding arrangements. AIG will also insure products that are under government restrictions (economic and foreign consideration). Policy terms range up to five years and $50,000 is the minimum premium.

Summary

The variety of export financing sources can be intimidating, and all sources are not applicable to all businesses. The size of the company, amount of the export transaction, type of products or services being exported, the country of destination, and even the company's state of residence, have a direct bearing on where to look for export funding. The sources covered in this chapter can be summarized as follows:

Trade credit   The use of letters of credit, banker's acceptances, and forfaiting by the exporter, working with his commercial banker, are the most common ways to convert foreign receivables into immediate cash for additional working capital.

Leasing   A small or midsized exporter can effectively use leasing to finance exports of capital goods either by leasing capital equipment itself, or by selling the foreign receivable to an international leasing company.

Eximbank   Eximbank supports several programs through bank guarantees or direct loans to the exporter or the foreign buyer. This government agency provides working capital funds to the exporter as well as medium and long-term financing for the foreign buyer.

The Private Export Funding Corporation   A private organization owned by several major banks and large corporations bridges the gap between what a commercial bank can do in export financing for the short-term, and what Eximbank can do for long-term credit.

Commodity Credit Corporation   A Department of Agriculture agency that issues buyer credits to economically depressed countries for the export of agricultural products. A special program, BICEP, subsidizes U.S. exporters to meet foreign subsidized competition.

The SBA   Though not very active in export financing, the Small Business Association does have a program for small exporters through bank guarantees or direct loans; but not in excess of $200,000. Recently, the SBA joined with Eximbank to participate in financing assistance of up to $1 million.

Eximbank's City-State Cooperation program   Started in 1989 as a marketing tool, several cities and a few states are beginning to assist smaller exporters in arranging financing as well as providing direct bank credit lines themselves.

The FCIA   By using insurance coverages provided by the FCIA, an exporter can reduce, or eliminate, most of the risks of selling or leasing to foreign buyers. Coverages can be obtained for both commercial and political risk.

Private insurance companies   An alternative to federal coverage, AIG additionally insures products that are under government restrictions and provides performance bid bonds.

Tax savings through foreign sales corporations

Chapter 3 mentioned foreign sales corporations (FSCs) as a method for reducing taxes on export sales. FSCs are a contrivance of congress to encourage American businesses, and especially smaller companies, to enter the export marketplace by providing a means to reduce the tax burden on income from such sales below prevailing tax rates for domestically generated income. The idea makes sense because the more goods and services exported, the less the trade deficit becomes, and this helps all American business. Unfortunately, as in everything else congress tries to do to help private enterprise, the complexities of operating FSCs preclude many smaller companies from using them. Still, for those who have embarked on an export program, FSCs have proven helpful and a legitimate tax saver.

An FSC is a separate company formed by the exporter (or others under contract), incorporated in a qualified foreign country, with an operating office in that country. Theoretically, this is an administrative and bookkeeping office. It prepares invoices to foreign customers for the exporter's sales and deposits collections in a local bank. When an exporter files its annual tax return, by employing complex formulae, it can exclude certain percentages of income from export sales from taxable income. The effect of using FSCs is a maximum tax reduction of 15 percent on export income.

There are both large FSCs—used by nearly all of the Fortune 500 companies—and small FSCs. To be classified as a small FSC, annual export sales of the parent company must be $5 million or less. To encourage smaller exporters to use FSCs, congress has simplified administrative procedures and reporting requirements. From a practical perspective, however, an exporter with less than $50,000 in export sales will find it too expensive to set up and maintain his own FSC. Several state and trade organizations have started their own FSCs called "shared FSCs" to fill this void, so that any company with any export business can now take advantage of this tax saving device. The major criteria for compliance with FSC regulations are:

1. The FSC must be incorporated in a qualified foreign country or U.S. possessions (excluding Puerto Rico).

2. The FSC must maintain an office in this non-U.S. location.

3. There must be at least one, non-U.S. resident on the FSC board of directors.

4. The FSC must maintain accounting records at its office.

5. The exporter must incur specifically defined costs through the FSC and these costs must be reflected on the books of the FSC. A large FSC must incur these costs offshore. A small FSC is allowed to incur the costs within the United States.

6. A large FSC must pay all FSC administrative expenses from a foreign bank account. A small FSC can use a U.S. bank account.

Furthermore, customer collections deposited in a local foreign bank can be repatriated to the U.S. tax-free, and treated as a dividend deduction by the parent company. Pragmatically, the FSC office does not have to prepare customer invoices. These can be prepared in the United States through the company's normal accounting channels. A monthly summary of paid customer invoices is then forwarded to the FSC and maintained as an accounting record in its office.

Smaller exporters find that it is not practical to set up a foreign office, staff it, and maintain local accounting records. A local FSC management company can handle these administrative details at a very low cost for any small exporter. Most large U.S. banks, law firms, and accounting firms with foreign offices provide this service. There are also independent FSC management companies located in nearly all qualified countries that are managed by Americans, who are more than willing to do the same thing.

Perhaps you don't want to limit your exploitation of global markets to exporting from the United States or your products or services do not lend themselves to the export marketplace. Enormous financial benefits can accrue to smaller companies willing to take the next step in international trade; that of establishing a physical presence overseas with a plant, warehouse, or sales office. There are a number of financing sources to assist in this endeavor. Some are U.S.-government sponsored, some are promoted by foreign governments and banks, and some are private. The next chapter examines methods for financing such expansion with U.S. or foreign sources of financing.

13

Financing overseas expansion

EXPORTING GOODS AND SERVICES IS AN EXCELLENT METHOD TO BECOME familiar with the global marketplace. An understanding of financing techniques unique to exporting provides the cornerstone to an active sales program for tapping foreign markets. Those companies with the foresight to recognize the necessity of becoming competitive worldwide in order to remain competitive at home will be the high flyers of the future. It usually isn't too long after companies enter the global marketplace through the export door that they recognize the benefits of establishing a physical presence overseas.

Large corporations learned years ago that exporting their products and services wasn't enough to maximize their worldwide market potential. They recognized that foreign competitors were expanding their profitability and growth by investing in real estate, facilities, markets, and going businesses right here in their own backyard. The isolationist philosophy so long promoted by American politicians and corporate leaders just wouldn't work in a free market when everyone else in the world followed global expansion opportunities. Consequently, industry giants such as GE, ITT, the automobile companies, Kodak, IBM, Bechtel, Fluor, and the aerospace companies, quickly learned how to establish their own plants, warehouses, sales offices, and shipping centers in foreign lands. Now, the time is right for small and midsized companies to follow the lead of their big brothers and begin to practice international trade with the same finesse and financial acumen as their European, Asian, Middle Eastern and Latin American competitors.

Cultural and language differences, marketing strategies, human resources development, and foreign legal and tax implications all enter into the equation for success in competing at the international level. Without adequate financing support, however, none of the other moves are possible. This chapter outlines several of the unique financing programs, methods, and support arrangements American and foreign sources provide for those ready to take the next step in the world of international trade. These sources break down into three categories:

1. Foreign banks.
2. U.S. and foreign government agencies, private international development institutions, and international development banks.
3. Joint ventures, partnerships, and other business sources.

Additionally, certain U.S. tax considerations must be recognized when structuring the financing and when aligning a company's ownership holdings.

Foreign banks

Foreign banks are as different from American banks as night is from day. Restrictive legislation and archaic accounting practices hampering U.S. banks in their efforts to be creative in structuring international financing packages are absent in most other Western countries. Off-balance sheet financing has been used by English, German, French, Italian, Israeli, and Japanese banks for years to further the global interest of their respective national companies without risking deterioration of the bank's capital ratios. But American banks remain locked in their traditional roles as depositories of money from individuals, companies, and the government. Although it is true that the large money center banks are now involved in everything from soup to nuts—and want to be involved in more—their lack of creativity, outdated accounting principles, and government regulations continue to prevent the level of financing assistance available from foreign banks.

Foreign banks are either clearing banks or merchant banks. Some banks have two divisions, each performing its own function. In other cases, the two activities are entirely separate. Clearing banks are similar to U.S. commercial banks. They act as a depository, they buy and sell their own government's treasury paper, they make loans to domestic companies and individuals, and they transact other business within the context of domestic banking activities.

Although similar to investment banks, merchant bank activities go far beyond those of their U.S. counterparts. For generations, merchant banks have transacted international business. They were originally formed by business people, not bankers, to handle the credit and other financing of merchant customers and suppliers. Eventually, they found themselves doing more financing and investing than merchant trading. Today, merchant banks form the backbone of international finance. Large American investment banks, such as Goldman Sachs and Morgan Stanley, are beginning to catch up, but the larger merchant banks from England and Japan continue to dominate in the international arena.

Usually, the first stop to make when considering opening a presence in a foreign country is at one of the major international merchant banks. Americans find it easier to deal with English banks because of the language symmetry. County NatWest, S.G. Warburg, Barclays de Zoete Wedd, Hong Kong and Shanghai Bank, Midland Bank, Charterhouse, and Lloyds Merchant Bank are some of the more popular ones. Divisions of Credit Suisse (Switzerland), Sumitomo (Japan), and Banque Indosuez (France) are also fairly easy for Americans to work with, depending on the type of investment and where it will be located. These merchant banks all understand the intricacies of international financing schemes and are creative in structuring a package to fit the deal. Most have offices in the United States, usually staffed by Americans, so getting off the ground with one of them is not difficult. Even if a merchant bank feels it can't finance your deal directly, it will put you in touch with other foreign sources more amenable to the task.

A word of caution in dealing with merchant banks. LBOs are not as common overseas as they are in the United States, so if you are planning to establish a foreign presence through an acquisition, be aware that typical, U.S. LBO financing will probably not be available. The easing of securities rules on the London Stock Exchange has resulted in what is called the "Big Bang," and creative public issues should probably fill the LBO void. This does require giving up part of your equity however, along with the costly process of preparing and underwriting an issue, and the administrative costs of compliance reporting.

As the globalization of markets continues into the nineties and beyond, merchant banks will undoubtedly assume a major role in financing worldwide expansion. Stock exchanges in London, Tokyo, and New York will become more integrated and interactive in new issues and trading of existing equity and debt instruments. Public issues will assume a global flavor with the issuer no longer restricted to segmented market demand. Business owners and financial officers will have a much wider choice of banking associations with commercial lenders and investment and merchant banks. The trend has already begun with major investments by foreign corporations in American businesses accomplished through merchant banks. Many foreign banks now have active offices in the United States, soliciting American customers as well as foreign businesses. With greater flexibility in accounting, banking regulations, and creative financing, American companies have already discovered that foreign banks are easier to work with. They have also learned that foreign banks offer more creatively structured debt instruments than their U.S. counterparts. Appendix K lists the U.S. addresses of several of the more active foreign banks.

Financing an overseas expansion through foreign banks is not the only, nor necessarily the best, source of funding, however. There are a number of U.S. government agencies, private organizations, and other sources that compete with banks from any country. The rest of this chapter examines several of these nonbank sources providing the business owner or financial manager a wide range to choose from.

Overseas Private Investment Corporation

The Overseas Private Investment Corporation (OPIC) is a self-sustaining agency of the U.S. government. The purpose of OPIC is to promote private sector economic growth in developing countries through investment by U.S. companies. About 100 developing countries fall under OPIC's jurisdiction. These are the only countries in which OPIC can assist U.S. investors. Several times each year, OPIC reclassifies which countries qualify for assistance, depending on the current status of development within the country and government-to-government trade agreements. Anyone interested in the current listing should contact the OPIC office directly.

OPIC tends to direct its efforts primarily to smaller businesses. In addition to an investor information service and a network of investor missions to assist smaller businesses identify foreign opportunities, OPIC provides medium to long-term project financing and political risk insurance. It does not insure against commercial risk such as FCIA, but will provide coverage for currency inconvertibility, insurrection, civil strife, revolution, war, and foreign expropriation risks relating to an American company's investment on foreign soil.

Both the insurance and finance programs are available to new foreign ventures for U.S. businesses that are commercially and financially sound (OPIC likes a 60/40 debt to equity ratio) and for the expansion of American businesses with existing locations overseas. There is one stipulation, however, the project being financed or insured must assist in the social and economic development of the host country and be consistent with the current economic and political interests of the United States.

OPIC financing can be used only for projects or other ventures in which there is a significant equity and management participation by American businesses. Management of the project must have a proven record of competence and success in another similar business or one related to the one being financed. Management must also have a significant continuing financial risk in the enterprise. "Significant" means 25 percent or more. Political risk insurance coverage is limited to the U.S. equity participation in the venture.

OPIC financing programs

OPIC finances medium and long-term projects in three areas:

1. Energy or energy related projects (water systems, electric utilities, oil and gas drillings, processing products for local consumption, and alternate energy sources).

2. Projects offering significant trade benefits or development of the infrastructure for the host country.

3. Projects sponsored by small businesses or co-ops in those countries where the per capita income is greater than $3,800 (the current measure of the stage of development of the country).

OPIC provides nonrecourse loans, and therefore, must be assured of the economic and financial soundness of the project, including, but not limited to, the ability of the company to repay the loan. The beauty of financing with OPIC is that once a venture is judged financially sound with competent management, the company will not be required to pledge any additional general credit. For example, if you want to start up a manufacturing plant in Honduras and put up 25 percent of your own equity in the deal, OPIC will coordinate with Eximbank and private foreign and U.S. banks to finance another 25 percent, which will probably require collateral of some form. OPIC then finances the remaining 50 percent without requiring additional collateral from the business. Occasionally, OPIC will consider non-project financing and take the role of a secured creditor, but it prefers the other route.

The project could be owned entirely by an American company but OPIC encourages joint ventures or other participatory arrangements with local corporations or citizens. Wholly owned government projects are not eligible and even 51 percent government owned projects are frowned upon. This is a good idea anyway from a business perspective. In some countries, such local participation is required to get permission to make the investment in the first place. For expansion projects of existing businesses, OPIC loans up to 75 percent of the cost. For new projects, it limits its participation to 50 percent. These ratios can vary, however, depending on the country, political considerations, and current U.S. government policy.

OPIC finances projects in two ways: by direct loans to the business and by guaranteeing bank loans. Direct loans are limited to those projects sponsored by a small business and currently range from $200,000 to $4 million. Occasionally, OPIC takes an equity position through a variety of convertible bond issues which it can then sell to companies or citizens in the host country. Most guaranteed loans are for major projects or larger companies. They can range up to $50 million, or even larger in some cases. Unless a small business participates with other American investors in a large project, such as taking a part interest in a manufacturing plant or participating in the construction of an electric utility plant, it will probably not qualify for the guarantee program.

International leasing

If you want to start up or expand a leasing company located overseas, OPIC provides political risk insurance coverage similar to that for other projects, and also participates in the financing of the leasing company. It does this through both direct loans and guaranteed bank loans. OPIC's loan limit is $1 million with a medium-term maturity to any American owned or controlled foreign leasing company defined as a small business. It also guarantees foreign bank loans to foreign leasing companies having a significant American interest, for up to seven years. The amount varies with the country and type of leases used.

Small Contractor Guarantee Program

One of the biggest problems for a small contractor doing work overseas is to provide a bank guarantee or surety bond to guarantee his performance against the contract. Many American contractors fail to consider overseas projects simply because they cannot get such a performance bond/guarantee or, if they can get one, it is too costly. OPIC's Small Contractor Guarantee program fills the void. To qualify, the contractor must not be one of the ''Fortune 1000.'' OPIC provides a performance guarantee to banks to support a standby letter of credit, which can then be used as a performance bond. OPIC covers all risks up to 75 percent of the credit unconditionally. Coupled with an OPIC insurance policy under the contractors and exporters insurance program, this percentage can be raised to 90 percent, leaving only 10 percent risk open for a bank or surety company.

Private international venture capital funds

In late 1989, the Eastern Bloc began to unravel. The Polish and Hungarian governments actively solicited American private investment in industrial and commercial enterprises. The idea was twofold, to attract foreign investment to shore up sagging economies and to provide Poland and Hungary with hard currency to purchase much needed goods and services from European and other Western countries. OPIC attempted to interest 40 American companies in forming a venture capital group to invest in production plants and other facilities similar to the African Growth Fund, which is currently investing capital in poor countries in sub-Sahara Africa. Subsequently, congress allocated $240 million to the Polish-American Enterprise Fund and another $60 million to the Hungarian-American Enterprise Fund to supplement private capital. OPIC guarantees the private investment portion against political risk in the event the countries revert to the orthodox socialist system.

As the Eastern Bloc, the USSR, China, and certain African and Latin American countries continue the evolution to market economies, additional U.S. government-supported programs similar to the Polish experiment, and the African fund will undoubtedly flourish. A business owner who aligns himself with other companies anticipating the opening of these new markets can only benefit in the long run. Establishing close ties with OPIC is a good way to get in on the ground floor when the next venture capital fund evolves.

U.S. Agency for International Development

The U.S. Agency for International Development (USAID) is a government-to-government agency whose mission is to assist foreign governments in economically disadvantaged areas stimulate economic growth, promote higher standards of living, and improve foreign exchange earnings. As a government-to-government agency, it does not provide financing direct to American companies investing overseas. It is included here, however, because, in an indirect way, American companies can benefit from USAID intervention in and support of a desired foreign investment. USAID programs are administered by 70 offices worldwide. Special private sector offices offer assistance to private businesses, which includes:

- Financial assistance to the host country for short-term stabilization and economic recovery to finance imports of raw materials and intermediate goods for the private sector.

- Improving the business climate by supporting host country policy reforms and incentives to restore domestic business confidence, rationalize interest and foreign exchange rates, attract foreign investment, upgrade the infrastructure (roads, port facilities, irrigation projects, free zone facilities), and develop new trading programs.

- Funding programs that upgrade human resource skills and managerial capabilities, overcome technical marketing and export obstacles, and capitalize financial intermediaries that provide credits to businesses in the host country. This includes capital for private sector development banks and other credit facilities for small and medium-sized businesses.

An American company can take advantage of USAID funding indirectly by investing in an area of the host country or in a project approved by USAID for financial assistance. A U.S. company is often given preference over other outsiders at the bidding stage or when trying to penetrate a specific market if a local project is financed with USAID money.

For example, one of my small contractor clients was a subcontractor on an electric utility project in North Yemen. Part of his contract was to provide most of the equipment (which was all manufactured by GE) to be installed at the site. When USAID learned that my client, along with several European firms, were competing for the project, they encouraged the North Yemenese to accept our bid since the equipment to be installed was American made and the installation would be done by an American company. We landed the job, and subsequently, when disputes arose concerning payments, USAID intervened, influencing the Dutch prime contractor to acquiesce to our requirement for L/C drawdowns at the time of shipment from New York.

Since 1984, USAID has been very active in supporting economic development of the private sector in the Caribbean and Central America under the Caribbean Basin Initiative (CBI) program. Under this program, USAID, through its Private Enterprise Bureau, participates in medium and long-term loans to joint ventures between an American company and a host country company or government agency. These loans are specially tailored for each case. For an application and current criteria contact the Enterprise Bureau directly. If you are considering investing in this part of the world, by all means, contact the Washington office of USAID to learn of current arrangements before searching elsewhere for financing.

International development banks

International development banks (IDBs) actively provide funding for the economic development of a country's infrastructure and its private sector. These banks are either privately owned by one or more large, multinational commercial banks, local businesses, local banks, or host country governments. Development banks have been popular with Europeans and Japanese companies for years. Smaller American businesses are just beginning to exploit these sources, however. Each IDB has variations in eligibility requirements and types of financial assistance, but they are all similar. Additionally, four super IDBs fund local IDBs and also offer direct financing to businesses. These four "super" banks are the Asian Development Bank (for the Pacific Rim), the African Development Bank and Fund (for Africa), the Inter-American Development Bank (for Latin America), and recently, the European Bank for Reconstruction and Development in Eastern Europe. Though each have slightly different programs, they are similar enough to use one—the Asian Development Bank—as an illustration of what can be done. Appendix L contains their addresses together with a selection of several local IDBs.

The Asian Development Bank (ADB) was established in 1966 by a consortium of 47 member countries located throughout the Asian Pacific region. Its stated purpose is to accelerate economic and social growth by promoting financial and technical assistance for projects contributing to the economic development of the region. The ADB supports two programs: (1) financing assistance to private businesses and private banks and (2) funding through intermediaries (financial institutions who provide medium to long-term financing as their principal endeavor, such as local development banks, some commercial and merchant banks, leasing companies, and venture capital firms).

The ADB offers direct financial assistance to private companies with medium and long-term loans without government guarantees. It will also participate in the underwriting and investment in a company's equity securities. Private sector companies can also apply for grants for project-related feasibility studies. The ADB program for assistance to local banks and sponsors of projects involving venture capital, leasing, factoring, investment management, and commercial finance encourages development throughout the region. Intermediary funding consists of credit lines for small to medium-sized new ventures and expansion of existing businesses. The ADB also encourages intermediary participation in the equity funding of new businesses by providing equity lines to those financial institutions.

Eligible projects include new or expanded productive facilities in energy, manufacturing, transportation, forestry, fisheries, mining, tourism, health, and agriculture. The production of luxury items might be eligible if these products are produced primarily for export. The projects should use domestic raw materials, provide jobs, and employ modern management techniques. Export products or other vehicles that encourage additional foreign investment in the region are favored. To qualify for assistance, a company can be local or foreign owned. It can be partially owned by a government but it must be run on a commercial basis. The ADB, as well as other "super" IDBs, are very active in providing financing assistance for the privatization of government-owned businesses.

The ADB restricts its total financial assistance loans and equity to no more than 25 percent of the total cost of the project. Loans range from $2 million to $30 million, except under unusual circumstances. Intermediary participation increases the amount. The ADB will not invest equity funds in excess of 25 percent of the capital of the business. The bottom limit is $100,000, and the ADB will not be the largest single investor.

The ADB also assists in structuring syndicated and co-financing arrangements. Collateral must be provided for all loans. Commitment fees are 1 percent per annum on the undisbursed loan balance. Front-end fees and legal fees are also charged. The repayment period cannot exceed 12 years. Interest rates are based on the London Inter Bank Offering Rate (LIBOR). Currency denominations can vary. Once the project is completed, the ADB will sell its equity investment at a fair price, preferably to nationals, although other buyers will be considered.

Non-regional member countries of ADB include: Austria, Belgium, Canada, Denmark, Finland, France, Germany, Italy, Japan, Korea, Netherlands, Norway, Spain, Sweden, Switzerland, the United Kingdom, and the United States.

Other U.S. government agencies

There are several U.S. government agencies that provide assistance to American firms interested in investing in foreign businesses or projects. Some programs offer technical or commercial assistance. Others offer financing assistance. Many federal Departments—Commerce, State, Defense, and so on—have their own programs but they are too specialized to include here. There are only a few major ones.

Department of Commerce

The Department of Commerce offers support to American companies making investment proposals to foreign countries or that have specific difficulties arranging foreign purchases. The Active Match Program assists companies in locating foreign suppliers for import needs and in sourcing potential foreign joint venture partners. No direct funding is available for these purposes, but the advice is free. The Commerce Department has become especially active in the Caribbean Basin Initiative through its CBI ombudsman. This official acts as a high-level expediter and facilitator when projects get bogged down in bureaucratic red tape. The department also actively assists American companies in locating opportunities in the Caribbean. Appendix J lists selective financing sources for CBI projects.

Department of State

The U.S. Department of State's Trade and Development Program (TDP) funds feasibility studies for Third World development projects that will eventually lead to the export of American goods to the host country. Projects include mining, agribusiness development, and infrastructure projects (energy, communications, port development, and so on). Though this is government-to-government funding, TDP also assists in co-financing studies leading to specific investment decisions.

Department of Agriculture

The Department of Agriculture assists U.S. businesses in identifying agribusiness investment opportunities overseas although it won't get directly involved in funding projects. Requests for assistance should be directed to the Private Sector Relations division of the Office of International Cooperation in Washington, DC.

Office of the U.S. Trade Representative

The U.S. Trade Representative (USTR) office is part of the Executive Office of the President. This office is responsible for coordinating U.S. trade policy with foreign governments. USTR is not directly involved in financing, but through programs negotiated with foreign governments, assists U.S. businesses investing in these host countries. Two of the most relevant programs are:

1. The Bilateral Investment Treaty (BIT) is with foreign governments to establish bilateral territories, export-import quotas, and industrial incentives to help U.S. companies trying to locate in the host country.
2. Guaranteed Access Levels for Textiles and Apparel negotiated with foreign governments to provide investment incentives for U.S. firms engaged in the textile and apparel industries.

International Finance Corp.

The International Finance Corp. is part of the World Bank. Among other activities, it coordinates and assists in arranging financing for U.S. and foreign joint ventures for projects located in several developing nations.

Countertrade

American businesses with substantial export programs are continually bombarded with customer requests for countertrade. Eastern Bloc nations, as well as countries in the rest of Europe and throughout the world, have used countertrade for years as a primary source of financing intercountry sales. American aerospace corporations could rarely sell either military or commercial aircraft to foreign governments without countertrade. The same holds true for many capital goods companies, pharmaceuticals, and more recently, large computer mainframe manufacturers.

Although not yet predominant, countertrade with Africa, Latin America, and China will undoubtedly flourish in the future. Yet, very few smaller U.S. businesses have even heard the term, much less have any idea how to use countertrade techniques. To become and stay competitive in the world economy, however, business owners and financial managers will have to educate themselves in this essentially non-cash form of international finance.

Countertrade applies most directly to exporting goods and services, but, once an overseas presence is established, especially a manufacturing or distribution facility, the international trader will have to learn countertrade if it wants to sell products in countries other than the host country or back to the United States. In fact, as we approach the next century, the probabilities are high that countertrade will be used more in this arena than as an export financing tool. Therefore, countertrade is an indirect approach to establishing a presence in a foreign country, and small and midsized business should consider using it as a financing vehicle.

Countertrade is a means of financing sales into a market that does not have hard currency (such as Eastern Europe or most of Africa and the Middle East) or is debt poor, such as most of Latin America. Financing through countertrade is relatively straightforward, though somewhat complex to administer. It generally involves one or a combination of six basic techniques: barter, compensation, counterpurchase, offset, buyback, or coproduction.

Barter and compensation

Barter is the oldest form of trade. Simply put, if I want to sell you 100 bags of flour and you don't have any money or credit but you have four cows with a value approximately equal to my 100 bags of flour, we merely trade one commodity for the other. I can then either use the cows myself or sell them to a farmer for cash.

Compensation is merely a modern form of barter. If, as an American producer, I want to sell 100 bags of flour worth $1,000 to you, a Venezuelan, for four cows worth 4,500 bolivars, we might contract with a trader in

Puerto Rico to take the cows and sell them on the open market for U.S. dollars. This deal is consummated in a single contract and involves a third party, often making the transaction cumbersome to administer. Neither barter nor compensation involves the transfer of cash between the two trading parties.

Counterpurchase

Counterpurchase is a variation on the barter theme that involves actual cash transfers. Using the 100 bags of flour example again, if I wanted to sell them to you, a cereal maker in Italy, you would arrange your own financing for the purchase of the flour, pay me in lira, and I, in turn, would purchase 50 cases of corn flakes from you for dollars. I would then turn around and sell the corn flakes to get my money back—hopefully at a profit.

Offset

Offsets are currently used primarily by large corporations manufacturing aircraft, military equipment, or large infrastructure equipment (turbines, boilers, smelting furnaces, and so on). The customer is normally a sovereign government, not a private sector customer. Offsets improve a customer's foreign exchange position. The deal normally involves a package of transactions, carried out over a defined period of time and theoretically, at least, compensates the acquiring or importing country for loss of jobs, currency, and local development of technologies.

For example, an American company, Amerco, wanted to sell 70 gas turbines to Ghana but the Ghanian government didn't have the dollars or credit to buy them, so the following deal was structured. Amerco financed the building of a plant in Ghana to process rubber, getting a 35 percent equity interest in the business for its investment. Rubber products are then exported from Ghana to Germany for deutsche marks, which are then used to pay for the gas turbines. Amerco then uses the deutsche marks to buy German components for its gas turbine assemblies. The Ghanian government has created jobs, foreign exchange, and a viable industry. Amerco expects to reap profits from its 35 percent equity ownership of the rubber company as the business grows. In addition, because Ghana is one of the countries eligible for USAID financing, most of the cost of building the rubber plant is financed by the U.S. government.

Buyback or co-production

A buyback is typically used in the turnkey construction of infrastructure projects such as power utilities, water-generating plants, and telecommunications networks. It can also be used in the turnkey construction of manufacturing plants. A buyback means that the contractor agrees to buy back a certain percentage of the production of the new facility that he builds. He then distributes the products at his own expense—and at his own profit. This arrangement has worked well in China, for example. When American companies sell turnkey manufacturing facilities to the Chinese, they agree to export a certain percentage of the production back to the United States or other hard-currency countries. This creates both an export market for the Chinese and transfers valuable technology to them. It also results in additional profits to the American company.

You might want to take an equity interest in the turnkey project or you might furnish management support to run the facility. In either case, the facility is usually co-constructed between your company and the foreign contractor. Running the facility becomes known as co-production because both parties are responsible for the production of the facility's products. Both parties benefit from the sale of products—the host country by sales within its borders and your company by exporting to the United States or other nations.

There's no question that countertrade is here to stay. Small and mid-sized companies are still learning how to use it as a financing technique. Most who have tried it, however, are convinced that, in one form or another, countertrade techniques make both export sales and establishing a foreign presence possible when other financing methods are cost prohibitive. In some cases, countertrade is the only feasible way to access a host country's markets.

If you decide to enter the countertrade arena, don't expect much, if any, support from the U.S. government. The government has taken a very negative position on countertrade. The Office of Management and Budget has stated that the U.S. government views countertrade as contrary to the best interests of the country and diametric to the free market philosophy. Fortunately, the OMB has also stated that the government will not oppose the use of these techniques as long as national security is not endangered.

The government might have a variety of reasons for not liking countertrade, but it seems clear that most of the strong opposition comes from the IRS. By trading goods for goods, taking part of a sell price in a co-production effort or disposing of traded goods through third parties in foreign countries, the IRS has a very difficult, if not impossible, task auditing the income of U.S. companies. There is nothing un-American about countertrade that I can see, however. In fact, it is a widely accepted, internationally practiced method of doing global business. American firms doing business overseas stand to lose the competitive race if they don't learn how to effectively use countertrade to at least partially finance operations.

Joint ventures with foreign nationals

There are a number of sound reasons to expand abroad through a joint venture with foreign nationals. Local customs, labor codes, tax and legal requirements, local marketing expertise, and political savvy all dictate joining up with a local individual or company to establish a foreign plant or office or to manage a project. In some countries, notably in the Middle East, a partnership with a national has become a prerequisite to getting a license to do business in the country. Beyond licensing requirements, cooperative financing with a local company remains a very pragmatic reason for joining forces.

Several financing programs for establishing a business or project are available from nearly every country in the Western world. The U.K., Germany, France, Sweden, Norway, the Netherlands, Italy, and Spain, all have government-sponsored financing schemes to assist start-up businesses. Money is not the problem in developed countries, the lack of specific technologies is. Although it certainly isn't as severe as in developing nations. Hardly without exception, financing assistance is not available unless a local company retains part ownership in the new business. Also, foreign banks, both commercial and merchant, usually support business development with a local partner in preference to full American ownership. Finally, many larger host country companies will finance the project themselves if allowed to participate in its ownership.

An example of the latter case occurred a few years ago when a client of mine, Mosti Automated Products, wanted to open a distribution center in Italy to stock automobile and machine parts imported from the United States for resale to North African and Middle Eastern countries. Mosti approached Fiat with a proposal that they join forces in the distribution center, with each owning 50 percent. Mosti wanted Fiat to provide all the financing for the center and in return, Fiat would be allocated 50 percent of the storage space for their own parts. In addition, Mosti's sales network in East Africa and Saudi Arabia would push Fiat spare parts. The deal went through without costing my client a penny in construction cost.

Another case occurred when Olstor, Inc. wanted to expand its market by building a paint factory in Saudi Arabia. The Saudi government required that any foreign investment be 50 percent owned by a Saudi. Olstor struck a deal with a Lebanese merchant, Jamal Greiu, who owned three other trading businesses in Saudi and qualified as a national. In exchange for the 50 percent ownership in the Olstor plant, Jamal arranged with the Saudi central bank, the Saudi Arabian Monetary Authority (SAMA), to provide 100 percent funding in long-term debt for the construction of the paint plant.

There are negatives in forming joint ventures with foreign nationals, however. Sharing the ownership of a facility also means sharing its profits, and the possibility of disagreements with a partner over operating policy. In most cases, these risks should be manageable and are a relatively small price to pay for entry into a lucrative new market.

International Executive Service Corps

The International Executive Service Corps (IESC) is a nonprofit organization funded partially by the U.S. government and partially by donations from American corporations. Originally, the mission of IESC was to assist in structuring joint ventures and partnerships between American companies and foreign nationals, principally in developing nations. Currently, the Corps' thrust is to assist American companies interested in establishing working relationships in a variety of different forms with foreign private and quasi-private businesses.

More than 10,000 retired American executives have volunteered through IESC to assist U.S. companies start an overseas operation. Volunteers are also active in consulting to foreign governments on a variety of projects. IESC volunteers trained in corporate and international finance can be an enormous help in locating the right financing for the project when just starting a foreign venture. The IESC also provides matching grants for feasibility studies of potential overseas investments.

Joint ventures with U.S. companies

Forming an operating partnership with a U.S. company is usually much less risky than going with a foreign national, especially if the partner has marketing, financial, or political connections in the host country. This works especially well if you are trying to sell patented technology or proprietary products to a large customer already established overseas. Increasingly, large customers are bankrolling an entire start up operation in exchange for marketing rights in countries not currently serviced. It's usually less expensive to have a subcontractor risk the labor, legal, tax, and management difficulties, even if it means financing the project.

A company can usually establish and finance a presence abroad through joint ventures or partnerships with companies already operating overseas. It is faster and less expensive than any other way. In fact, it remains one of the most widely used methods in manufacturing and distribution businesses. Two of the greatest advantages are: (1) It eliminates the need to comply with mountains of paperwork, substantial time and effort, and reporting restrictions required when using government financing of any type; and (2) it provides the smaller company with internal assistance in mastering the host country's legal and tax requirements for starting up a foreign operation.

Bank loan debt-equity swaps

Within the past seven years, some U.S. companies have utilized the complex method of debt-equity swaps to establish an international presence in Latin America. During the seventies, American banks made unwarranted loans to Latin American countries. The banks should have seen, but didn't, that there was little or no chance of ever being repaid by these undeveloped countries. The potential in Latin American financial markets led these banks to overlook the most fundamental axiom in the banking industry (at least since 1930): always collaterize a loan with more security than required to meet repayment schedules.

By 1980, several Latin countries were already in deep financial trouble, and by the mid-eighties it became clear that few, if any, would ever meet the repayment schedules negotiated, and renegotiated, with the banks. Several banks eventually reserved against these bad loans and took a severe hit in their earnings. The loans were not written-off, however. To this day, the banks publicly announce that they will eventually collect all their money via government bailouts and swaps.

Beginning in 1985, a few American banks began swapping their defaulted loans to Latin American governments for equity investments in Latin American companies and other properties. The scheme was to reduce or eliminate the debt by exchanging it with the central bank of the host country for local currency and then investing this currency in local businesses and properties. The program never succeeded, however. Debtor nations realized that issuing new currency to buy the debt would add to an already impossible inflation problem. The banks wanted prime real estate and profitable businesses and, of course, both were is short supply.

Several larger corporations began to purchase Latin debt in the secondary markets. They made the swaps with Latin governments, and by getting in on the ground floor, managed to finance their foreign acquisitions at a substantial saving.

As time passed, other, smaller American manufacturers began using this secondary market to accomplish the same feat. The company first purchased the debt instrument in the secondary market at a substantial discount from its face value, say 50 percent. It then offered to exchange this debt with the foreign government for local currency to be used to build or purchase a plant or other facility. The rate of exchange might be, for example, equivalent to 80 percent of the debt. The resulted in a presence in the host country for half the cost of a straight investment. Granted, its own money had to be used to acquire the debt on the secondary market and it probably supported its own start-up expenses, but it was still an inexpensive way to get established overseas.

Swapping activity has continued, though somewhat sporadically. Recently, the secondary debt market has picked up, and with Brazil, Ecuador, and other Latin American countries beginning to stabilize their political and economic conditions, swapping should increase in popularity.

Obviously, debt-equity swaps are a complicated maneuver and not to be engaged in by companies without the financial management talent to handle the deal. On the other hand, for those companies who want to establish a presence in a debt-poor Latin American country and have the financial acumen to manage this technique, debt-equity swaps continue to be an increasingly attractive financing alternative.

Technology licensing

For some businesses, and in some countries, the nature of the product, local restrictions governing foreign investments, or lack of management talent might preclude establishing either an export program or a physical presence overseas. Yet, penetration of the global market could open new opportunities or even become essential to a company's survival. Technology transfers through foreign licensing agreements can provide the key to unlock the door to future international trade. Technology licensing has been used extensively in developing markets, in Eastern Europe and in the USSR for many years.

The major advantage of licensing over exporting or direct foreign investment is that it provides an entree to global markets without requiring any financing. The biggest disadvantages are the enforcement of audits and royalty payments and the risk of losing control over the technology, the production, and the marketing of proprietary products. For many companies, however, the latter presents less of a problem as newer technologies are developed domestically to replace those licensed overseas. Additionally, the ease of entry through technology licensing can frequently outweigh the risks.

Franchising

A close cousin to licensing, franchising affords a company the same opportunity to enter the global arena without incurring the headaches and cost of raising significant capital. Most of the larger companies who have franchised overseas for years—MacDonalds, Burger King, Radio Shack, and so on—do assist the franchisee finance his start-up either through leasing arrangements or short-term working capital loans. While some franchisers provide this financing through their own financial services subsidiaries, many merely refer the franchisee to known sources of leasing and other financing. Franchising overseas can be difficult if you are not already in the franchise business domestically. It is usually wiser to enter foreign markets through other channels.

Foreign trade zones

Foreign trade zones (FTZs) have been used for years throughout the world as a means of moving goods between countries. FTZs allow the use of a third country as an intermediary stop without the imposition of customs duties. Though not a method of financing, per se, it is a convenient way to save costs, as well as adding to the available money a firm has for operations. There are currently 141 FTZs in the United States and only South Dakota, West Virginia, and Idaho do not have at least one.

FTZs can be used for storage, distribution, assembly, light manufacturing, product modifications, or transshipping. One of the most interesting applications of FTZs is as an intermediate stop for a company to add value to its products as they move from an overseas manufacturing location to the ultimate customer, also located offshore.

For example, assume you have a plant in Ireland manufacturing washing machines. You want to ship the machines to a customer in Jamaica. The machines could be assembled in Ireland and shipped direct to Jamaica. However, the freight would be substantially less if you could ship only the components, and perhaps some subassemblies part way, say to the United States. There, they could be assembled and the final product shipped to Jamaica. Ordinarily, customs duties would have to be paid coming into the United States. Insurance, taxes, and additional paperwork would be imposed to get them shipped to Jamaica. If the products reside in an FTZ, however, no duties are paid, no tax liability is incurred, and no additional insurance is required. The FTZ is treated as a foreign port, and the U.S. government keeps its hands off. This can amount to substantial cost savings. It also allows the American parent company to utilize American labor and management for the final assembly of the goods.

Tax implications

As noted in chapter 3, the U.S. government has enacted tax treaties called Tax Information Exchange Agreements (TIEAs) with many countries around the world. The primary purpose of TIEAs is to provide the taxing authorities of both countries free access to information and transactions of companies doing business in their respective countries. Though clearly an infringement on the privacy of American citizens doing business overseas, a TIEA assures the IRS that their auditors can track the worldwide income and expenses of American companies and individuals. To sweeten the pie, the IRS allows expenses incurred by American taxpayers attending business meetings and conventions in TIEA countries to deduct their expenses without regard to the more stringent rules generally applicable to foreign conventions. Documentation to substantiate the expense must be produced, however, when a return is audited.

The U.S. Treasury has the lead responsibility for negotiating bilateral TIEAs between the IRS and foreign governments. Any country with a TIEA qualifies as an eligible site for a Foreign Sales Corporation (FSC). In addition, an American company doing business, or wishing to do business, in a Caribbean country that has executed a TIEA, could qualify for financing under the IRS's Puerto Rican Section 936 program.

Section 936 financing companies

Under Section 936 of the Tax Code, American companies that derive a significant portion of their income from Puerto Rican activities are considered "936 companies." A 936 company is effectively exempt from U.S. income tax on income derived from Puerto Rican activities. If the company repatriates this income to the United States, a "toll gate" tax of 10 percent is imposed by Puerto Rico, but still nothing from the IRS. As long as the funds remain in Puerto Rican banks or are reinvested in the commonwealth no tax is paid to anyone.

Large deposits of 936 funds remain in Puerto Rican banks. These funds are referred to as "qualified possession source investment income." Under the Tax Reform Act of 1986, Puerto Rico can use these funds as collateral to make loans for qualified projects in any country falling under the Caribbean Basin Initiative—assuming the country has signed a TIEA with the IRS. Through 1988, the countries that have signed up for participation in the 936 program were Jamaica, Barbados, Grenada, and Dominica. St. Lucia is awaiting legislation from its own government to join the throng. Other countries will undoubtedly participate in the future.

Currently, the Puerto Rican government is establishing a private Caribbean Basin Initiative Fund through private investment banks to provide a vehicle to invest 936 funds in eligible countries. Underwriters will be hired to sell notes and stocks of the fund to investors and expect to raise $60 million in capital. It is expected that loans from the fund will be secured, at least in part, by a combination of hard security, guarantees, and insurance coverage. OPIC and the Government Development Bank of Puerto Rico expect to participate in providing such collateral. These loans carry very favorable interest rates resulting from the tax-exempt status of the fund, which are similar to the municipal revenue bonds examined in chapter 8. There is a catch, however. To qualify for these funds, the project, located in an eligible country, must be complementary with Puerto Rico. In other words, the project must produce goods or services from which Puerto Rico will benefit in some direct or indirect way.

Controlled foreign corporations

A controlled foreign corporation is one in which U.S. shareholders own more than 50 percent of the corporation's voting interest for at least one day during the taxable year. A proportionate share of the controlled foreign corporation's income must be included in the tax return of U.S. shareholders as "subpart F income," exclusive of FSC income. A U.S. shareholder is any U.S. individual, partnership, corporation, estate, or trust who owns 10 percent or more of the foreign corporation's voting interest. Subpart F income is defined as the sum of the following:

1. income from the foreign company;
2. income from the insurance of U.S. risks;
3. personal holding company income;
4. income of the foreign corporation multiplied by the international boycott factor as determined under Section 999; and
5. any illegal payments paid by, or on behalf of, the foreign corporation to government employees or agents (an obvious attempt to enforce provisions of the Foreign Corrupt Practices Act).

These income items are included only for that portion of the taxable year during which a U.S. shareholder held controlling interest. If it's one month, then 1/12 of the annual income items are included. To be eligible for the foreign tax credit as described in chapter 3, a U.S. shareholder must make the election to be taxed as a domestic corporation on the undistributed earnings of the controlled foreign corporation.

When structuring a foreign subsidiary, it is imperative to consult with competent tax advisors. IRS rules governing foreign holdings of American taxpayers can become extremely complex as can foreign tax considerations. Any American company going abroad for the first time should carefully weigh both U.S. and foreign tax implications to be certain of taking advantage of all tax breaks allowed.

Foreign personal holding company

A foreign corporation is classified as a foreign personal holding company under the following circumstances:

1. At least 60 percent (50 percent after the first year) of its gross income consists of dividends, interest, royalties, annuities, rents

(unless 50 percent or more of total gross income), gains in stock and commodity transactions, income from personal service contracts, and other specified types of income.

2. More than 50 percent of the corporation's outstanding stock is owned directly or indirectly by five or fewer U.S. citizens or residents.

A U.S. shareholder of a foreign personal holding company is subject to a tax on both the distributed and undistributed income of the foreign company. The tax is imposed on all income as if it had been actually received as dividend income. This is a blatant attempt to eliminate "tax haven" countries from a business owner's estate plans. Properly structured, however, the use of such tax havens can continue to provide a shelter for offshore income.

Dividends and interest received by the foreign company from certain related foreign corporations are exempt, providing: (1) the company paying the interest or dividends is related to the recipient; (2) it is created or organized under the laws of the recipient's country; and (3) it has a substantial part of its assets used in its trade or business located in the same foreign country. Tiered foreign subsidiaries meeting these requirements are excludable from foreign personal holding company rules but could be subject to the foreign controlled corporation rules. Again, competent tax advice is crucial.

Summary

This chapter and the preceding chapter have outlined several financing schemes to get started in international trade. Some are geared strictly to exporting from the United States; others are restricted to establishing a physical presence on foreign soil; and still others provide government-to-government financing, which indirectly flows to an American start-up enterprise. Technology licensing and franchising don't require any seller financing. Joint ventures and countertrade techniques involve little, if any, outside financing. Many of the financing sources are government agencies or government-supported organizations.

Unfortunately, for business owners just getting started in international trade, a quick reference to determine which financing technique is best for his company just isn't possible. There are too many options and combinations. The size of the company, types of products or services offered, specific foreign markets sold into, continuing changes both in U.S. and foreign government political and economic policies, competitive market forces, the impact of economic timing on financial markets, and rapidly changing domestic and foreign tax laws preclude the business owner from having the luxury of picking and choosing from a predetermined list of sources. Each situation is different. With the rapidly changing economic and political climates in Europe, Latin America, the Middle East, Africa, and the Pacific Basin, a financing scheme that might work today, could be obsolete tomorrow.

For these reasons, when the time seems right to enter the global marketplace, consult competent outside counsel—tax advisors, international lawyers and consultants, and global accounting firms. These are the people who have up-to-date contacts in financing circles. Following their advice and direction can usually make the difference between success or failure in international trade. The fees they charge for these services are nearly always substantially less than the cost of going global alone and paying for the inevitable trial and error mistakes.

One thing a business owner can do on his own before engaging outside advisors, however, is to research as carefully as possible the current status and available mechanisms for raising capital through the U.S. government and other domestic agencies. Several valuable books are available that can help, and government publications abound. Even multinational accounting firms publish periodic bulletins covering changes in tax, legal, and financing rules for international trade—and they are free for the asking.

14

Special techniques for troubled companies

TacChap Health Products Corporation manufactured personal health care and grooming products for women. The company had been profitable for several years with annual sales approaching $14 million. The company's founder and CEO, Robert Morlak, was nearing his 60th birthday when he suffered a mild heart attack. His doctors warned him to slow down, and Robert heeded the medical advice by hiring a chief operating officer, John Olsen, to manage the day-to-day running of the company. Backing off the firing line for two years, Robert's rude awakening occurred one February with a call from his commercial banker notifying him that his operating line was at its limit and that the bank had decided to cut his borrowing base back from 80 percent of receivables to 60 percent. Two days later, the asset based lender who held a mortgage of $12 million on the company's real estate and a long-term note of $4 million, notified Robert that, because he had missed three consecutive month's debt service payments, they would be forced to call the loan. They were, however, willing to restructure it for three more years for a premium of $500,000 and interest at prime plus 5 points!

Although sales remained level, the new chief operating officer had completely botched up the financial side of the business in Robert's

254

absence and now TacChap was on the verge of bankruptcy. When major trade creditors began demanding C.O.D. deliveries, Robert panicked and called me in to help restructure the company's debt.

As the door to the nineties swings open, much of the business and financial community is in financial disarray. The high-leverage acquisition craze of the eighties has left both large and small companies alike saddled with unmanageable debt levels. Equally high-leveraged and overextended construction activity is forcing developers to grope for ways to stay solvent. A staggering stock market has eaten away at potential capital formation. Financial institutions of every type and size, commercial banks, investment banks, venture capital firms, and asset based lenders, reeling from collapsing loan and investment portfolios are cutting off business credit and pressuring leveraged debtors for help, when there is no help to give. It is not surprising then that debtors are overflowing the bankruptcy courts seeking protection.

Small consolation can be derived from realistic forecasts for the 1990s. An increasing number of domestic and global economic indicators point to a deepening national recession and the potential for a serious collapse of the global financial system. With the continuing decrease of American capital accumulation, a heavy stream of debt service payments flowing out of productive resources, and both the business community and the federal government becoming increasingly dependent on Japanese, German, and Middle East money to rescue failing domestic economic policies, business owners must move quickly to restructure financially unstable companies.

As traditional financial resources dry up and fierce global competition presses in from all sides, the only sensible course of action for sustained survival and future prosperity is to reduce debt, trim management and operating fat, dispose of resource-draining products and customers, and sell unnecessary assets as soon as possible. In other words, restructure your company to increase cash flow.

The principal means to accomplish this end is to institute austerity programs based on the sound financial and economic principles practiced decades earlier. Companies must quickly reach the point where total debt does not exceed what the company is worth on the market, as measured by what a buyer would pay for it if the company was offered for sale.

It will do little good to appeal to your commercial bank for relief. By taking the initiative yourself, however, you will go a long way toward winning approval from lenders and investors, which should encourage them to help in restructuring your company's balance sheet. The first steps should be to trim the operating fat by purging unprofitable or conflicting product lines and to convert unneeded assets to cash.

Purging unprofitable product lines

With the exception of very small service businesses, every company, even a retail store, has products or product lines that are unprofitable or drain cash or other resources from the principal products of the company. A retail store might carry inventory that hasn't turned over in years, yet continues to take up space, personnel to manage, and robs the business of much-needed cash. A manufacturing company might produce a dozen different product lines of which two or three account for 80 percent of the company's profits. A service business might offer to perform services at the customer's location at a cost of two, three, or four times as much as it would cost if done in house.

To eliminate unnecessary product lines, a company must know what profits are made on each of its lines and what assets are needed to produce the products. When cash flow is good, many companies ignore basic cost systems and dismiss the importance of accounting for product line profitability as a luxury reserved for larger companies. In difficult times, however, when cash is tight and a business owner must reduce debt significantly or perish, allocating costs and assets to product lines is no longer a luxury; it is a necessity. Now is the time to implement a basic cost system that segregates costs and assets.

Cost accounting became a dirty word with high tech, high flying, rapid-growth companies. Though a cost accounting system has always been required for government contracting, ignorance of the art of cost accumulation and allocation by the financial community—who hold the purse strings for many companies—has mothballed this valuable management tool, especially in the manufacturing sector.

When debts pile up and cash becomes a scarce commodity, the wolves begin to howl at the door. You must return to basics if your company is to survive. The two most fundamental principles in any business are to know how much each product costs and to produce and/or sell only those products that fit the company's primary mission. A basic cost accounting system can provide the data needed to identify those products that are losing money and draining the business of cash. An owner can then either raise prices, if that is possible, or get rid of the products.

Disposing of products or product lines that do not support the primary mission of the company is a bit more difficult. Suppose, for example, a company whose primary objective is to manufacture wooden tables and chairs begins to divert its resources by producing aluminum doors and windows and plastic toys. During boom times, such diversification seems to make sense. It is a good way to spread the risk of economic cycles for different products. When a company is strapped for cash, however, it is always safer, more profitable, and diverts less cash to stick with the basic product lines, and this company should return to manufacturing wooden tables and chairs.

There are several ways to generate cash by purging products or product lines. In many companies, different product lines require different assets to support the lines: Machinery and inventory to produce the products, equipment to transport and store them, and possibly even a building to house the assets. The ideal way to purge a product line is to find a buyer for all the assets that support that line. Selling an entire product line, including the assets supporting it, or a complete operating division or subsidiary, is often referred to as a "spin-off."

Spin-offs

Raising cash through a spin-off is very much like selling a company. The sale not only includes the product's engineering drawings, name, and patent (if any), but also its raw material, work-in-process, and finished goods inventory; its customer list, order backlog, and receivables; any machinery, equipment, or vehicles associated with the line, including testing equipment; and land and buildings, if there is a separate facility for the line. A buyer might even want to hire the production and supervisory workers or sales personnel responsible for the product line.

Because a spin-off is a sale of assets by a company, the same bulk sales laws that apply to the sale of all of a company's assets are applicable to a spin-off. The tax recognition of capital gains and ordinary income is also the same. Of course, because the company is the seller, the gain must appear on the company's tax return. In addition, the built-in gains provisions, as noted in chapter 3, might apply if an S corporation election has been executed.

Spinning off a product line, especially if the products are profitable, can be a viable way to raise capital in a distress situation. When a business owner is behind the eight ball and his first priority is to raise cash to liquidate trade debt or to meet debt service payments, spinning off a product line has three advantages:

1. Additional borrowings from banks or other sources are not necessary. Borrowing additional funds might not be a viable alternative anyway.

2. Generally, if the product line has commercial value, its selling price will exceed the cost of its supporting assets. This premium represents incremental cash that would probably not be realized simply by continuing to sell the products in the marketplace.

3. Once the product line and assets are gone, additional cost-cutting moves can be engineered, such as personnel reductions, selling or

leasing excess production and storage space, and reduced personal property taxes.

Finding a buyer for a product line is not as difficult as it might seem, assuming the markets are growing, or are at least stable. Frequently, a competitor planning to expand its operation will find it less expensive and easier to buy an existing product line than to buy an entire company or develop the products internally. A customer who wants to expand through vertical integration might be eager to acquire a source of supply for its components, subassemblies, or spare parts. It's even possible to interest the supervisory personnel or workers that produce the products. It is certainly one way to save their jobs, and can be easily accomplished through an Employee Stock Ownership Plan (ESOP).

Partial liquidations

A partial liquidation is another way to raise cash for financially troubled companies. This process also involves selling off assets allocated to a specific product line, but at liquidation prices rather than as a going business. A partial liquidation can also be used to sell unused or obsolete assets, generally at an auction. A partial liquidation differs from a spin-off in three ways:

1. Once the assets are sold, the products or product lines associated with these assets are no longer produced.
2. The sell price of the assets will not reflect any value attributable to a going business and, therefore, will be lower than with a spin-off.
3. With no production or sales, supporting personnel can be terminated.

In some cases, machinery, equipment, vehicles, and inventory can be sold piecemeal on the open market in what is referred to as an "orderly liquidation." This takes time, however, and a distressed company seldom enjoys this luxury. Therefore, even though the selling prices are lower than could be realized with an orderly liquidation, most companies find a liquidation auction the best way to raise capital in a hurry. An auction of inventory and hard assets can be accomplished in about four months from start to finish. An auction requires three things:

1. A qualified auctioneer to manage the advertising and mechanics of the auction.
2. A location to hold the auction.
3. The minimum price the seller is willing to take for each asset sold.

There are a number of qualified, reputable auctioneers throughout the country. Two of the best ways to find auctioneers, however, are through auction advertisements in city newspapers and through asset based lenders (ABLs). Auctioneers tend to specialize, however, so it's important to find one who handles large sales of the type of assets you are selling.

Auctions are always advertised in newspapers in the cities in which the auctions are held. It doesn't take much research to locate the auctioneer who holds the greatest number of auctions in your area for the type of assets you have—just read the newspapers. If newspaper advertising doesn't work, try contacting one of the larger asset based lenders for advice. Two national auction companies you might try are Plant & Machinery, Inc., Houston, Texas, for manufacturing equipment and vehicles and Traimon Auction Co., Inc., Philadelphia, Pennsylvania, for real estate.

If you are currently indebted to an asset based lender, its loan officer can certainly recommend an auctioneer it uses for liquidations on foreclosure. It is always a good idea to research one or two on your own, however, for comparison. Auctioneers who work with specific ABLs often work side deals with the lender that might preclude getting the maximum prices at an auction. Also, auctioneers charge different fees.

The normal auctioneer fee runs between 7 and 10 percent of the gross proceeds of the auction. This is in addition to their out-of-pocket expenses for advertising, travel, cleanup, and crane rental (if necessary) expenses. Unless watched closely by the seller, for sales under $1 million, these miscellaneous expenses can easily run more than the auctioneer's fees. The arrangements for any auction must be negotiated; nothing is fixed. Once the parties reach accord on the terms of the auction, a contract is executed. Your banker or asset based lender will certainly want to approve the terms of this contract although, by law, except for a foreclosure, the seller and the auctioneer must negotiate their own terms.

The auction should be held at the same location that houses the assets. In a partial liquidation, however, a seller might not want to cast negative aspersions on the balance of the business by holding an auction on the company's premises. In this case, a nearby warehouse or vacant building can be rented. This will require moving the assets to the auction site, however, and that means extra cost.

The best way to establish minimum auction prices for each of the assets is to rely on the judgment of the auctioneer. Auctioneers deal with auction values for a living and should know what prices the assets will bring in the current market. It is always a good idea to cross reference this judgment, however, by checking with your asset based lender, who also keeps records of current hard asset liquidation values.

Any gain on the sale of assets during a partial liquidation will be taxed to the company as either capital gains or ordinary income, depending on the character of the asset. If, for some reason, the proceeds of the liquidation sale are distributed to the corporation's shareholders, however, this distribution might qualify as a tax-free exchange for the shareholders stock. As described in chapter 3, specific criteria must be met in order to qualify, including the adoption of a reorganization plan and the corporation's ceasing to conduct the trade or business actively conducted by the company for five years before the distribution.

Raising cash through either a spin-off or a partial liquidation results in trimming back the company's business and, in many cases, this might be impractical and actually hurt the company rather than help in the bailout. A better way to raise cash without contracting any of the business might be through a sale and leaseback of assets.

Sale and leasebacks

There are two ways that the sale and leaseback of hard assets can help a financially troubled company:

1. If the assets are not pledged to a bank, their sale and leaseback can provide significant working capital.
2. If they are pledged as collateral to a loan, a sale and leaseback can provide cash to pay down the debt.

Although unusual, it is possible for a company to be debt poor and yet have assets that are not pledged against a loan. Hotels are a good example. The building itself normally secures a mortgage loan leaving the kitchen, bar, air conditioning, telephone, and other equipment free and clear. The owner can then sell these assets to a leasing company. In most manufacturing or retail companies, however, all of the hard assets are pledged as collateral to a loan. To enact a sale and leaseback arrangement, it's first necessary to get approval from the secured lender. This normally isn't a problem providing that the proceeds of the sale are applied against the outstanding debt.

Typically, an agreement for the sale and leaseback of business machinery and equipment contains several pages of items. Each piece of equipment can have a different useful life. Some might be old, some new; some might have a normal useful life of 10 years, some perhaps only three. Because of the variations in ages, lives, and replacement costs of various assets, the term of the lease might be variable, with each item returned to the lessor as its useful life expires. A more common arrangement, however, stipulates a fixed monthly, quarterly, or annual lease payment against the total list of items. As one item wears out, it is replaced with a new one, purchased by the lessor, and the lease payment either increases or decreases for the incremental cost. Such a lease is normally written for five years with automatic renewal by the lessee.

The obvious danger in this type of lease is that monthly payments can go on forever, and the business owner will never own the assets. The advantages for a financially troubled company usually outweigh this disadvantage, however. To make the transaction economically feasible, the monthly lease payments must be less than the replaced debt service. The lender must either be paid off entirely with the proceeds of the sale, or the debt service for the balance of the loan must be restructured over a longer period of time. The total of the lease payments and the remaining debt service payments will then be less than the original debt service. Without restructuring the loan, there is no advantage in a sale and leaseback. Chapter 9 described how Quantum Hotel Associates used a sale and leaseback to restructure its debt to get the company through a short-term cash bind when business dropped. A similar scheme was employed by Brad Schoon to salvage his fitness and health clubs.

Golden Palm Health and Racquet Clubs, Inc. had been a profitable chain of four exercise facilities for several years and was purchased by Brad Schoon in 1979. During the ensuing eight years, newer health clubs emerged as strong competitors and the Golden Palm clubs began losing revenues rapidly. Each club included a fruit bar and small restaurant, which continued to break even, but with membership sales down, the debt service on Brad's acquisition loan was draining cash from working capital needs. When he finally exhausted his bank operating line, Brad began the inevitable personnel layoffs and the stretching of trade payables. Still, the cash flow failed to cover debt service and working capital needs.

Brad's request to the commercial bank for an increase in his operating line proved fruitless and the insurance company holding the mortgages on all four facilities wouldn't budge. Brad knew that if he didn't do something fast, the bankruptcy court was right around the corner. He called me in to help him restructure his balance sheet and to try to locate additional capital. The first step was to sell off all the unused furniture and exercise equipment stored in the basement of one of the clubs. That cash kept Golden Palm liquid until we could structure a sale and leaseback of the operating equipment.

My first call was to Leaseamerica Corporation of Cedar Rapids, Iowa, a leasing company specializing in long-term sales and leasebacks. The deal worked as follows:

Long-term loan balance outstanding to Aetna Insurance Co.	$9,404,122
Current annual debt service to Aetna	1,150,245
Lease with Leaseamerica covering all club furniture, fixtures, and equipment	$7,600,000
Annual lease payment	612,456

With the $7,600,000 payment for the sale of the assets, Brad paid $5 million down on the long-term debt. He used $2,600,000 for additional working capital, which was enough to update some of the equipment, redecorate the clubs, and implement a strong advertising campaign. In about 12 months, membership sales began to increase.

Simultaneously, we renegotiated the long-term debt balance of $4,404,122 on a new amortization schedule for 30 years. The reduction in debt service didn't get Brad completely out of the woods, but it did give him enough breathing space to weather the competitive storm and survive.

A sale and leaseback arrangement won't work for every company. On the other hand, with sufficient hard assets in the business, whether they are pledged to secure long-term debt or not, a sale and leaseback refinancing scheme might help solve the cash problem, at least until the business can be turned around.

Partial sale to employees

Selling part of the equity in the company to employees is one of the best ways to raise capital in a financially distressed company. Although employees seldom have enough equity cash to buy a share in the company outright, financing is relatively easy to arrange. The most popular method is through an Employee Stock Ownership Plan (ESOP). Not only can an ESOP be used to acquire a product line, subsidiary, or division through a spin-off, it can also serve as a vehicle to buy equity in an existing company.

An ESOP is a formal employee profit-sharing plan, drawn up by an attorney, just like a pension plan. The company contributes cash or other property to the plan either in lieu of, or in addition to, other employee benefit programs. These contributions to the ESOP are tax deductible to the corporation. As the cash accumulates, the ESOP buys shares in the company. The ESOP actually owns the shares, and the employees, in effect, own the ESOP. Obviously, this is merely a tax gimmick endorsed by the IRS. You could just as easily give the employees company stock, but if you did, this would be taxable income to the employees. So even though the company provides the cash for the employees to buy its shares, convoluted tax laws make the ESOP a more popular way for employees to acquire equity ownership in their own company, tax free.

An employee benefit, however is not the only advantage in using an ESOP. An ESOP can also be used by the employees to raise additional capital outside of the company's contributions to acquire part, or all, of the equity of their company. Whether the ESOP buys a minority interest in the company or completes a total management buyout, lenders lean over backwards to finance the deal. The reason is simple. Interest charged to the ESOP on borrowed funds used to acquire shares in the company is only taxable to the lender. Not only is an ESOP a tax-free way to provide employee benefits and a tax-free way for employees to own shares in the company, it also provides low-tax interest income to financial institutions. To qualify under the Code, corporate contributions must be:

1. Paid in cash directly to the participants; OR
2. Paid to the ESOP and subsequently distributed in cash to the participants within 90 days after the plan year ends; OR
3. Used to repay an ESOP loan.

There are additional restrictions:

1. The company contributions to the ESOP must be allocated to each of the participants' accounts, and this allocation must be made on the same basis as the pro rata share of each participants' annual compensation to the total compensation paid.
2. Compensation in excess of $100,000 per annum is excluded from this calculation.
3. All participants must have nonforfeitable rights.
4. Employer securities must remain in the ESOP for seven years, except for:
   - ~ death, disability, separation from service, or termination of the plan, in which case, securities can be withdrawn by the participant; or
   - ~ transfer of a participant's employment to an acquirer corporation; or
   - ~ disposition of the selling corporation's stock in a subsidiary when the participant continues employment with the subsidiary.

Notwithstanding these minor restrictions, an ESOP offers a tax-free method for the corporation to provide additional employee benefits and it gives the employees a viable vehicle to acquire a share of the company. Cash raised through a partial sale of the equity in the company can then be used to reduce outstanding debt.

Using the bankruptcy code

A filing under Chapter 11 of the federal Bankruptcy Code is a drastic step not to be taken lightly. In some cases, a company can be so financially strapped, however, that none of the methods mentioned previously will work. The only remaining option is to seek protection from creditors by filing for bankruptcy under Chapter 11. A Chapter 11 filing won't solve any financing problems, and it certainly won't create any additional capital sources. There are two ways, however, that a Chapter 11 can assist in restructuring a company's debt: by using the threat of filing for bankruptcy protection and by threatening to liquidate once in bankruptcy. Before getting into the mechanics of using the Bankruptcy Code, it might be helpful to distinguish between a Chapter 11 filing and other forms of bankruptcy. Later in this chapter, the personal risks to a business owner filing a Chapter 11 are also examined.

Types of bankruptcies

Excluding railroads, insurance companies, banks, savings and loans, and similar financial institutions, stock and commodity brokers, and municipalities—which fall under specialized bankruptcy proceedings—there are four types of bankruptcies.

Chapter 7—Liquidation bankruptcy A Chapter 7 filing is the form of bankruptcy most people think about when they hear the word bankruptcy. A Chapter 7 filing can be initiated by the business itself or by its creditors. A trustee appointed by the court has control of the assets of the business. A business can continue to operate under Chapter 7 in special circumstances, but generally, the trustee's primary function is to sell its assets and distribute the proceeds to creditors. The sale is normally performed at an auction, and the entire bankruptcy proceeding can usually be completed in 90 days. Obviously, Chapter 7 won't generate operating cash.

Chapter 11—Reorganization bankruptcy A Chapter 11 filing means that the creditors of a company cannot take any action to force payment of debts while the company works out a plan of reorganization. This plan, which must be court approved, allows the company to settle its debts and eventually come out of bankruptcy. Once the plan is accepted by the court (and the creditors), the company's obligations are limited to only those that appear on the schedules accompanying the reorganization plan. Even though a trustee is appointed by the court, the business owner actually continues to control and operate the business—but with court approval of all major activities—while the reorganization plan is being worked out. If the company and the creditors are unable to agree on a plan of reorganization, the court has the option of converting a Chapter 11 filing to a Chapter 7 and liquidate the business.

Chapter 12—Family-farmer bankruptcy   Chapter 12 is a relatively new feature of the Code and applies only to a family owned business with at least 50 percent of its income from agriculture. The total debt cannot exceed $1.5 million. Although the trustee monitors payments to the creditors while the debtor continues to operate the business, he does not control the debtor's assets.

Chapter 13—Wage earner bankruptcy   Chapter 13 is designed for individuals with a steady source of income. Debt cannot exceed $450,000, of which unsecured debt cannot be more than $100,000. The debtor presents a plan to the court for paying off his other debts and, if approved, makes regular payments to a trustee, who then disburses the funds to creditors. The debtor controls his own assets. Normally, it takes about three years of payments before the total debts are discharged.

Using the threat of filing

When a corporation, partnership, or a proprietorship is on the brink of filing for protection under the Bankruptcy Code, he has an amazing amount of leverage in dealing with creditors, especially unsecured creditors. No creditor wants to see a company file bankruptcy because he knows that chances are very low that he'll recover much more than 5 or 10 cents on the dollar. If the company has purchased materials, supplies, or other goods from a creditor for several years, or if its annual purchases are fairly sizable, a creditor knows that he is further ahead by either negotiating a long-term payment schedule with the company or settling for some fraction of what is owed. If he expects to continue supplying the company in the future, it just makes sense to recoup any losses through additional business or higher prices later on. With this type of leverage, a business owner should be able to negotiate an arrangement to reduce his cash outflow, thus allowing more for debt service to secured lenders.

This tactic won't work very well with the IRS, however. A company has no leverage at all in dealing with this agency. The IRS has no interest in seeing the company survive. It has no interest in collecting more taxes on income in the future. It has no interest in the social consequences of a company folding. All the IRS wants is its money, and if that means liquidating the company, so be it! State and municipal taxing authorities aren't much better, although in some communities, a business owner might have enough political clout to stave them off, at least for a while.

An owner might consider negotiating with trade creditors to take future shipments of raw materials on consignment and pay for the goods only when they are converted to finished goods and sold. An owner might even be able to convince employee groups, such as a union, to loan money to the company on a term-loan unsecured note. From the employees' point of view, almost anything is better than going into bankruptcy with the possibility of losing their jobs.

Using the threat of liquidation after filing

Once a company has filed under Chapter 11, a different set of circumstances arises and a different type of leverage exists. At this point, a business owner can threaten to take the company into liquidation rather than working out a reorganization plan. Secured debt holders such as banks or ABLs retain the highest position in the priority of creditors under the Bankruptcy Code. They have the least to lose if you do file under Chapter 11. They know that if there is any chance at all of the company reorganizing and coming out of bankruptcy, they will get paid in full. A Chapter 7 liquidation, however, is a different matter entirely; especially if the bank debt is secured with equipment, machinery and vehicles, or with inventory. Seldom, if ever, does a liquidation sale yield selling prices even close to the secured value of these assets. And all lenders know this.

Therefore, once in Chapter 11, a business owner has a significant amount of leverage in dealing with lenders and other secured creditors simply by threatening to liquidate the company. This leverage can usually be parlayed into a renegotiated loan agreement with significantly reduced debt service. The term of the loan can be extended; there can be a moratorium on principal payments; there can be a moratorium on both interest and principal payments for several months or years; short-term debt can be converted into long-term debt; or there can be complete refinancing, with the secured creditor trading some of the debt for an equity share in the company.

This latter step, trading debt for equity, can also work with unsecured creditors, such as employees, or a collective bargaining unit. It becomes more difficult to interest a trade creditor in a swap, however. They generally feel that they are better off remaining on the outside.

The risks of a Chapter 11 filing

Even though a Chapter 11 filing can be used to restructure a financially distressed company, you need to be aware of two legal points unique to bankruptcy law. The Bankruptcy Code embodies a set of laws completely independent of those we all live under every day. A fundamental principle in our legal system is that an individual is presumed innocent until proven guilty. Just the reverse occurs under bankruptcy law; an individual is presumed guilty until proven innocent. Once a Chapter 11 has been filed, it is the court's duty, under law, to protect and save the company—not the business owner—which leads to the second point.

Under the protection of the bankruptcy court, the company, prodded by creditors and the trustee, has the right (it's really an obligation) to recover what are called "preferential payments" from anyone considered an insider. If the debtor is a corporation, an insider is defined as any director or officer of the corporation, any person in control of the corporation (such as a general manager), a partnership in which the debtor is a general partner, or a general partner of the debtor, or a relative of the general partner, director, officer, or person in control (such as a spouse or child). This clearly means that the owner of a closely held business is an insider.

Preferential payments are any payments made to an insider while the corporation is insolvent (liabilities exceed assets) for up to 12 months prior to filing. By definition, the company is considered insolvent for 90 days prior to filing. Under the bankruptcy laws, any payments for any reason made to an insider during the 12-month period prior to filing (assuming the company is insolvent during this period) or any payments made in the 90 days preceding filing—whether or not the company is actually insolvent during that period—must be repaid by the individual to the company. This means salaries, bonuses, dividends, travel expense reimbursements, insurance premium payments, pension plan contributions, and any other payments made by the company to, or on behalf of, the insider. An insider cannot win. These payments must be returned. Even the company's owner has no right to them. That's how an individual is presumed guilty under the bankruptcy laws. So think twice before electing a Chapter 11 to solve your financial problems. You could end up much worse than you were before.

Summary

This chapter covered some of the ways to generate cash through restructuring a financially troubled company. They don't all work in all situations, however. Some companies are so far in the hole that nothing can bail them out, and a complete liquidation is in order. Most, however, with some creative effort by the owner, can be saved, even if it means running the severe risks of a Chapter 11. In summary, a distressed company can generate extra cash or restructure its debt by:

1. *Selling a product line, division, or subsidiary.* Spinning off part of the company to an employee group or an outsider can bring free cash into the company for debt reduction or working capital.

2. *Selling unused equipment or inventory at a liquidation sale.* A partial liquidation can also raise capital, but the prices obtained at an auction are substantially less than if each asset were sold separately.

3. *A sale and leaseback of assets.* A sale and leaseback is ideally suited to businesses with substantial hard assets, such as a hotel or a manufacturing company. This procedure can provide cash for debt reduction, working capital, or both.

4. *A partial sale to employees.* Using an ESOP to finance the sale of a minority equity share to employees can bring in extra cash without incurring any more debt. This also has the advantage of improving employee participation in solving a company's problems.

5. *Using the Bankruptcy Code.* A threat to file Chapter 11 can often bring concessions from unsecured creditors by extending payment terms or by negotiating a debt-for-equity swap. After filing, the same leverage can be brought against secured creditors. Preferential payment laws make a Chapter 11 filing a risky venture, however.

There is nothing easy about raising capital in a financially troubled company. The more distressed the circumstances, the harder it is to save the company. Many times, more than one road must be taken. Combinations of cost-cutting, product purging, and restructuring are often necessary. If the owner of a financially troubled company can begin taking appropriate actions in time, most businesses can survive. But it takes imagination, perseverance, and above all else, the nerve to take the risk.

Appendix A

Associations, bureaus, and agencies for financing assistance

NATIONAL ASSOCIATION OF SMALL BUSINESS
Investment Companies
1156 15th Street NW, Suite 1101
Washington, DC 20005

NATIONAL VENTURE CAPITAL ASSOCIATION
1655 North Fort Myer Drive, Suite 700
Arlington, VA 22209

U.S. SMALL BUSINESS ADMINISTRATION
Office of Business Loans
1441 L Street NW, Room 804
Washington, DC 20416

U.S. DEPARTMENT OF COMMERCE
Economic Development Administration
Credit and Debt Management Division
14th and Constitution Avenue NW, Room 7839
Washington, DC 20230

SECURITIES AND EXCHANGE COMMISSION
Office of Small Business Policy
Division of Corporate Finance
450 Fifth Street NW
Washington, DC 20549

WESTERN ASSOCIATION OF VENTURE CAPITALISTS
3000 Sand Hill Road, Building 2, Suite 215
Menlo Park, CA 94025

Appendix B

Investment banks and venture capital firms

ACQUIVEST GROUP, INC.
1 Newtown Executive Park
Suite 204
Newton, MA 01262

ADVEST INCORPORATED
6 Central Row
Hartford, CT 06103

ALLIED CAPITAL CORPORATION
1625 I Street, NW, Suite 603
Washington, DC 20006

ALLSTATE INSURANCE CO.
Allstate Plaza E-2
Northbrook, IL 60062

AMERVEST CORPORATION
10 Commercial Wharf West
Boston, MA 02110

AMEV CAPITAL CORP.
1 World Trade Center, 50th Floor
New York, NY 10048

ATLANTIC AMERICAN CAPITAL, LTD.
Lincoln Center, Suite 851
5401 West Kennedy Boulevard
Tampa, FL 33609

ATLANTIC VENTURE PARTNERS
P.O. Box 1493
Richmond, VA 23212

BANCBOSTON CAPITAL CORP.
100 Federal Street
Boston, MA 02110

BANKAMERICA CAPITAL CORPORATION
555 California Street, 42nd Floor
San Francisco, CA 94104

BEAR STERNS & COMPANY
Investment Banking Division
55 Water Street
New York, NY 10041

BLAKE INVESTMENT GROUP
1101 30th Street NW, Suite 101
Washington, DC 20007

BNE ASSOCIATES
Bank of New England
60 State Street
Boston, MA 02109

BRADFORD ASSOCIATES
22 Chambers Street
Princeton, NJ 08540

BUTLER CAPITAL CORP.
767 Fifth Avenue, Sixth Floor
New York, NY 10153

CAPITAL CORPORATION OF AMERICA
225 South 15th Street, Suite 920
Philadelphia, PA 19102

CARL MARKS & CO, INC.
77 Water Street
New York, NY 10005

CHARLES DeTHAN GROUP
51 East 67th Street
New York, NY 10021

CHARTERHOUSE GROUP INTERNATIONAL
535 Madison Avenue
New York, NY 10022

CHASE MANHATTAN CAPITAL MARKETS
1 Chase Manhattan Plaza, 3rd Floor
New York, NY 10081

CITICORP VENTURE CAPITAL, LTD.
Citicorp Center
153 E. 53rd Street, 28th Floor
New York, NY 10043

CONNECTICUT NATIONAL BANK
Investment Banking Division
1604 Walnut Street
Philadelphia, PA 19103

CONTINENTAL ILLINOIS VENTURE CORP.
231 South LaSalle Street
Chicago, IL 60697

DAIN BOSWORTH, INC.
100 Dain Tower
Minneapolis, MN 55402

DILLON REED & COMPANY, INC.
535 Madison Avenue
New York, NY 10022

DJS GROUP
745 Park Avenue, 21st Floor
New York, NY 10155

DREXEL BURNHAM LAMBERT, INC.
55 Broad Street
New York, NY 10004

E.F. HUTTON LBO, INC.
1 Battery Park Plaza
New York, NY 10004

EAB VENTURE CORPORATION
90 Park Avenue
New York, NY 10016

FIDELITY BANK
Investment Banking Division
Broad & Walnut, Sixth Floor
Philadelphia, PA 19109

FIRST CHICAGO VENTURE CAPITAL
1 First National Plaza
Suite 2628
Chicago, IL 60670

FIRST CONNECTICUT SBIC
177 State Street
Bridgeport, CT 06604

FIRST INTERSTATE CAPITAL CORP.
515 South Figueroa Street
Los Angeles, CA 90071

FLEET GROWTH INDUSTRIES, INC.
111 Westminster Street
Providence, RI 02903

FOOTHIL CAPITAL CORPORATION
2049 Century Park East
Los Angeles, CA 90067

FOUNDERS VENTURES, INC.
477 Madison Avenue
New York, NY 10022

FRONTENAC CAPITAL CORP.
208 South LaSalle Street
Suite 1900
Chicago, IL 60604

GENERAL ELECTRIC VENTURE CAPITAL
3135 Easton Turnpike
Fairfield, CT 06431

GOLDER, THOMA & CRESSEY
120 South LaSalle Street
Chicago, IL 60603

HAMBRECHT & QUIST
235 Montgomery Street
San Francisco, CA 94104

HAMBRO INTERNATIONAL VENTURE FUND
17 East 71st Street
New York, NY 10021

HILLMAN VENTURES, INC.
2000 Grant Bldg.
Pittsburgh, PA 15219

HOWARD, LAWSON & CO, INC.
2 Penn Center Plaza
Philadelphia, PA 19102

INTERFIRST VENTURE CORPORATION
P.O. Box 83644
Dallas, TX 75283

ITC CAPITAL CORPORATION
1290 Avenue of the Americas
New York, NY 10104

JAMES RIVER CAPITAL ASSOCIATES
9 South 12th Street
Richmond, VA 23219

JOHN HANCOCK VENTURE CAPITAL
Management, Inc.
John Hancock Place, 57th Floor
Boston, MA 02117

KEELEY MANAGEMENT COMPANY
2 Radnor Corporate Center
Radnor, PA 19087

KIDDER PEABODY & COMPANY
Investment Banking Division
Mellon Bank Center
Philadelphia, PA 19102

LEPERQ DE NEUFLIZE & COMPANY
345 Park Avenue
New York, NY 10154

MANUFACTURERS HANOVER VENTURE
Capital Corp.
140 East 45th Street
New York, NY 10017

MARYLAND NATIONAL BANK
Investment Banking Group
P.O. Box 987
Baltimore, MD 21203

MELLON BANK
Corporate Finance Group
Mellon Bank Center
Philadelphia, PA 19102

MENLO VENTURE
3000 Sand Hill Road
Menlo Park, CA 94025

MERIDIAN VENTURE PARTNERS
259 Radnor-Chester Rd.
Radnor, PA 19087

MIDLAND CAPITAL CORPORATION
950 Third Avenue
New York, NY 10022

NARRAGANSETT CAPITAL
40 Westminster Street
Providence, RI 02903

NORWEST VENTURE CAPITAL
MANAGEMENT
1730 Midwest Plaza Bldg.
801 Nicollet Mall
Minneapolis, MN 55402

OXFORD PARTNERS
Soundview Plaza
1266 Main Street
Stamford, CT 06902

PAINE WEBBER VENTURE MANAGEMENT
100 Federal Street
Boston, MA 02110

PENNWOOD CAPITAL CORPORATION
645 Madison Avenue
New York, NY 10022

PHILADELPHIA CAPITAL ADVISORS
Philadelphia National Bank Building
Broad & Chestnut Streets
Philadelphia, PA 19107

PNC VENTURE CAPITAL GROUP
Fifth Avenue & Woods Streets
Pittsburgh, PA 15222

PRU CAPITAL, INCORPORATED
1 Seaport Plaza, 31st Floor
199 Water Street
New York, NY 10292

QUINCY PARTNERS
P.O. Box 154
Glen Head, NY 11545

ROSENFELD & COMPANY
625 SW Washington Street
Portland, OR 97205

ROTHSCHILD, INCORPORATED
Rockefeller Plaza
New York, NY 10020

RUST VENTURES LP
114 West Seventh Street
Suite 1300
Austin, TX 78701

SALOMON BROTHERS, INC.
1 New York Plaza
New York, NY 10004

SECURITY PACIFIC CAPITAL CORP.
4000 MacArthur Boulevard, Suite 950
Newport Beach, CA 92660

SEIDLER AMDEC SECURITIES, INC.
515 South Figueroa Street
Los Angeles, CA 90071

SMITH, BARNEY, HARRIS, UPHAM
1345 Avenue of the Americas
New York, NY 10105

SPROUT CAPITAL GROUP
140 Broadway
New York, NY 10025

SUMMIT VENTURES
1 Boston Place
Boston, MA 02108

TA ASSOCIATES
45 Milk Street
Boston, MA 02109

TDH II LIMITED
c/o K.S. Sweet Associates
P.O. Box 6780
Radnor, PA 19087

TUCKER ANTHONY AND RL DAY, INC.
120 Broadway
New York, NY 10271

UNION VENTURE CORPORATION
445 South Figueroa Street
Los Angeles, CA 90071

WARBURG, PINCUS VENTURES, INC.
466 Lexington Avenue
New York, NY 10017

WELLS FARGO EQUITY CORPORATION
1 Embarcadero Center
San Francisco, CA 94111

WELSH, CARSON, ANDERSON & STOWE
45 Wall Street, 16th Floor
New York, NY 10005

WILLIAM BLAIR VENTURE PARTNERS
135 South LaSalle Street, 29th Floor
Chicago, IL 60603

WISSAHICKON PARTNERS
19 Vandeventer Avenue
Princeton, NJ 08542

Appendix C

Foundations awarding larger grants and low-cost loans

Foundation	Program Related Type of Businesses
BUTLER MANUFACTURING COMPANY FOUNDATION BMA Tower P.O. Box 917 Penn Valley Park Kansas City, MO 64141	Agribusiness
THE EDNA MCCONNELL CLARK FOUNDATION 250 Park Avenue, Room 900 New York, NY 10017	Education related
FINANCIAL EXECUTIVES RESEARCH FOUNDATION 10 Madison Avenue P.O. Box 1938 Morristown, NJ 07960	Research in finance
THE XEROX FOUNDATION P.O. Box 1600 Stamford, CT 06904	Science and technology

THE JOYCE FOUNDATION 135 South LaSalle Street Chicago, IL 60603	Conservation
THE FORD FOUNDATION 320 East 43rd Street New York, NY 10017	Urban development, public policy, international economic issues
CHARLES STEWART MOTT FOUNDATION 1200 Mott Foundation Building Flint, MI 48502	Environmental
ADRIAN & JESSIE ARCHBOLD CHARITABLE TRUST Chemical Bank Administrative Services Department 30 Rockefeller Plaza, 60th Floor New York, NY 10012	Health care
THE ROBERT WOOD JOHNSON FOUNDATION P.O. Box 2316 Princeton, NJ 08543	Personal health care
ROCKEFELLER BROTHERS FUND 1290 Avenue of the Americas New York, NY 10104	International trade and finance

Flow Through

Foundation	Type of Businesses
THE ARCA FOUNDATION 1425 21st Street NW Washington, DC 20036	Aid for Central America, Community Development, Environmental
WHITEHALL FOUNDATION 249 Royal Palm Way, Suite 220 Palm Beach, FL 33480	Life Sciences

Appendix D

Underwriters handling initial public offerings

(IPO) (from *Institutional Investor*)

ADVEST, INC.
280 Trumbull Street
Hartford, CT 06103

ALEX, BROWN & SONS, INC.
135 East Baltimore Street
Baltimore, MD 21202

A.G. EDWARDS & SONS
1 North Jefferson Street
St. Louis, MO 63103

BATEMAN EICHLER, HILL RICHARDS
700 Flower Street
Los Angeles, CA 90017

BLUNT ELLIS & LOEWI INC.
111 East Kilbourn Street
Milwaukee, WI 53202

BUTCHER & SINGER, INC.
211 South Broad Street
Philadelphia, PA 19107

DAIN BOSWORTH
100 Dain Tower
Minneapolis, MN 55402

DEAN WITTER REYNOLDS, INC.
2 World Trade Center, 65th Floor
New York, NY 10048

DONALDSON, LUFKIN & JENRETTE
140 Broadway
New York, NY 10004

FIRST BOSTON CORP.
Park Avenue Plaza
55 East 52nd Street
New York, NY 10055

FURMAN, SELZ, MAGER, DIETZ & BIRNEY
230 Park Avenue
New York, NY 10169

GOLDMAN SACHS
85 Broad Street
New York, NY 10004

HAMBRECHT & QUIST, INC.
1 Bush Street
San Francisco, CA 94104

INTERSTATE JOHNSON LANE
2700 NCNB Plaza
Charlotte, NC 28280

KIDDER, PEABODY & CO., INC.
10 Hanover Square
New York, NY 10005

LEGG MASON WOOD WALKER, INC.
Legg Mason Tower Building
111 South Calvert Street
Baltimore, MD 21202

MERRILL LYNCH CAPITAL MARKETS
World Financial Center
North Tower
New York, NY 10281

MONTGOMERY SECURITIES
600 Montgomery Street
San Francisco, CA 94111

MORGAN STANLEY
1251 Avenue of the Americas
New York, NY 10020

PAINEWEBBER
1285 Avenue of the Americas
New York, NY 10019

PIPER, JAFFRAY & HOPWOOD
222 South 9th Street
Minneapolis, MN 55402

PRESCOTT, BALL & TURBEN
1331 Euclid Avenue
Cleveland, OH 44115

RAYMOND, JAMES & ASSOCIATES, INC.
880 Carillon Parkway
St. Petersburg, FL 33716

ROBERTSON, COLMAN & STEPHENS
1 Embarcadero Center
San Francisco, CA 94111

RONEY & CO.
1 Griswold
Detroit, MI 49226

SHEARSON LEHMAN HUTTON, INC.
American Express Tower C
World Financial Center
New York, NY 10285

SMITH BARNEY, HARRIS UPHAM & CO.
1345 Avenue of the Americas
New York, NY 10105

THOMSON MCKINNON SECURITIES, INC.
Financial Square
New York, NY 10005

WHEAT, FIRST SECURITIES, INC.
707 East Main Street
Richmond, VA 23219

WILLIAM BLAIR & CO.
135 East LaSalle Street
Chicago, IL 60603

YOUND, SMITH & PEACOCK
3443 N. Central Avenue
Phoenix, AZ 85012

Appendix E

Asset based lenders

CONGRESS FINANCIAL CORPORATION
American City Building
Columbia, MD 21044

GENERAL ELECTRIC CREDIT CORPORATION
Eastern Corporate Finance Dept.
3003 Summer Street
Stamford, CT 06905

GLENFED CAPITAL CORPORATION
Carnegie Center
Princeton, NJ 08540

ITT CAPITAL CORPORATION
1400 North Central Life Tower
St. Paul, MN 55101

SECURITY PACIFIC BUSINESS CREDIT, INC.
45 South Hudson Avenue
Pasadena, CA 91101

FIDELITY CAPITAL
Fidelity Bank Building
Broad & Walnut Streets
Philadelphia, PA 19109

Appendix F

SBIR federal agency release and closing dates

(Fiscal Year 1990 Calendar)

Agency	Release Date	Closing Date
Agriculture	7/1/90	9/1/90
Commerce	11/1/89	1/31/90
Defense	10/1/89	1/5/90
Education	1/15/90	3/16/90
Energy	10/23/89	1/23/90
Health & Human Services:		
Public Health Service/Health Care Finance Administration	10/1/90	12/8/89
Office of Human Development Services	11/6/89	1/12/90
Public Health Service	1/15/89	4/15/90
		8/15/90
		12/15/90
Transportation	2/12/90	5/1/90
Environmental Protection Agency	11/8/89	1/16/90
National Aeronautics & Space Administration	4/9/90	6/14/90
National Science Foundation	4/5/90	6/18/90
Nuclear Regulatory Commission	1/19/90	3/28/90

Appendix G

Associations, bureaus, and agencies for international trade

COUNCIL FOR EXPORT TRADING COMPANIES
1200 19th Street NW, Suite 605
Washington, DC 20036

OVERSEAS PRIVATE INVESTMENT CORPORATION
1615 M Street NW
Washington, DC 20527

U.S. AGENCY OF INTERNATIONAL DEVELOPMENT
Office of Small and Disadvantaged Business
Utilization/Minority Resource Center
1100 Wilson Boulevard, Room 1400-A
Rosslyn, VA 22209

U.S. DEPARTMENT OF COMMERCE
International Trade Administration
14th and Constitution Avenue NW, Room 1128
Washington, DC 20230

U.S. DEPARTMENT OF COMMERCE
Office of Trade Finance
14th and Constitution Avenue NW, Room 4420
Washington, DC 20230

U.S. DEPARTMENT OF COMMERCE
United States and Foreign Commercial Service
14th and Constitution Avenue NW, Room 3012
Washington, DC 20230

U.S. SMALL BUSINESS ADMINISTRATION
Office of International Trade
1441 L Street NW, Room 501-A
Washington, DC 20416

WORLD BANK
1818 H Street NW
Washington, DC 20433

FOREIGN CREDIT INSURANCE CORPORATION
40 Rector Street
New York, NY 10006

Appendix H

Credit reports on entities in foreign countries

Agency	Country
ASSESSORIA EMPRESARIAL E INFORMACOES COMERCIALES Rua Brigaderio Tobia-577 6th Floor, Suite 605 Sao Paulo, Brazil CEP 01032	Brazil
AFRIC GESTION 95 Rue d'Azilal Casablanca, Morocco	Morocco
AFRIQUE SERVICE—AFSER 08-P. B. 18 Abidjan, Ivory Coast	Gabon, Ivory Coast, Senegal, Togo
AFRO-ASIAN TRADING OFFICE Sulieman Al Hamad Building 4th Floor Flat #27 King Abdul A 212 Street P.O. Box 587 Jeddah, Saudi Arabia	Saudia Arabia, United Arab Emirates

ALPHA M. I.   Greece
3 Aghiou Constantinou Street
Athens 101 Greece

AMALGAMATED TRADES PROTECTION LTD.   Most Countries
(A.T.P. International)
Sutherland House
70/78 Edgware Road
Staples Corner
London NW9 7BT, U.K.

ANDRES F. ARCHIBOLD S.A.   Panama
Apartado 6369
Estafeta Balboa
Panama 5

ANTONY FORNE JOU   Andorra
Carrer Les Canbals 13,
Zalet Forne
Andorra La Vella

ARGUS INFORMATION SERVICE   Afghanistan, Cyprus, Egypt,
15 Archbishop Makarios Avemue   Iraq, Israel, Jordan, Kuwait,
Nicosia, Cyprus   Malta, Oman, Qatar, Saudi Arabia,
                                        Sudan, U.A.E., Yemen Arab Republic

ASIA MERCHANTIE AGENCY (H.K.) LTD.   Burma, China (PRC), Hong Kong,
1301-3 Chiao Shang Building   India, Indonesia, Korea, Morocco,
92-104 Queen's Road   Malaysia, Philippines, Singapore,
Central, Hong Kong   Sri Lanka, Taiwan, Thailand

ASOCIACION DE CEDITO C POR A—ACCA   Dominican Republic
Apartado Postal #988
Zona Postal 1
Santo Domingo, Dominica Republic

ASSOCIATED CREDIT BUREAU   Philippines
Room 306 Pilar Building #2
507 Gastambide Street
Sampaloc Manila 2906
Philippines

ATLAS CREDIT MARKETING SERVICES   Bahrain, Cyprus, Jordan,
117 Athalassa Avenue   Yemen Arab Republic
P.O. Box 2136
Nicosia, Cyprus

"AUDIRRIESGOS" AUDITORES DE RIESCO   Colombia
ASOCIADOS
Carrera 9, No. 17-47 OF. 404
Apartedoa Aereo 8182
Bogota, Colombia

AUGUSTTO J. AMADOR   Costa Rico
Apartedo Postal 2-810
San Jose, Costa Rico

AUSTRALIAN MERCANTILE BUREAUX   Australia, British Pacific Islands,
& AGENCY LTD—AMBA   Fiji, French Pacific Islands, Nauru,
363 Kingsway 1st Floor   New Zealand, Papua New Guinea,
P.O. Box 291   Solomon Islands, Tahiti
Caringbah N.S.W. 2229, Australia

B.C.A.—BERMUDA CREDIT   Bermuda
P.O. Box 280
Hamilton 5, Bermuda

BRASINFORM, LTD.   Brazil
Rua 24 de Maio, 188
3 Andar 5/304
01041 Sao Paulo
Brazil

BURGEL GMBH—CENTRALE DER   Austria, Belgium, Canada, Denmark,
VERINGTEN AUSKUNFTEI   Finland, France, Germany, Iran,
Elisabethstrasse 14   Ireland, Italy, Liechtenstein,
Postfach 310   Luxembourg, Morocco, Netherlands,
D-5100 Aachen, West Germany   Netherlands Antilles, Norway,
                                              Portugal, Saudi Arabia, Spain,
                                              Sweden, Switzerland, Turkey,
                                                   U.K., Yugoslavia

IRVING C. BYINGTON   Colombia
Avenue Jimenez 7-25
Ofic. 1025
Apartado Aereo 45-62
Bogota, Colombia

CABINET ZEMOUCHI   Algeria
5 Rue Mahmond Bendali
Algiers, Algeria

CANADIAN CREDIT REPORTING, LTD.   Canada
2175 Sheppard Avenue East
Suite 305
Willowdale, Ontario M2J 1W8
Canada

CENTRO INFORMATIVO DE CREDITO—C.I.C.   Nicaragua
Apartado Postal 2391
Managua, Nicaragua

CHINESE UNITED CREDIT CENTER   Taiwan
7th Floor, KUO Hwa Building
#154 Po Ai Road
Taipai, Taiwan

CLEMENT H. DANA   Lebanon
Commercial & Financial Service
136 Robeiz Street
P.O. Box 11.436
Beirut Lebanon

COMMERCIAL BANK OF ETHIOPIA   Ethiopia
P.O. Box 255
Addis Ababa, Ethiopia

C.C.C.—COMMERCIAL CREDIT CENTRE   Fiji, Papua New Guinea,
89 Robertson Road   Samoa
G.P.O. Box 926
Suva, Fiji

COMPANIA ARGENTINA DE SEGUROS DE   Argentina
CREDITO A LA EXPORTACION S.S. (C.A.S.C.)
Sarmiento 440, 4o Piso
1247 Buenos Aires, Argentina

CONTINENTAL CREDIT CO.   Guatamala
12-Calle 6-27
Zpna 1-2o Piso
P.O. Box 579
Guatemala City, Guatemala

CREDIT BUREAU PORT OF SPAIN   Trinidad & Tobago
P.O. Box 31
23 Chacon Street
Port of Spain, Trinidad W.I.

CREDIT CONSULTANT, (JA) LTD.   Jamaica
P.O. Box 131
Kingston 10, Jamaica

CREDIT EXCHANGE AGENCY, LTD.   Japan
(Shingo Kokansho Co., Ltd.)
22-1 Chome, Azuchi-Machi
Higashi-Ku
Osaka, Japan

CREDIT INFORMATION   Iceland
(Upplysningar Um Lanstraust)
Laufasvegur 36
P.O. Box 515
Reykjavik, Iceland

CREDIT REPORT S.A.   Peru
Jiron Zepita No. 423 Of. 303
Edificio Ferrand
Casilla 208
Lima, Peru

DUN & BRADSTREET   Most Countries
Dun & Bradstreet International
One World Trade Center, Suite 9069
New York, NY 10048

GENERAL CREDIT   Bahamas, Trinidad
Columbus House
East & Shirley Street
P.O. Box N 7343
Nassau, N.P., Bahamas

CHARLES GONSALVES   Guyana
4 D'Urban & George Street
P.O. Box 663
Georgetown, Guyana

ROBERT GREGG   El Salvador, Guatemala, Honduras
Apartado Postal CC-208
San Salvador, El Salvador

THE GUARDIAN MERCANTILE AGENCY   Brunei, Malaysia
G.P.O. 2669
116-B Jalan Tuanku
Abdul Rahman
Kuala Lumpur 01-07, Malaysia

J. CH. HEAVE   Suriname
P.O. Box 1015
Parimaribo, Suriname

INFAE   Ecuador
Informes Agencieas Estudios
Edif. "Benalcazar Mil" Apto. 1101
Apartado 1321
Quito, Ecuador

INFO CHECK   United Kingdom
Shaibern House
28 Scrutton Street
London EC2A 4RQ, U.K.

INFORMCONF   Paraguay
Fulgencio R. Moreno 536
Asuncion, Paraguay

INFORM CREDIT S.A.   Mexico
Lopez 15-309 y 310
Aparetado Postal 572
Mexico City, Mexico

INTERNATIONAL CREDIT AND TRADE   Singapore
Information Agency Pte. Ltd.
Suite 507, 5th Floor
Katong Shopping Center,
Singapore 1543

KOBMANDSTANDENS OPLYSNINGSBUREAU A/S   Denmark
Gammel Mont 4
Post Box 2187
1117 Copenhagen K, Denmark

KOREA CREDIT GUARANTEE FUND   Korea
Credit Informations Dept. I
Dae Woo Building
C.P.O. Box 1029
Seoul 100, Korea

C. LOYNES COMMERCIAL REPORTS   South Africa
P.O. Box 3488
Capetown, South Africa

MIDA INFORM PRIVATE LTD.   India
P.O. Box 7690
Shankar Lane
Kandivi,
Bombay 400 067, India

MOPE LTDA.   Portugal, Cape Verde
Agencia Informadora Comercail
Rue Rodrigue Sampaio 52-h
Lisbon, Portugal

OIKOS   Chile
Estudios Economicos e Informes
   Crediticios
Miraflores 686-DPT 901
Casilla 359-V
Santiago, Chile

PIGUET AFRIQUE CENTRALE   Burkina Faso, Cameroon,
B.P. 1470   Congo, France, Gabon,
Doula, Cameroon   Ivory Coast, Monaco, Togo

G.A. ROE & SONS LTD.   Belize
6 Fort Street
Belize City, Belize

S.A.M. IMPORT AND EXPORT   Mauritius
Commercial Reporting Service
P.O. Box 37
Qatre Bornes, Mauritius

SOCRAT (PVT) LTD.   Zimbabwe
P.O. Box A 60
Avondale
Harare, Zimbabwe

Appendix I

Country categories for OECD arrangement on officially supported export credits*

The interest rates on Eximbank's loans are determined by the classification of the country to which the export will be shipped. Eximbank uses the following country classification adopted in the OECD Arrangement on Officially Supported Export Credits. Not all of the countries listed are eligible for Eximbank Financing, however.

Rich Countries

Andorra	Finland	Liechtenstein	Spain
Australia	France	Luxembourg	Sweden
Austria	Germany	Libya	Switzerland
Bahrain	Greece	Monaco	United Arab Emirates
Belgium	Iceland	Netherlands	United Kingdom
Bermuda	Ireland	New Zealand	U.S.A.
Brunei	Israel	Norway	U.S.S.R.
Canada	Italy	Qatar	Vatican City
Czechoslovakia	Japan	San Marino	
Denmark	Kuwait	Saudi Arabia	

*Source: Export-Import Bank of the U.S.

Intermediate Countries

Albania
Algeria
Argentina
Bahamas
Barbados
Belize
Botswana
Brazil
Bulgaria
Chile
Colombia
Costa Rica
Coted'Ivoire
Cuba
Cyprus
Dominican Republic

Ecuador
Fiji
Gabon
Guatemala
Hong Kong
Hungary
Iran
Iraq
Jamaica
Jordan
Kiribat
North Korea
South Korea
Lebanon
Macao
Malaysia

Malta
Mauritius
Mexico
Montserrat
Morocco
Namibia
Nauru
Netherlands Antilles
Nigeria
Oman
Panama
Papua New Guinea
Paraguay
Peru
Poland
Portugal

Romania
St. Kitts-Nevis
St. Lucia
Seychelles
Singapore
South Africa
Suriname
Syria
Taiwan
Trinidad & Tobago
Tunisia
Turkey
Uruguay
Venezuela
Yugoslavia

Poor Countries

Angola
Bangladesh
Benin
Bolivia
Burkina
Burma
Burundi
Cameroon
Central African Republic
Chad
China
People's Republic of the Congo
Egypt
El Salvador

Ethiopia
Gambia
Ghana
Guinea
Guinea-Bissau
Guyana
Haiti
Honduras
India
Indonesia
Kenya
Lesotho
Liberia

Madagascar
Malawi
Mali
Mauritania
Mozambique
Nepal
Nicaragua
Niger
Pakistan
Philippines
Rwanda
Senegal
Sierra Leone

Somalia
Sri Lanka
Sudan
Tanzania
Thailand
Togo
Uganda
Yemen Arab Republic
Yemen
P.D.R.
Zaire
Zambia
Zimbabwe

Appendix J

Selected sources of financing for Caribbean Basin Initiative Projects

Financing Source	Type of Assistance
OVERSEAS PRIVATE INVESTMENT CORP. 1615 M Street NW, Fourth Floor Washington, DC 20527	Loans and loan guarantees Political risk insurance
U.S. TRADE AND DEVELOPMENT PROGRAM Room 301 - SA - 16 U.S. DEPARTMENT OF STATE Washington, DC 20520	Reimbursable grant for feasibility studies
U.S. EXPORT-IMPORT BANK 811 Vermont Avenue NW Room 1229 Washington, DC 20571	Trade finance-loans for feasibility studies
PRIVATE ENTERPRISE BUREAU U.S. Agency for International Development Washington, DC 20523	Trade finance-loans for joint ventures with foreign firms

CARIBBEAN PROJECT DEVELOPMENT FACILITY International Finance Corp. The World Bank Washington, DC 20433	Arranges financing from multiple sources
LATIN AMERICAN AGRIBUSINESS DEVELOPMENT CORP. 225 Alhambra Circle - Suite 905 Coral Gables, FL 33134	Loans for agribusiness projects
INTERNATIONAL EXECUTIVE SERVICE CORPS Joint Venture Feasibility Fund Planning Office 440 Middlesex Road Darien, CT 06820	Matching grants for feasibility studies
GOVERNMENT DEVELOPMENT BANK San Juan, Puerto Rico	Loans
CARIBBEAN FINANCIAL SERVICES CORP. (CFSC) Chapel Street Bridgetown, Barbados	Equity participation
BANEX Apartado 798-3 1000 San Jose Costa Rico	Trade finance/long-term loans
BANCO CENTRAL DE COSTA RICO P.O. Box 10058 1000 San Jose Costa Rico	Trade finance/long-term loans through commercial banks
CORPORACION COSTARRICENSE DE FINANCIAMENTO INDUSTRIAL INTERNACIONAL (COFISA) APDO. 10067 1000 San Jose Costa Rico	Trade finance/long-term loans
PRIVATE SECTOR CORPORATION (PIC) P.O. Box 8609 1000 San Jose Costa Rico	Equity participation/ long-term loans

DEVELOPMENT FINANCE CORPORATION (SOFIHDES) 11 Harry Truman Blvd. Port au Prince, Haiti	Loans
FINANCIERA INDUSTRIAL Y AGROPECUARIA S.A. (FIASA) Avenida Reforma 10-00 01009 Guatemala	Loans
BANCO DE EXPORTACION Avenida la Reforma 11-49, Zona 10 Guatemala City, Guatemala	Trade finance
FINANCIERA GUATEMALTECA Avenida la Reforma 11-49, Zona 10 Guatemala City, Guatemala	Trade finance
FINANCIERA GUATEMALTECA 1A. Avenida 11-50, Zona 4 01010, Guatemala City	Equity participation, Loans Grants for feasibility studies
FINANCIERA INDUSTRIAL, S.A. 7A. Avenida 5-10, Zona 4 Torre II Centro Financiero 01004 Guatemala City	Loans
FINANCIERA DE INVERSION 10A. Calle 3-17, Zona 10 01010 Guatemala City	Loans
FIDE P.O. Box 2029 Tegulcigalpa, Honduras	Equity participation, Loans
FEPROEXAAH P.O. Box 1442 San Pedro Sula, Honduras	Equity participation/ Loans
FIA CENTRO COMMERCIAL Centroamerica Boulevard Miraflores Tegulcigalpa, Honduras	Equity participation/ Loans

FIDE Banco Central De La Republica Dominicana Avenue Pedro Henriques Urena Santo Domingo, Dominican Republic	Loans
TRAFALGAR DEVELOPMENT BANK The Towers, 2nd Floor 25 Dominia Drive Kingston 5, Jamaica	Equity participation/ Loans
DEVELOPMENT BANK OF THE NETHERLANDS Antilles Salinga 206 Willemstad, Curacao	Trade finance/Equity participation/Loans
KORPODEKO Breedstraat 39-C(p) Willemstad, Curacao	Equity participation/ Loans
GUYANA DEVELOPMENT BANK 126 Parade and Barrack Streets Kingston, Georgetown Guyana	Agribusiness loans
CREDIT DISCOUNT FUND Central Bank of Belize Public Building Belize City, Belize	Trade finance

Source: *1989 Guidebook*, U.S. Department of Commerce, International Trade Administration, U.S. and Foreign Commercial Service, The CBI Center, Room H-3203, Washington, DC 20230, October 1988.

Appendix K

Major foreign banks with offices in the United States

BANCA SERFIN, S.N.C.
88 Pine Street
Wall Street Plaza, 24th Floor
New York, NY 10005

BANCO DI NAPOLI
277 Park Avenue
New York, NY 10172

BANCO POPULAR DE PUERTO RICO
7 West 51st Street
New York, NY 10019

BANCO SANTANDER
375 Park Avenue, 29th Floor
New York, NY 10152

BANCOMER, S.N.C.
15 East 54th Street
New York, NY 10022

BANK BUMI DAYA
350 Park Avenue, 7th Floor
New York, NY 10022

BANK OF EAST ASIA, LTD.
450 Park Avenue
New York, NY 10022

BANK LEUMI TRUST CO. OF NEW YORK
579 Fifth Avenue
New York, NY 10017

BANQUE NATIONALE DE PARIS
499 Park Avenue
New York, NY 10022

BARCLAYS BANK OF CALIFORNIA
111 Pine Street
San Francisco, CA 94104

CHICAGO-TOKYO BANK
40 North Dearborn Street
Chicago, IL 60602

THE FUJI BANK AND TRUST CO.
1 World Trade Center, Suite 8023
New York, NY 10048

ISRAEL DISCOUNT BANK OF NEW YORK
511 Fifth Avenue
New York, NY 10017

KANSALLIS-OSAKE-PANKKI
575 Fifth Avenue
New York, NY 10017

KRUNG THAI BANK
452 Fifth Avenue
New York, NY 10018

LLOYDS BANK OF CALIFORNIA
612 S. Flower Street
Los Angeles, CA 90017

MITSUI MANUFACTURERS BANK
515 South Figueroa Street, 4th Floor
Los Angeles, CA 90071

Appendix L

Coordinating international development banks

ASIAN DEVELOPMENT BANK
2330 Roxas Boulevard
P.O. Box 789
Manila, Philippines 2800

AFRICAN DEVELOPMENT BANK AND FUND
B.P. No. 1387
Abidjan,
Ivory Coast

INTER-AMERICAN DEVELOPMENT BANK
808 17th Street NW
Washington, DC 20577

Bibliography

Axtell, Roger E., *The Do's and Taboos of International Trade*, New York: John Wiley & Sons, 1989.

Blum, Laurie, *Free Money for Small Businesses and Entrepreneurs*, New York: John Wiley & Sons, Inc., 1989.

Bremer, Claire, *Tailoring an IPO*, *Business Age* magazine, May 1989.

Curran, Dennis J., and Gabrielle A. Lucci, *The ABCs of FTZs*, *Business Age* magazine, May 1989.

Directory of American Firms Operating in Foreign Countries, published by World Trade Academy Press, New York.

Editors of *INC.* magazine, *The Best of INC. Guide to Finding Capital*, New York: Prentice-Hall, 1988.

Goldstein, Arnold S., *How To Save Your Business*, Wilmington, DE: Enterprise Publishing, Inc., 1983.

Guttman, H. Peter, *The International Consultant*, New York: John Wiley & Sons, Inc., 1987.

Hayes, Rick Stephan, *Business Loans: A Guide to Money Sources and How to Approach Them*, New York: John Wiley & Sons, Inc., 1989.

Heyman, John A., *Seeing Your Way Through a Blind Pool Merger*, *Business Age* magazine, May 1989.

Investment Climate in Foreign Countries, published by Dept. of Commerce, National Technical Information Service.

Mrkvicka, Edward F., Jr., *The Bank Book: How to Revoke Your Bank's "License to Steal"—and Save Up to $100,000*, New York: Harper & Row, 1989.

300

Manring, A.B., *Exporting From the U.S.A.: How to Enter the Export Market*, Vancouver, Canada: International Self-Counsel Press, Ltd., 1986.

Nicholas, Ted, *Where the Money Is and How to Get It*, Wilmington, DE: Enterprise Publishing, Inc., 1980.

Oxelheim, L., and C. Wihlborg, *Macroeconomic Uncertainty: International Risks and Opportunities for the Corporation*, Chichester, England: John Wiley & Sons, Inc., 1988.

Rossman, Marlene L., *The International Businesswoman: A Guide to Success in the Global Marketplace*, New York: Praeger Publishers, Greenwood Press, Inc., 1986.

Schaffer, Matt, *Winning the Countertrade War: New Export Strategies for America*, New York: John Wiley & Sons, Inc., 1989.

Shenkman, Matin M., *Real Estate After Tax Reform: A Guide for Investors*, New York: John Wiley & Sons, Inc., 1987.

Smith, Roy C., *The Global Bankers*, New York: E.P. Dutton, 1989.

Stevens, Mark, *Leveraged Finance: How to Raise and Invest Cash*, Englewood Cliffs, New Jersey: Prentice-Hall, 1981.

Summers, Mark S., *Bankruptcy Explained: A Guide for Businesses*, New York: John Wiley & Sons, 1989.

Sutton, David P., and M. William Benedetto, *Initial Public Offerings: A Strategy Planner for Raising Capital*, Chicago: Probus Publishing Company, 1988.

Venedikian, Harry M., and Gerald A. Warfield, *Export-Import Financing*, Second Edition, New York: John Wiley & Sons, 1986.

Wallace, Alan, *Europe 1992: Old World, New Market*, *Business Age* magazine, June 1989.

Weiss, Stuart, *Channeling Funds to Smaller Exporters*, *Venture* Magazine, September 1989.

Wells, L. Fargo, and Karin B. Dulat, *Exporting From Start to Finance*, Blue Ridge Summit, Pennsylvania: Liberty Hall Press, TAB Books, 1989.

Zimmerman, Mark, *How to Do Business With the Japanese: A Strategy for Success*, New York: Random House, 1985.

Index